THE
EVERYTHING
NEW NURSE BOOK
2ND EDITION

Dear Reader,

You have chosen a fine and noble profession. It will bring you great joy and satisfaction, and you'll experience your fair share of frustration as well. Nursing is a demanding and rewarding profession that is facing many challenges. The economic downturn with the recession of 2008 that lingers today caused many nurses to delay retirement or to return to work. This seemed to stall the pre-existing nursing shortage and caused many new grads to have a difficult time finding a job. This is temporary, and as the economy recovers, we will see a critical shortage of nurses develop.

This book is about all the things you didn't learn in school. There is only a little bit of theory to show you how to put it to use and make it work for you. I have drawn on my own experiences and those of many wonderful colleagues whom I have had the pleasure to know to provide you with some tips and helpful hints to survive your first year as a nurse.

I wish you all the best in your new career, and I hope that you find great success and happiness along the way.

Kathy Quan, RN, BSN, PHN

Welcome to the EVERYTHING® Series!

These handy, accessible books give you all you need to tackle a difficult project, gain a new hobby, comprehend a fascinating topic, prepare for an exam, or even brush up on something you learned back in school but have since forgotten.

You can choose to read an Everything® book from cover to cover or just pick out the information you want from our four useful boxes: e-questions, e-facts, e-alerts, and e-ssentials.

We give you everything you need to know on the subject, but throw in a lot of fun stuff along the way, too.

We now have more than 400 Everything® books in print, spanning such wide-ranging categories as weddings, pregnancy, cooking, music instruction, foreign language, crafts, pets, New Age, and so much more. When you're done reading them all, you can finally say you know Everything®!

QUESTION

Answers to
common questions

FACT

Important snippets
of information

ALERT

Urgent
warnings

ESSENTIAL

Quick
handy tips

PUBLISHER Karen Cooper

DIRECTOR OF ACQUISITIONS AND INNOVATION Paula Munier

MANAGING EDITOR, EVERYTHING® SERIES Lisa Laing

COPY CHIEF Casey Ebert

ASSISTANT PRODUCTION EDITOR Jacob Erickson

ACQUISITIONS EDITOR Lisa Laing

SENIOR DEVELOPMENT EDITOR Brett Palana-Shanahan

EDITORIAL ASSISTANT Ross Weisman

EVERYTHING® SERIES COVER DESIGNER Erin Alexander

LAYOUT DESIGNERS Erin Dawson, Michelle Roy Kelly, Elisabeth Lariviere, Ashley Vierra, Denise Wallace

Visit the entire Everything® series at *www.everything.com*

THE
EVERYTHING®
NEW NURSE
BOOK

2ND EDITION

Gain confidence, manage your schedule,
and be ready for anything!

Kathy Quan, RN, BSN, PHN

Avon, Massachusetts

An Everything® Series Book.
Everything® and everything.com® are registered trademarks of F+W Media, Inc.

Published by Adams Media, a division of F+W Media, Inc.
57 Littlefield Street, Avon, MA 02322 U.S.A.
www.adamsmedia.com

ISBN 10: 1-4405-2687-7
ISBN 13: 978-1-4405-2687-9
eISBN 10: 1-4405-2760-1
eISBN 13: 978-1-4405-2760-9

Printed in the United States of America.

10 9 8 7 6 5 4 3 2 1

Library of Congress Cataloging-in-Publication Data
is available from the publisher.

This publication is designed to provide accurate and authoritative information with regard to the subject matter covered. It is sold with the understanding that the publisher is not engaged in rendering legal, accounting, or other professional advice. If legal advice or other expert assistance is required, the services of a competent professional person should be sought.

—From a *Declaration of Principles* jointly adopted by a Committee of the American Bar Association and a Committee of Publishers and Associations

Many of the designations used by manufacturers and sellers to distinguish their products are claimed as trademarks. Where those designations appear in this book and Adams Media was aware of a trademark claim, the designations have been printed with initial capital letters.

This book is available at quantity discounts for bulk purchases.
For information, please call 1-800-289-0963.

Contents

Acknowledgments

When the first edition of this book was published, it was my first book, and it was an experience akin to giving birth the first time. This time around, it's like watching your child grow into adulthood with great pride and satisfaction.

I have to thank all of the many nurses I have encountered throughout my lifetime and my career for the good times and the bad, as they all helped to make this book a reality.

Many thanks to my family, who have always been there and supported me through all of the ups and downs of writing and revising this book. And to my friends, who have encouraged me to step out of my comfort zone and reach for my dreams.

My agent, Barb Doyen, has been there for me through the best and worst parts of writing and publishing. Thanks for believing in me and keeping me sane. And to my editors, who have been patient, understanding, and most of all extremely helpful in making this experience a positive one as we work together to produce a book that will be helpful and supportive for nurses everywhere.

Thanks so very much to you all!

The Top 10 Things for
New Nurses to Know

1. Nursing is one of the noblest professions.

2. Nursing involves a process of lifelong learning.

3. Once a nurse, always a nurse.

4. Nursing is a profession and not a gender.

5. Nursing combines the art of caring with the skills and technology of math and science.

6. Nursing is one of the most physically and emotionally demanding jobs.

7. Always set the bar high; expect professionalism.

8. If you've "burned out," you just need to find another niche as a nurse.

9. Nurses have been honored as the Most Ethical Professionals every year since 2002 by the Gallup poll.

10. Nurses make a difference in someone's life every day and are masters at the fine art of caring!

Introduction

WELCOME TO THE WORLD of nursing. As you embark on your new career, know that you have made a wise and wonderful choice to give of yourself to help make a difference in someone's life every day. Nursing is one of the most rewarding and yet challenging careers. It can be a thankless job and at the same time, nursing can bring you countless hours of joy and some of the most heartfelt love.

Nursing is one of the most physically and emotionally demanding careers. You will require a great deal of physical stamina and a strong sense of humor to perform your daily duties. Nurses combine the art of caring with a broad scientific knowledge base to provide care, promote wellness, and improve the lives of their patients. It takes strong communication skills, both written and oral, combined with a scientific mind and a warm heart and soul to form the foundation for a good nurse.

You will learn to laugh and to cry with your patients, to share their joys and disappointments and sorrows. They will all touch your life in very different ways and some will become a part of you forever. Nursing is a lifelong learning experience. As you approach your new career, you will discover just how much you didn't learn in school. This may frighten you and cause you to feel incompetent, give you much self-doubt, and even make you want to quit. Be patient, give yourself time (at least a year) to grow into your new role. You will learn something new every day. You will teach your patients how to improve their lives, to become responsible for their own outcomes, and to be independent in their own health care.

You will learn many new techniques and skills and nurture many talents and abilities, some of which you never knew you had. You will become competent and lose your fear and feelings of inadequacy as you grow into your new profession. You will also experience many negative aspects and encounter nurses who are burning out. Your enthusiasm could help them to rediscover why they chose nursing and how to make nursing important again in their own lives.

This book is based on the experiences of many nurses and is meant to help you to understand that you are not alone in your feelings at any stage of your career. Every nurse was once a new grad. Every nurse has had just as many firsts as you will: first shot, first birth, first death, first error, first patient, first special moment when it all makes sense. Share in their triumphs and failures as you grow into one of the finest professions.

Always smile and be honest. Consider how you would like to be treated if you were in this predicament, and never take care of someone in a manner less than what you would demand for your loved ones. Set the bar high and demand excellence; mediocrity is common, boring, and unacceptable. Be professional.

Always remember to recharge your own batteries. Take care of yourself so that you have the strength, stamina, and desire to care for others who need you. Learn from your mistakes and move on. Enjoy your career and always keep track of your accomplishments and successes. Find something positive about every day. If you ever lose track of why you became a nurse, think back to those moments and your doubts will fade. Good luck and thank you for becoming a nurse.

CHAPTER 1

What Is a Nurse?

A nurse is someone who cares for the sick and infirm. But a nurse is so much more. The nurse comforts the sick and dying and participates in the joy of birth. A nurse is your best friend when you lie awake in a hospital bed at night scared and lonely. A nurse may also seem like your worst enemy when he comes at you with needles and tubes to probe your body.

Definitions of Nursing

A nurse is a professional caregiver. Someone who advocates for patients' rights, promotes health, educates patients and families, and strives to eliminate pain and suffering. A nurse carries a large responsibility in the care and treatment of her patients. Nursing is one of the most rewarding professions and yet at times can be one of the most frustrating and thankless. A nurse is a highly skilled individual who learns to combine the scientific aspect of health care with the fine art of caring.

The following definitions will provide you with an understanding of the basic levels of the nursing profession. They will serve as building blocks for determining what education is required, what roles are open to each level, and how to explore opportunities for advancement.

- **Nurse:** someone who cares for the sick and infirm. A nurse is a member of the health care team and provides different kinds of health care to patients based on the nurse's level of education.
- **Registered Nurse (RN):** a nurse who has graduated with a diploma or a degree (Associate Degree in Nursing [ADN] to PhD) from a state-approved nursing program, passed the state board examination for professional nurses, and has been granted a license by the state to practice professional nursing in that state. RNs with advanced degrees and certificates will have increased options for their scope of practice.
- **Licensed Practical (or Vocational) Nurse (LPN/LVN):** a technical nurse who has graduated from a state-approved practical or vocational nursing program, passed the state board examination for practical nursing, and has been granted a license to practice in that state as a practical nurse. The LPN/LVN works under the supervision of an RN or a physician to provide patient care. With IV Certification, the LPN/LVN can perform certain aspects of IV care. The title of practical or vocational nurse varies by state law, but the role is essentially the same. Most states use the practical nurse title; California and Texas use vocational nurse.
- **Certified Nursing Assistant (CNA):** also known as a nurse's aide, is unlicensed. A CNA delivers limited care to patients under the supervision of licensed nurses. The CNA may take vital signs and assist

in activities of daily living such as giving baths, making beds, dressing, feeding, and positioning patients. The CNA completes a training course that includes classroom and clinical instruction. They are regulated by state agencies.

- **Scope of Practice:** each licensed or certified member of the health care team is allowed to perform certain duties based on the content and level of education received, the license or certificate granted, and the specifics of the laws and regulations of the state in which they are practicing.
- **Nurse Practice Act (NPA):** the group of laws in a state that protect the public health. It defines the scope of practice for nurses in that state. The Nurse Practice Act also includes the requirements for education and licensing, as well as disciplinary and punitive measures for unsafe practice. It is the responsibility of every nurse to know the responsibilities and limitations outlined in the NPA of the state(s) in which the nurse practices.
- **State Board of Nursing:** the governing board in each state that oversees the statutory laws that comprise the NPA for that state. This board is responsible for protecting the public by determining who is competent to practice nursing in that state and suspending or revoking the license of anyone who is deemed incompetent.

For additional information and definitions, please refer to Appendix A. There are many other members of the health care team. In some settings, medical assistants, CNAs, and other non-licensed personnel may be referred to as "the nurse." While they play an important role in health care delivery, confusing their role with that of the nurse is a practice that is misleading and at the very least should be discouraged.

Roles for Nurses

There are several roles for nurses. One role is the practical nurse, sometimes referred to as the technical nurse. This is the LPN/LVN. The other is the professional nurse. This is the RN. Both play an essential part as members of the health care team. Their roles and responsibilities vary. An RN can perform any of the duties of an LPN, but the reverse is not true.

In some instances, an LPN/LVN's skills at specific tasks may be more refined than those of her supervising RN. This can often be the case because the LVN has the primary responsibility for performing bedside nursing and tasks, while the RN is given a supervisory responsibility for the patient's care and often forgoes the hands-on practice of direct patient care.

FACT

RN training involves more science, math, patient assessment, critical thinking, and theoretical aspects. This includes the nursing process, which encompasses the whole patient and his response to his illness as well as patient treatment.

Both the LPN and RN combine the knowledge they acquired in school with their own art of compassion and caring to provide excellent care. Beyond the basics of science and the treatment of disease that both LPNs and RNs receive, LPN training is primarily focused on bedside nursing and performing tasks such as changing dressings and Foley catheter care.

LPN/LVN Training

The technical nurse attends a vocational school. Some community colleges and adult education schools provide LPN training. This is usually a one-year to fifteen-month program that includes classroom as well as clinical hands-on instruction. After graduation, the nurse must sit for a board exam to become licensed to practice.

Professional organizations have been battling for years to make a distinction between nurses who have been educated at minimally the baccalaureate level as being *professional nurses* and those with a diploma or ADN nursing education being *technical nurses*. Those without a BSN would be given a grace period to acquire the degree or an option to work at a newly designated level. There was also a movement to eliminate the LPN role altogether.

Studies have repeatedly shown that patient mortality rates and quality of care are directly related to the level of education of the nursing staff, and the American Association of Critical-Care Nurses (AACN) believes that quality care hinges on having a highly educated workforce.

The wax and wane of the shortage of nurses has prevented further implementation of these distinctions. But when employers have an opportunity to pick and choose among qualified candidates, the hiring trend moves toward the higher-educated nurses.

RN Training

The RN has several options for education. Each level of education prepares the student for the role of a professional nurse. All nurses will sit for the same RN board exam in order to become licensed as a registered nurse. However, there are distinct differences in the programs and the level of preparation they provide. Consequently, salaries and opportunities for advancement are often tied to the level of education.

Diploma Nurse Program

The Diploma Nurse program was once a primary option for RNs, but it is rapidly disappearing. This is because nurses no longer work primarily in a hospital setting. There are only about twenty-five such programs left in the United States today. These programs provide nurses with a three-year, non-degreed nursing education. Diploma programs are usually associated with a teaching hospital and nurses reside in a dormitory setting. They attend classes in the hospital and work regular shifts on the floors of the hospital to obtain their hands-on clinical training. Today many diploma programs have combined with ADN programs at community colleges or offer practical or vocational nursing.

Associate's Degree

Community colleges provide an Associate Degree in Nursing (ADN) program option for RNs. This is typically a two-year associate's degree program. It includes the same general education/liberal arts courses required for any associate's degree. For nurses, the curriculum will include math (minimum: algebra) and science (chemistry, physics, anatomy, and physiology and microbiology). The nursing courses include classroom instruction and hands-on clinical courses that may be provided at institutions available within the community.

Bachelor's Degree

The third option is a four-year program, a Bachelor of Science in Nursing (BSN) in which the nurse completes all the general requirements for a bachelor's degree with all the above math and science, as well as a comprehensive program in nursing. The nursing courses cover the same materials as the other programs but add a more intense study of the nursing process, nursing theory and models, and leadership skills. It is also a springboard for advanced degrees. As such, a BSN is often required for leadership roles and management positions in the nursing profession. In some cases, the RN must make a commitment to obtain a master's degree in nursing within a timeframe. This is becoming more common again because of the shortage of nurses and the need to allow those with less education to advance more rapidly.

Advanced Degrees

Advanced degrees for nurses include fields such as a master's or PhD in nursing, health care, and health care administration. A Master in Business Administration (MBA) in health care or health care administration is also a popular choice for nurses with an inclination for business and managing health care organizations such as home health agencies, clinics, and hospitals. Advance practice nurses, such as NPs, nurse midwives, nurse anesthetists, and clinical nurse specialists, minimally require an MSN.

Opportunities for Nurses

Health care as a whole is one of the fastest growing career opportunities worldwide. Combined with the growing shortage of personnel, nurses are in high demand and will remain so for at least another ten to twenty years. Part of the reason for the shortage is the ever-expanding opportunity and accompanying need for nurses. Nurses no longer work primarily in hospitals, nursing homes, doctor's offices, and clinics. These will continue to be major employers for nurses, but as new opportunities arise because of constant changes in the workplace, nurses are leaving these sites.

New nurses are also exploring the opportunities that have grown out of advances in technology and medicine. Community-based nursing is on the rise as the trend for treating patients in their homes in lieu of hospitalization increases. Home health and hospice fields will continue to grow faster than many other nursing fields over the next decade.

FACT

Expanding nursing roles for RNs are in areas such as information technology, forensics, telemedicine, prisons, geriatric day care, assisted living facilities, schools, research, home health, private duty, hospice, holistic care, and the military. Many corporations are now hiring an on-site nurse to assist with employee health issues.

Health Care Reform and the Nursing Profession

The Patient Protection and Affordable Care Act, also known as Health Care Reform of 2010, will help to advance the nursing profession in multiple ways. When President Obama was campaigning for office in 2008, the American Nurses Association (ANA) chose to endorse him because he took the time to listen and learn about the issues facing nurses today and promised to work to improve as many as he can.

By expanding access to health care coverage for millions more Americans, one of the biggest impacts of this act has been, and will continue to be, using nurses to provide more care and patient education to help reduce the high costs of health care, as well as expand the availability.

Nurse practitioners have long been used to help provide primary care in areas such as women's health, pediatrics, and family medicine, especially under HMO (i.e., managed care) insurance plans, and in low-cost community- and retail-based clinics. Many more NPs are going to be needed in the future to meet the need of the public for health care. As nurses leave other roles to become NPs, replacement nurses will be needed to fill their vacancies.

ESSENTIAL

With a focus shift to preventive care and wellness, all nurses will take on more responsibility for educating patients to assist them in taking more responsibility for their own health care and outcomes.

The Affordable Care Act also designates funding increases to provide for educational assistance for nurses at all levels from LPN to PhD RN. A major focus of the funding will be on educating nurse educators so that more nurses can be educated rather than turned away because of the lack of nurse educators.

Funds will also be directed to the Nursing Workforce Diversity Program to improve cultural diversity among nurses. In addition, funds will be added to the Nurse Education, Practice and Retention grant program to update the quality component, help nurses obtain a stronger background in quality improvement, and help implement mandated quality improvement across the health care delivery process.

LPN/LVNs

Most of these new opportunities for nurses require an RN and often a BSN, but some areas do offer opportunities for LPNs as well. Sometimes these are limited roles, such as in home health care, hospice, and private duty, where the LPN can perform certain tasks such as Foley care, venipuncture for lab specimens, wound care, ventilator care, and basic bedside nursing.

One expanded role for LPNs is IV care. IV Certification at present is an additional optional course of study in most states. Each state's Nurse Practice Act for LPNs spells out the level of IV care that this certification covers. In most instances, dressing changes, hanging new bags, and possibly adjusting the rate of flow is about all that is allowed. New laws are being legislated in some states to allow LPNs to flush central lines and perform central-line care. Inserting IV lines is not likely to become standard practice for LPNs in most states.

ALERT

Be sure that you have a clear understanding of the policies of your employer as well as the Nurse Practice Act in the state in which you practice. Never rely on the culture of what is acceptable in your facility as the final rule. You are responsible for knowing the law and abiding by it. If some administrator or a physician has bent the law for the convenience of the facility, you can be held liable.

Advance Practice Nurses

Advance practice nurses (APNs) hold advanced degrees and/or certifications in specialties that include certified registered nurse anesthetists (CRNA), certified nurse-midwives (CNM), certified diabetic educators (CDE), clinical nurse specialists (CNS), and nurse practitioners (NP) in such areas as palliative care, pediatrics, geriatrics, family practice, women's health, and mental health. There are many more areas of specialization and more to come in the future. Nurse practitioners work under the supervision of a physician. In most states, they can prescribe medications and non-complex treatments. They assess patients and can perform many procedures that are normally performed only by physicians, such as pap smears.

Pending legislation at the state and national levels may pave the way for even more changes in the range of opportunities for advance practice nurses. When Medicare and/or Medicaid reimbursement to nurse practitioners becomes possible everywhere in the United States, the Advanced Practice Registered Nurse (APRN) role will expand further, especially in rural areas where access to physician care is limited. NPs will serve to supplement the care. In particular, case management of patients with palliative care and mental health issues could once again be reimbursed when this legislation is passed and implemented.

Additional Opportunities

Nurses can be childbirth educators and lactation consultants, flight nurses, and legal nurse consultants. They can specialize in managed care, infection control, IV infusion, nutrition support, diabetes education, oncology, cardiology, and heart catheterization, and in case management of catastrophic illness and workers' compensation cases.

In some instances, nurses holding a BSN can now become instructors in vocational and ADN programs. Generally, nurse educators must hold a master's or PhD in nursing or education. In fact, even in vocational and ADN programs, the minimum requirement has been for a master's-prepared nurse educator. However, with the shortage of nurses and the need to increase enrollment in nursing programs, the BSN-prepared nurse now has more opportunities to teach.

Responsibilities of Nurses

All nurses provide direct patient care as directed by a physician. Both LVNs and RNs can take orders directly from physicians. In some states, however, the LVN must have the RN cosign any verbal orders the LVN takes. The LVNs can carry out the orders and report to the RN any significant findings or response to treatment. The RN would then assess the patient and report to the doctor. All verbal orders must be read back and verified.

All nurses promise to do no harm to any patient and are expected to uphold fundamental responsibilities to help to prevent illness and restore health, to help to alleviate pain and suffering, and to promote health. Nurses should also follow a code of ethics for nurses as set and frequently revised by the ANA. The International Council of Nurses (ICN) has also written a code of ethics for nurses that expands on the ANA's code.

FACT

For the exact content of the codes of ethics, please refer to the organization's website. The ANA website is *www.nursingworld.org*, then search for "Code of Ethics." The ICN website is *www.icn.ch/about-icn/code-of-ethics-for-nurses*.

Highlights of the responsibilities and guidelines for the ethical and legal practice of nurses as outlined in these codes are:

- The nurse is expected to provide care for a patient with respect for his human dignity and uniqueness as an individual regardless of race, creed, gender, socio-economic status, or the nature of the illness.
- The nurse is responsible for safeguarding the patient's right to privacy by honoring the confidentiality of information related to the patient.
- The nurse is responsible for protecting her patient and the public from health and safety issues affected by illegal, incompetent, and unethical practices.
- The nurse is responsible and accountable for her own nursing actions and judgments, as well as for those she is supervising.
- The nurse is responsible for maintaining her own nursing competency.

- The nurse is responsible for making informed decisions about her own skills and abilities, as well as for those to whom she might delegate responsibility. The nurse is expected to seek consultation if necessary before accepting or delegating the responsibility for any aspect of a patient's care.
- The nurse is expected to participate in the nursing profession's ongoing efforts and activities to expand the core of research-based knowledge for nurses.
- The nurse is expected to participate in the nursing profession's efforts to implement and improve the standards of nursing care.
- The nurse is expected to participate in the nursing profession's efforts to maintain conditions of employment, including equitable socioeconomic standards, which allow for delivery of high-quality nursing care.
- The nurse is responsible for participating with the nursing profession in protecting the public from misinformation and misrepresentations.
- The nurse is expected to participate and collaborate with other members of the health care team and community in promoting local and national efforts to meet the health care needs of the public.

The nursing profession is not to be taken lightly, nor to be entered into on a whim. Nurses render health care not only to the individual patients, but also to their families and to the community. Nurses are expected to coordinate the efforts of everyone involved to enhance the health and well-being of their patients. Nurses are responsible for respecting human rights. These include the right to life, the right to dignity, and the right to respect.

Nursing as a Profession

Nursing at all levels, whether you are an LPN, RN, or an APRN, is a profession. Achieving this status has been a hard-fought battle, but is one that all nurses must continue to fight with the goal to attract more capable young people into the profession. Nurses are overworked and underpaid. That is a fact, but salaries are increasing and work conditions are improving.

Professional Appearance

All nurses need to strive for maintaining a professional appearance at all times. Caps and white starched uniforms may be a thing of the past, but there is no excuse for not dressing appropriately. No matter what setting you work in, clean, professional attire must be worn. Wearing clean surgical scrubs and lab coats go a long way toward distinguishing men and women as health care professionals.

Gender issues cause male nurses to be mistaken for doctors and females accepted as nurses, even when they are doctors. Wearing identification tags and making a gentle correction could quickly clear up any misunderstandings. There is no reason to become indignant when people make incorrect assumptions.

ALERT

Remember that you represent the nursing profession at all times—whether at work or at play. Your attire, hygiene, actions, and demeanor are always on display. This can be an intense responsibility and unfair at times, perhaps, but something you must be aware of. Would you want *you* taking care of *your* loved one?

In addition to representing the nursing profession, whether on or off duty, you represent your employer. How you appear and act reflects on the employer's business. If you conduct yourself professionally and present a professional demeanor, you will command the respect you deserve from your employer, your coworkers, your patients, their families, and your community.

If you look and act the role, your patients will have much more respect for you as a professional. You will be better able to convince them that what you are telling them is in their best interest. You will gain your patients' confidence and be better able to educate them and advocate for them.

Hair

Your personal grooming issues affect infection control. Having your hair fall into your field of vision in the middle of a procedure can be a cause for concern. Not only does hair falling in your face present the potential for you to make a mistake, but it can also contaminate your clean or sterile field. Having to brush your hair aside can cause you to break technique, contaminate yourself, or require you to remove yourself in the middle of a procedure to wash and re-glove. All these put you and the patient at risk.

Fingernails and Jewelry

The Centers for Disease Control (CDC) issued warnings about the use of artificial nails and most hospitals and clinics now prohibit their use. This standard has not been adopted in all areas of health care. Nurses who work in areas where this standard has not been addressed should review the literature and research the topic for themselves.

Long fingernails, whether natural or artificial, and jewelry, such as rings, have long been known to harbor bacteria even with the best hand washing efforts. Using gloves can alleviate the infection risk, but the practical approach is to keep nails short, to keep hair short or pulled back, and to limit or omit jewelry in the workplace. This is not only for the patient's protection but also for your own.

Fragrances

Another consideration is the use of scents. Whether wearing scented shaving lotions, perfumes, hair products, or mouthwash, nurses should remember that they work with sick people. The sense of smell of an ill person may be more acute because of medications, such as chemotherapy. The sensitivity to smells may also be heightened due to allergies, migraines, and other aspects of illness and intolerance. Less is more. Please be considerate of other's inability to cope with what you might think smells terrific.

Smoking

Smoking is another consideration. If you smoke, you smell of smoke. Your skin, your hair, your clothing can reek no matter how well you try to mask it. Sometimes the masking only increases the potency of the smell. Just because you are not smoking in the presence of patients doesn't mean your smoking is not a problem. Everywhere your cigarettes have been the smell of smoke has been too. Your car, your purse, your pockets will all smell of smoke. Be aware of this and try to minimize the experience for others.

Legal Issues

As a licensed nurse, your responsibility is to promote health and well-being. Under the Nurse Practice Act for your state, you will find a section that deals with disciplinary measures. Here, you will most likely find that not only will you be punished by the laws of your state for a criminal act, such as a DUI, but that your nursing license is subject to suspension or revocation. This is true even though you were not on duty at the time of the DUI.

The commission of other criminal acts, not limited to malpractice issues or the illegal use of drugs, can also result in the suspension or revocation of your nursing license. These can include things such as writing bad checks, shoplifting, fraud, etc. Remember, you are a professional person and you are expected to conduct yourself in a professional manner at all times.

A Brief History of Nursing

There have been caregivers throughout human history. Where there is illness, you will find a caregiver of some sort in the picture. In reality, the first nurses were men who were caregivers in ancient Rome. Florence Nightingale elevated the role of caregiver to that of a professional nurse during the Crimean War in 1854, when she brought standards of care and infection control to wounded soldiers. She started a school for nursing, but it was not the first school.

The Beginning

In 1836, a secular movement began when the Reverend Theodor and Friederike Fliedner established a three-year course for nurses at their school in Kaiserwerth, Germany. Florence Nightingale visited this school in 1851. Graduates could dispense medications and nurse the ill and convalescing patients back to health. Sixteen hundred nurses had been trained there and at various Kaiserwerth motherhouses throughout the world by 1864. Kaiserwerth had a motherhouse as far away as Milwaukee, Wisconsin.

Modern nursing began early in the nineteenth century in Europe with the Protestant Deaconess Movement. The deaconesses cared for the sick and infirm and were housed in motherhouses, where they received room and board but no pay for their work (similar to a monastic system).

Florence Nightingale (1820–1910)

Florence Nightingale was from a well-to-do family in Britain, and, after receiving an extensive education, she decided to devote her life to caring for the sick. She volunteered to go to Crimea in 1854 to work in the Turkish hospital in Scutari. The conditions appalled her. The barrack's hospital was dark, poorly ventilated, and overrun with vermin. Nurse Nightingale taught the few trained nurses and orderlies there how to clean and disinfect the facility. Because of her early infection control measures, the death rate fell from 40 percent to 2 percent within six months.

After the war, Nightingale returned to London and wrote about her adventures and findings. She also started her own school for nurses. Her book, *Notes on Nursing*, was published in 1859 and is still required reading in most nursing programs.

The Beginning of Nursing in America

Nursing in America was still in its infancy at the start of the Civil War in 1861. As the war began, the only nurses in this country were members of religious orders, such as the Catholic Sisters of Mercy and the Sisters of Charity. They were quickly overwhelmed by the numbers of war casualties and the army was ordered by the U.S. government to establish a nursing service. Dorothea Dix, who was sixty years old and had devoted her life to the reform of insane asylums, was picked to lead the nursing efforts for the war.

Nurse Dix set some rigid standards for the women who volunteered for the nursing service. She took in no one under thirty years of age and all applicants had to be plain looking. The uniform was a plain black or brown dress with no bows or hoops. The women wore no curls or jewelry. For the most part, the nurses worked in hospitals far from the battlefields. However, a young woman named Clara Barton took to the battlefields to bring her nursing skills to the wounded. She went on to found the American Red Cross.

Other famous nurses at the time were Mary Todd Lincoln, who worked as a volunteer nurse in Union hospitals, and Louisa May Alcott. Ms. Alcott wrote about her experiences as a Civil War nurse in her book, *Hospital Sketches*.

Harriet Tubman, a famous runaway slave, also served as a nurse in the Civil War. She was awarded a government pension in 1892 for the work she had done on the Sea Islands in South Carolina. Walt Whitman, the author and poet, was a nurse and medic at the time as well.

CHAPTER 2

Why Become a Nurse?

Nursing offers one of the fastest growing career opportunities today. The entire field of health care is expanding, while growth in many other fields is slowing. There is a shortage of nurses worldwide. According to the U.S. Bureau of Labor Statistics, by the year 2012 the United States will need more than one million new and replacement nurses.

Pros and Cons

The fact is that nursing is one of the most rewarding professions for those who love people and love helping people. The roles for nurses are always expanding, which keeps the field new and exciting. Technology and advances in medical science offer new and challenging opportunities to work on the cutting edge of science. There are an unlimited number of career choices in nursing.

There are drawbacks. Nursing is sometimes a thankless job. Patients don't always say "thank you." The job is physically, emotionally, and mentally challenging. Patients need nurses on weekends and holidays and at all hours of the day and night. But for every difficult day, there is always one experience that tugs at your heart and shows you that it is all worth it.

Why Not Become a Doctor?

This is the burning question that at least one of your loved ones will probably ask you and not just once, but many times over. You may even ask it of yourself. The answer, however, will be a personal one and one with many different twists and turns. The fact is that you want to be a nurse. A doctor is not a nurse. Just like a police officer is not a firefighter. You are comparing apples with oranges despite the fact that they are both highly regarded professions in the health care industry.

Is It Better to Be a Doctor?

Those who choose medicine as a career do so because they want to help people but more so because they want to be involved in the diagnosis and treatment of disease. They want to be part of the act of curing someone. Doctors have the advantage of having a longer-term relationship with a patient than most nurses. Doctors will see the patient from the initial diagnosis through to the cure or through the course of long-term treatment. They receive their emotional rewards when the patient is cured or learns to cope with an illness and make the appropriate lifestyle changes.

Nurses are a part of this process as well, except that they never diagnose. (The exception to this rule is the nurse practitioner, who has been specifically trained to diagnose and prescribe medications and treatment for illnesses in patients.) Nurses collaborate with the physician and coordinate the scientific information about the disease with the patient's signs and symptoms and his ability to cope, understand, and respond to the treatment. The nurse usually has a more limited experience with the patient according to where she practices (i.e., hospital, clinic, or home health setting). This might be a two- to four-day hospital stay and the nurse has a short time to participate in the care. Consequently, the nurse may not see the full or end results of her efforts.

ESSENTIAL

The health care team is comprised of doctors, nurses, therapists, social workers, nursing assistants, pharmacists, and a whole ancillary of non-licensed personnel.

What Nurses Do

Nurses look at the patient as a whole and they make a nursing diagnosis with regard to the disease and what else is needed to help the patient cope and respond to the treatment and maximize outcomes. This includes lifestyle issues, nutrition, hygiene, as well as knowledge deficits. Armed with all this information, the nurse sets out to educate the patient about his illness, the treatment modalities necessary, and the expected response or outcome. The nurse also helps the patient understand any possible side effects and untoward signs and symptoms that should be reported to the doctor.

FACT

Nurses work independently to provide case management, develop care standards, and improve the quality of patient care. Nurses also educate patients and family members in aspects of preventive health and wellness, taking responsibility for the patients' own health, and promoting awareness of health care issues.

Physicians have little training in most of these areas. They aren't trained in the nursing process and they don't make nursing diagnoses. Many a nurse has gone on to become a doctor and they bring together the best of both worlds. However, in the course of treating patients, often their skills as nurses are minimized and even lost due to a physician's time restraints.

Why Do You Want to Be a Nurse?

When someone asks you why you would *want* to be a nurse, the answer is that you *want* to make a difference in the quality of someone's life every day.

Nursing is a highly skilled profession. You need the ability to understand math and science, as well as have great compassion for people. You need a strong desire to want to make a difference in the quality of a person's life.

You will learn to glean your rewards from seeing how you've helped someone, even if just a little. You will take with you a satisfaction that you have given it your best shot and tried everything you know how to do, even if you think you've failed.

But what if you can't handle the sight of blood? What if needles terrify you? What if you can't stand the smell of hospitals? What if you pass out at the sight of an open wound? What if you gag at the sight of excrement and bodily secretions? These are definitely challenges you will have to face. Your strong desire to be a nurse can help you to come to grips with your fears and aversions.

Those who can't understand your desire to be a nurse will wonder why in the world you would *want* to deal with these things. Or why you would *want* to take math and science courses beyond what was required in high school. You know why you want to be a nurse, even if you can't put it into words. Getting back to those difficult questions, let's explore them one at a time.

What If You Can't Handle the Sight of Blood?

In the past, the blood you've been exposed to is usually either yours or that of a close friend or loved one. The sight of your own blood has usually involved pain. Your body's response incorporates a natural defense mechanism and you may feel faint or nauseated as a result.

When a friend or loved one is injured, your emotional response incorporates this mechanism and you may have the same type of response. This is not to say you won't have the same response to a stranger's blood, but it should be less of an issue. It is something that you can and will develop a level of tolerance to given time. Additionally, as a nurse, you will often automatically move into an "emergency/help mode," and you won't really have time to worry about your own response.

QUESTION

What if I'm squeamish?
Most nurses do have either a weak stomach or an aversion for something involved in patient care. Overcoming this is an acquired art. Give yourself some time and try some of the tips and tricks discussed in this chapter.

What If Needles Terrify You?

Again, as a nurse, you won't be on the receiving end. Learning to handle and use hypodermics and IV needles prior to injecting or inserting into a patient will help you have a new respect for needles. As an instrument to help you assist the patient in getting well or alleviating pain, needles will take on a different meaning to you.

In fact, your own fears will help you to be a better nurse. You'll wield the needles with more compassion, and you'll be sure to take the time to help the patient tolerate the procedure better.

What If You Can't Stand the Smell of Hospitals?

First, your intolerance to the smell of hospitals is probably linked to a scary or unpleasant experience in a hospital. As a student and then as a nurse, your experience will be on a different level. Also, like anything else, the more time you spend around an odor, the less you can smell it. At first, you may find that everything smells like the hospital, and then it will begin to fade. As you spend time in the hospital and understand what makes some of the smells, your fears will fade as well.

FACT

One way of dealing with unpleasant smells is to use a little camphor or eucalyptus oil on the tip of your nose to mask the smell until you become more comfortable in a hospital setting.

There is a common misperception that the smells are emanating from sick people, but, in fact, it is usually a combination of cleaning chemicals, food odors, plants and flowers of all varieties, a multitude of perfumes and body scents, and all the people congregating in a space that has no open windows.

What If You Pass Out at the Sight of an Open Wound?

In the past when you were exposed to an open wound, it was probably a wound on yourself or a friend or loved one. Again, your emotional response combined with your body's defense mechanisms was most likely causing you to faint.

If someone else has already seen the wound you are about to go and re-dress, ask that person what it looks like. If you already have a vision in your mind, you'll be more prepared for what you find. Surprises can make the experience a lot worse. Read the chart. What was the latest description? Are there any photos in there? Be prepared and it won't be as bad as you anticipated.

Wounds, especially large, infected ones, are not a favorite of any nurse. Wound ostomy nurses who specialize in wound care seem to be more tolerant and can even discuss them over meals; but in general, this is something that you will develop your own way of coping with.

What If You Gag at the Sight of Excrement and Bodily Secretions?

It's usually the smell of these secretions that will cause you to gag. If you can do something to avoid or mask the smell, it helps. Breathing through your mouth helps. You can also cough. It's impossible to cough and gag at the same time. Pop a strong peppermint candy or potent piece of gum in your mouth just before you tackle the job.

Your main concern will be helping the patient retain some dignity. Just get in there and do what you have to do. Turn your head away, close your eyes and relax for a second, and remind yourself that you can do this! Comforting and reassuring the patient will get you through it.

Remember, many a nurse has discreetly gone straight from the patient's room to the bathroom when it's all said and done. Nurses are not robots. Don't let your fears keep you from becoming a nurse. You will learn to cope.

Gender Issues in Nursing

One of the most important things to remember about nursing is that it is a profession, not a gender. Stereotypically, however, nurses are most often portrayed as females in the media. As efforts succeed to break down this gender barrier, more men are becoming nurses. The opportunities for men are as widespread as they are for women, but the battle continues to eliminate the feminine image.

FACT

Men represent about 9 percent of the total workforce of nurses in the United States today. In the military, however, more than 32 percent of the nurses in the three branches (army, navy, and air force) are men.

In 1901, when the U.S. Army Nurse Corps was formed, men were excluded from nursing in the military; only women could be nurses. This rule remained in effect until after the Korean War in the early 1950s. During this time, men who were RNs could join the armed forces and many were drafted, but they did not serve as nurses in the military. Men were also excluded from the American Nurses Association (ANA) from its beginning in 1917 until 1930.

Ironically, in other countries throughout the world, men have been nurses for centuries. The first male nurses were in the Roman Empire in the third century as members of the Parabolani brotherhood who cared for the sick and dying in Alexandria during the plague. During the Crusades, several groups of knights cared for the sick and their injured comrades and were involved in building and managing hospitals in these times.

During the Civil War, both the Union and Confederate armies had men serving as nurses and medics. For example, Walt Whitman, famed poet and author, served as a volunteer nurse in a hospital in Washington, D.C. Historically, however, the nurses you hear about from this time were the women volunteers who helped care for wounded soldiers on the battlefields and in the hospitals.

Men are drawn to nursing for the same reasons women are. The only significant difference is that men can be physically stronger than women and, as such, are often called upon more often to help lift and turn patients. This task can interfere with completing their assignments and it requires a strong sense of teamwork to keep this from becoming a problem.

FACT

Hospitals have historically prevented men from working in OB/GYN and women's health departments, but even that is changing. There remains an attitude that patients have to be forewarned and given a choice whether to accept a male nurse. As health care workers help to educate the public that there is no difference, a nurse is a nurse, even these subtle biases will be a thing of the past.

Men are often asked the question of why they did not become a doctor instead. Again, nursing is a different profession from medicine. The implication that somehow medicine is nobler or that nursing is a waste of your talents and intelligence is a huge issue for all nurses.

Sexual orientation implications have also been a factor in keeping many men away from nursing. There has long been a misconception that male nurses are predominantly homosexual. In reality, most male nurses are heterosexual and regardless of sexual orientation, men go into nursing today for the same reasons many women do; for example, the flexibility it offers for spending time with family while working three, twelve-hour shifts a week. Other professions often demand a nine-to-five, forty-hour schedule, which prevents parents' participation in their child's life through school events and youth sports.

The nursing shortage has helped to ease many of these gender biases, as well as helped to increase salaries that will attract both men and women. Statistically, men seem to be drawn to the technical specialties in nursing, such as anesthesia and intensive care, to the fast-paced life in the ER, and to the autonomy of the nurse practitioner role. As more young people learn about the growing career opportunities the nursing field has to offer, you will see many more males entering the field.

Nursing as a Second Career

September 11, 2001, struck a chord in many adults and made them explore why their profession didn't provide satisfaction in their lives and how they could make a difference in the lives of others. The recession that began in 2008 also influenced many as they began to look for something more meaningful to do with their lives. Because of all of this, a significant number of people have found themselves looking for a new career in nursing. Some had never considered nursing before and others were finally fulfilling a lifelong dream to become a nurse.

New Nurses with Previous Degrees

In general, these new nursing students already have a degree and are pursuing an accelerated BSN, MSN, or PhD program. These programs have existed for some time but are rapidly increasing now. There are over 230 accelerated nursing programs across the United States, and the number grows each year.

Graduates of these programs are highly sought after by employers. In general, these second-career nurses are older and more seasoned workers. They are quick on-the-job learners, more motivated, and more mature. Their clinical skills are strong and their critical thinking skills are very sharp. Their previous education and job skills add tremendous insight into the nursing profession from many different angles. They've been around the block and understand more about working with others and office politics. On top of all these qualities, they will possess a BSN or perhaps an advanced practice RN degree.

Typically, the second-degree nursing student has higher academic expectations and standards, and is more competitive and less intimidated about challenging instructors. This makes them better students and the majority pass the NCLEX-RN (National Council Licensure EXamination for RNs) exam on the first try.

These accelerated degree programs are usually very intense and can be completed in as little as twelve to eighteen months. Most students already possessing a non-nursing degree will have completed the liberal arts courses in the arts and social sciences. Many will not have the natural sciences such as anatomy and physiology or microbiology. Some will need chemistry and a higher math. Consequently, these courses are offered more readily so that students can complete these prerequisite courses in a timely manner prior to beginning their nursing education.

If an accelerated program proves to be too intense, these students have the option of transferring into the more traditional program to earn their BSN. This typically takes two years. Financially, this is often the choice many students will make because of the high costs of accelerated programs.

Employers who have learned the value of hiring these second-degree nurses will often offer tuition reimbursement incentives in exchange for postgraduate employment.

Non-Degreed Second-Career Nurses

Not all students seeking a second, third, or even a fourth career in nursing possess a non-nursing degree. Some are high school graduates who have been in the workplace for a number of years, or they are re-entry moms who are also ready to pursue their dream of becoming a nurse now that their children are older.

The same as those with prior degrees, these non-degreed nursing students tend to be eager to accept the challenges of an education with very high expectations. These students are also more mature and highly motivated. Their prior work experience also provides them with a variety of backgrounds and expertise that ensure a solid foundation for their new career.

These nursing students have the same choices and career advancement options as their new high school graduate classmates. Many choose to begin with an ADN program or an LVN/LPN course. Statistically however, most will eventually pursue a BSN.

ESSENTIAL

The one downside to the second-career nurse is that he enters the workforce at an older age and therefore will have a shorter time to devote to the nursing profession. One of the ongoing causes of the current nursing shortage is an aging population of nurses. However, the valuable experiences and strong clinical skills they bring to the profession far outweigh this disadvantage.

The Nursing Shortage

There have been a number of shortages of health care workers throughout history. The current nursing shortage is worldwide, and it is a serious one. Factors contributing to the shortage include an aging workforce, a decline in enrollment in nursing programs, a significant growth in the population, and the fact that the baby boom generation is rapidly approaching both retirement and an age where they will require more intense health care services.

The Baby Boom

The baby boom bubble holds a major key to understanding how this shortage came about and why it is so critical. From 1946 to 1964, the post–World War II years, the number of babies born exploded. In the United States alone, approximately 76 million baby boomers were born during this time. The 1990 census reported a population of 77 million boomers. (This includes immigrants and subtracts deaths.)

In the eleven years immediately following the baby boom, 1965–1976, there was a significant decline in the number of births. This group is often referred to as the baby busters and more recently, Generation X. At the time of the 1990 census, there were 44 million baby busters (including immigrants and subtracting deaths). There was a small baby boom from 1976–1981, and as those known as Generation Y come of age, there will be a slight improvement in the ratio of workforce to baby boomers.

As the baby boomers age and retire, the number of available replacements significantly declines. By 2011, the first of these boomers turned sixty-five. By 2020, half of the current RN workforce will reach retirement age.

Compound this decline in new members available for the workforce with the fact that by 2008, the number of jobs for RNs grew by 23 percent (according to the U.S. Bureau of Labor Statistics). By 2018, the U.S. Bureau of Labor Statistics reports that there will be a need for more than 580,000 new and replacement nurses, and by 2020, that number will rise to 800,000. The average age of new nurses graduating today is thirty-one. This means these new nurses will have a shorter time span in the workforce, and with the ever-increasing need for more nurses, this shortage is not going to be short-lived.

FACT

According to a report published by the American Association of Colleges of Nursing (AACN), over 54,991 qualified applicants to BSN and graduate nursing programs were turned down for admission for the 2009–2010 school term. The reasons cited continue to be the same problems seen for at least a decade: insufficient qualified nursing faculty, lack of classrooms and clinical space, too few clinical preceptors, and budget constraints.

As anyone can imagine, this shortage already has had and will continue to have a huge impact on health care. Staffing shortages have caused a great deal of job dissatisfaction for nurses everywhere, not just in hospitals. This dissatisfaction has led to burn out and nurses leaving the nursing profession altogether. Obviously, this doesn't help solve the shortage.

Shortage Temporarily Stalled

The recession of 2008 and the years leading up to it caused a significant economic hardship for all Americans. Retirement funds in 401Ks, IRAs, and so on incurred huge losses, making it impossible for many nurses to retire. Job losses for spouses caused many retired or semi-retired nurses to return to the field. Hospitals grabbed them up and soon new grad nurses began to find it difficult to get jobs, especially in the large metropolitan areas.

Travel nursing took a huge hit, especially in the larger markets, as well as in many of the smaller ones. Where nurses had become accustomed to demanding salaries and perks, suddenly, without the high demand, they found themselves taking the best jobs they could get and settling in. Sign-on bonuses became a thing of the past. And employers found themselves in the power seat again.

With mandates to improve quality of care or face fines, hospitals cut back on hiring nurses who had little to no experience, and they began to demand higher-degreed nurses as well. Additionally, the use of unlicensed assistive personnel (UAPs) has seen a generalized decline in favor of experienced nurses.

Nasty rumors began to emerge that no new nurses could find jobs and there was no longer any shortage of nurses. Consequently, students began to look for other career options. The danger with this is that, as the economy recovers and older nurses have the opportunity, they will retire. This may result in a mass exodus of nurses and create a nursing shortage of critical levels over a very short period of time. Despite a slowdown, the need for new and replacement nurses for the future continues to grow. While it is true that some new grads are currently having a difficult time finding a job, not all of them are (see discussion in Chapter 4).

What Can Nurses Do to Help?

One of the most important things that nurses need to continue to do is band together to advocate for their own cause. Legislators working with nursing organizations have passed laws in a number of states to reduce the patient-to-nurse ratio. This is a Catch-22 situation that forces hospitals to close beds if they don't have enough staff to care for the patients. However, it reduces the potential for harm to patients when inadequate staffing is allowed to continue.

Patients are being made responsible for their own health care issues. In past years, a patient might spend several days in the hospital for a minor illness or injury. Today, patients continue to be sent home much sooner with instructions for self-care. A whiny hypochondriac might spend a few hours in an emergency room, but won't necessarily be admitted without due cause, thereby wasting valuable time and resources. The Patient Protection and Affordable Care Act signed into law in 2010 includes several provisions to help address the shortage of nurses. This includes increased funding for educating nurse educators. Time will tell whether Congress repeals the entire act, or serves to fix the problems and leaves alone the essential parts of this law.

In the United States today, emphasis continues to be placed on promoting preventive care as well as general health and wellness. A holistic approach including diet, exercise, personal hygiene, and lifestyle issues presents nurses with an expanding role in patient education and the promotion of healthy living. Nurses continue to be more specialized and skilled, and are asked to assume many roles within that specialization to improve patient outcomes and quality-of-care issues. For example, an RN is no longer just highly skilled in handling an acute illness and all the tubes and machines involved in helping the patient get better. Now he is involved in discharge planning for that patient as well. This requires educating the patient and family in the nature of the illness, how to prevent a recurrence, when to report symptoms to the doctor, and how to arrange follow-up care at home. The nurse has to understand the reimbursement issues for the patient's insurance or Medicare, what community resources are available, and how to set in motion all the aspects of care to prevent re-hospitalization.

Hospitals and other health care facilities have begun to really listen to their staff, not only about how to recruit, but more important, how to retain the staff they have invested time and money in. Split shifts, job sharing, and more flexibility with schedules seem to be important issues for nurses, especially those with families. Nurses need to step up and offer suggestions and get involved in the process to improve working conditions and staff retention.

CHAPTER 3

How to Become a Nurse

There are a number of ways in which you can become a nurse. The one most highly recommended is to obtain a minimum of a Bachelor of Science in Nursing (BSN). Studies have shown that patients experience better outcomes and a decrease in mortality rates in situations and environments where they are cared for by a higher number of BSN-prepared nurses. Therefore, the American Association of Colleges of Nursing (AACN) advocated for two-thirds (66 percent) of the nursing force to be composed of BSN- and MSN-prepared nurses by 2010. Although this goal was not reached, it continues to be a primary focus of the AACN.

Prepare in High School

Nursing is a highly skilled profession that is based on a strong understanding of physical sciences, such as chemistry and physics, and life sciences, such as biology, microbiology, anatomy, and physiology, as well as math and computer skills.

Social sciences, such as sociology and psychology, will also play an important role in the holistic approach to patient care. Cultural differences, coping mechanisms, and emotional issues all affect the patient's ability to understand and make the necessary lifestyle changes to prevent illness and promote health.

Nurses also need a strong sense of compassion and empathy and a desire to help people and alleviate pain and suffering. As a nurse, you will need to be emotionally stable and able to help patients and families cope with illness, pain, suffering, birth, loss, and death.

Entrance Exams

Nursing schools will require a variety of entrance exams. Almost all schools require one of the College Board exams, such as the Scholastic Aptitude Test (SAT) or the American College Test (ACT). In addition, many nursing schools may now require one of several nursing entrance exams, such as the NET, the TEAS, or the HESI A2. The College Board exams test language and math skills and branch into essay exams in specific areas of study, such as foreign language, sciences, and history.

The nursing entrance exams test skills in math and reading comprehension and the rate at which you read. A proficiency level in algebra is expected as well as a reading comprehension at a minimum tenth-grade level. Algebra is required for tasks such as adjusting and verifying medication administration scenarios. The reading comprehension at a tenth-grade level is necessary for comprehending most science textbooks.

In addition to testing math, reading, and reading comprehension, these tests may include such things as your test-taking skills, learning style, decision-making skills, and personality traits. They are used to help predict not only if you can pass the prerequisites and nursing classes, but also how likely you are to become licensed as and remain a nurse. They are used to rank you in the admissions process.

If you are in school, work with your guidance and career center counselors to determine a course of study that prepares you for a career in nursing. Utilize the resource materials available on the Internet and in your school or public library to determine which entrance exams are needed. Locate practice test materials or live opportunities to determine your abilities to excel on these exams.

Computer Skills

Basic computer skills are essential to almost any career now, and nursing is no exception. You will need word processing skills and a good understanding of how to research topics on the Internet in order to survive college or vocational school. Health care is rapidly becoming automated, from programmable pumps for IVs to computerized medical records. A comfort level in utilizing computers is essential for anyone pursuing a nursing career today.

Be an Aide First

It used to be optional to become a nurse's aide first, but today, many nursing schools require applicants to have had some experience in the health care field. Even for those schools that don't require it yet, employment or volunteer work in a related health care facility may make the difference between being accepted and having to be placed on a waiting list to reapply to an overcrowded program.

Becoming an Aide

Basic training to be a nurse's aide is usually available through an adult education program in your community. Some community colleges and vocational schools also offer CNA training. Each state regulates nurse's aides and the certificate programs. Nurse's aides are not licensed medical personnel. The training usually takes six to nine weeks and provides 120–150 hours of classroom and hands-on instruction.

Nurse's aides are allowed to assist in the care of patients in such tasks as taking and reporting vital signs and activities of daily living (ADLs), such as feeding, bathing, oral hygiene and nail care, dressing, transferring, and walking.

This experience will offer you exposure to patient care and the basics of bedside nursing. You will see nurses in action and gain an inside edge in better understanding the roles and functions of the health care team.

Advantages of Being an Aide

One of the advantages this experience provides is that it helps candidates to find out for themselves whether nursing is what they imagined it to be. It also provides potential nursing students with a firsthand sense of what nurses actually do and what their responsibilities are and gives a better understanding of the need for a strong background in science and math. Those students with health care experience tend to be more successful in nursing programs.

The primary advantage to the student is that he or she can work part-time as an aide while attending nursing school. As an aide, the student can earn a reasonable wage in an environment that understands the need for flexible options and scheduling around their classes. Although many schools may discourage students from working, this is often not possible financially. Working as an aide also gives students access to their most valuable resource: nurses.

Choosing the Program for You

Deciding where to enter the nursing field is a personal choice. Many factors may influence your decision, including, but not limited to, financial considerations, family situations, and a choice of how much responsibility you want to have. Professional and educational goals will determine which program is right for you.

In choosing the program that meets your goals, you will need to know where you think you would like to work and the amount of supervision or autonomy you need or want to have. You will also have to explore such factors as the financial requirements and the amount of time you want to devote to a nursing program at this point in your career.

Most employers offer some kind of tuition reimbursement to help their nurses advance their education. In most cases, this assistance requires an employment commitment, but some employers are becoming creative in their recruitment efforts and will pay off this commitment to another facility in order to entice a nurse to hire on. Be careful what you might have to commit to in order to receive financial aid.

QUESTION

Should I decide ahead of time what kind of nurse I want to be or what area I'd like to work in?
If you have an idea whether you would like to work strictly as a bedside nurse, in the ICU, or in pediatrics or become the CEO of a hospital, this information will help guide you as you select the program you want to enter. But most student nurses fall in love with a specialty many times over during their clinical rotations.

Being a Technical Nurse (LVN/LPN)

Many nurses begin and end their career as a technical or bedside nurse. They make some of the most excellent nurses because they love providing this level of care.

The LVN/LPN program prepares you to provide basic nursing and to perform specific tasks under the supervision of an RN or a doctor. These tasks may include such things as wound care, tube care (e.g., gastrostomies, tracheostomies, and jejunostomies), Foley catheter insertion and care, enemas, medication administration, and venipuncture. With additional certification, IV care is an expanded role and one that is being redefined to encompass ever-greater responsibility. Many states are phasing out LPNs, and, in these areas, LPNs can usually only work in long-term care settings.

For others, becoming an LVN/LPN is a stepping-stone. After a twelve- to fifteen-month program and successfully completing the NCLEX-LPN board examination, the LPN can practice as a nurse while pursuing further education to become an RN. There are a rapidly growing number of LPN-RN and even LPN-BSN programs available that provide educational credits for professional experiences and afford nurses a somewhat accelerated program for advancing their education.

Becoming an RN

Nursing students today are being encouraged to obtain a BSN. As health care becomes much more technical and specialized, employers are seeking out BSN-prepared nurses. The nursing shortage and health care reform are forcing nurses to think outside the box and provide higher-level, higher-quality care to their patients in a shorter time. The BSN program is more intellectually challenging and better prepares nurses to adapt to and seek out these expanding roles.

There are three options for becoming an RN: the diploma, the associate's degree, and the bachelor's degree. Advance practice nurses hold a master's degree in nursing.

A Diploma Program

Diploma programs are rapidly disappearing. There are fewer than fifty programs nationwide. These are typically three-year programs primarily run in a hospital setting. Students work in the hospital and accumulate an intense hands-on experience. The students earn a diploma, not a degree. However, an option to go from RN to BSN is available to qualified diploma nurses.

Associate's Degree

The next option is a two-year degree program in which the student earns an associate's degree in nursing. The ADN program combines general education liberal arts studies with the sciences, nursing procedures, and an introduction to nursing theory and sometimes leadership. There are also an expanding number of ADN-BSN programs available for continuing the education process.

Bachelor's Degree (BSN)

The third option is a four-year program in which the student earns a bachelor's degree in nursing. This combines a program of liberal arts and sciences with studies of nursing theory and leadership, as well as clinical skills. Critical thinking skills and the ability to organize, prioritize, plan, and think on your feet are more refined in the BSN program.

Pay scales vary from one employer to another in regard to level of education. Most employers do pay more for more education, while others do not. As more employers demand a BSN, the pay scale should begin to change for all RNs. The fact that some employers have gotten away without paying more for more education seems to stem from a situation unique to the employer and its ability to recruit and hire nurses, but it is a disservice to all nurses everywhere. This has served as a deterrent to many nurses who have questioned the need for more education if they don't get paid for having it.

There has also been a history of much debate over whether the BSN education actually provides far less clinical experience than the diploma or ADN programs do. The pros and cons of clinical versus theoretical preparation can be argued to death. What it really boils down to is the role each nurse is filling and whether she is prepared for that role and how she affects the quality and outcomes of patient care. Many studies by health care quality organizations, such as the Agency for Health Care Research and Quality (AHRQ), over the last ten to fifteen years have shown that patients cared for by nurses with a BSN or higher education have a lower mortality rate than if their nurses were diploma or ADN prepared.

Online Education

Online education options are available for all levels of health care workers. However, these programs are not for everyone. In general, they require an intense level of self-motivation and self-discipline. Some programs offer an opportunity to earn your entire nursing education from an online venue. Be aware that most of these programs are not accredited. For the rare one that may be, the student is advised to carefully consider his personal ability to translate what he has learned in pictures, written instructions, and videos into an ability to perform the skill in a work environment. This may work well for some but not for everyone. Certainly, nursing requires hands-on practice and education.

Even in BSN programs where clinical experiences may be forgone in favor of spending more time on the theoretical, students usually have the opportunity to see a procedure "live" even if they don't actually get an opportunity to perform it personally.

ESSENTIAL

Non-clinical classes online may be the way to go for many students. But try out one or two first to see how you fare. Some people swear by them and others can't learn that way at all.

A program that consists of 100 percent online education may afford students more flexibility in completing courses in their own time frame, but are they sacrificing skill?

One of the factors influencing an online program's accreditation is whether it requires some additional onsite clinical preparation, which is required to sit for the NCLEX.

The LVN/LPN-BSN, RN-BSN, and BSN-MSN online programs, on the other hand, are for nurses who have been practicing and have hands-on skills. Make an informed decision about any online nursing program.

Finding the Right School

Once you have narrowed down the type of nursing program you want, it's time to find the school that provides it for you. And, of course, you have more choices to make. Do you want to go away to school or stay near home? Do you want to go to a big school or a smaller one? Does the school offer small-sized classes with individual attention if you need it? Sometimes the choices will be made for you because either you can't find a program near your home or you can't go away to school for any number of other reasons.

You can find lists of nursing schools online or in the library or career center. Here are three of the most popular and useful sites for researching nursing schools:

- *www.petersons.com* (Peterson's College Guides)
- *www.nsna.org* (National Student Nurses' Association)

- *www.discovernursing.com* (Johnson & Johnson's site for all things nursing)

Some of the other factors that might be very important to you include the NCLEX pass rate over at least the last five years, the average class size, and whether the faculty is expected to continue practicing nursing. If you have all PhD professors who haven't touched a patient in ten years, you might not be getting the most current clinical education.

Small classes can be intimidating to some because it's not easy to be invisible. Your instructor is going to know everyone's name and who's missing from a class. Yet, in a big school, beginning nurses can get lost in the shuffle, never to appear again. Larger schools will have more fiscal resources, but a smaller environment might be better for you. These are all things you will have to weigh.

Check the class schedule and see how many facilities are used for clinical rotations. How many clinical rotations does the school offer? Read the bios of the faculty. How diverse is their makeup? Is a labor/delivery nurse teaching the clinical rotation through ICU?

FACT

Whatever educational program you choose to enter, one of the most important factors is making sure that the program is accredited by the National League for Nursing Accrediting Commission (NLNAC). You must attend an accredited school in order to take the licensing nursing board exams. Be aware that there are nursing schools that are not accredited. Visit NLNAC's website for further information at *www.nlnac.org.*

Other things to consider are the ethnic makeup and social diversity and how you fit into the picture. You want to feel comfortable. If you're an older student, are all your classmates going to be brand new high school graduates? If you are devoutly religious and politically conservative, will you feel out of place in an extremely liberal environment? If you're going to reside on campus, you want to have the best options for getting a great roommate.

Visit the campus if possible, or ask to have a nursing student contact you so you can get a feel for the social culture, learning environment, and atmosphere of the school. Visit the school library, technology labs, and bookstore. Thumb through the textbooks. If you're going to live on campus, how convenient are the amenities that are important to you, such as churches, shopping, laundry, and recreational venues such as movie theaters and sporting events? How accessible is transportation? Will you have a car? What about parking? How much is transportation back home? How many times will you want to go back and forth for holidays, spring break, and summer?

What about other costs? How much is tuition? What can you expect to spend for books? Don't forget lab fees, parking fees, and student fees. The cost of uniforms and nurse's shoes will add up too. Do you need to order them from the school or purchase on your own? You'll also need bandage scissors, a stethoscope (a five-way is best), and a watch with a second hand that you can read easily.

Financial Aid

Next you need to figure out how to pay for your schooling. How far will your college savings account go? How much can you afford? How much will you need to supplement? Are you eligible for scholarships or grants or will you need education loans?

ALERT

There are a large number of scams and con artists out there who will promise you the moon to help you finance your education. The truth is you can do anything a professional financial counselor can do and even more. You might find a seminar given by counselors helpful, but take all the information they give you and run straight to your computer to begin the search yourself.

Everyone has to complete a Free Application for Federal Student Aid (FAFSA) to determine financial aid eligibility. All schools will need this information for their financial aid departments. You can complete this online at *www.fafsa.ed.gov*. Be sure to read the overview information first to understand the process and to help you avoid scams. The FAFSA will determine your financial need and expected family commitment. If you are eligible for federal grants, you will be directed as to how to apply.

Remember, you have to complete all the forms yourself. Your best friend in this process is going to be the financial aid officer at your potential school because she/he will decide what aid you will be awarded. Scams about moving funds and making your income or your family's look smaller are ploys that are well known to financial officers, and using these ploys may adversely affect your aid.

After you have completed your FAFSA, you should explore a few other sites for general financial aid information to help you understand what is actually available and how to avoid the scam artists. Helpful sites include:

- *www.collegeboard.org*
- *www.fastweb.com*
- *www.nursingscholarship.us*

Other resources you should check out include your school, your employer or your parents' employers, community service organizations and clubs in your hometown (especially any that you or your family members participate in), and churches and businesses in your community. Remember that the employer may require specific employment commitments in return for any monies you receive.

In addition to scholarships and grants, you can apply for low-interest education loans. There are several types of these, and you'll probably be required to complete a short online course from your school before you can complete the application. The purpose is to have you sign an acknowledgment that you understand that you have an obligation to repay these loans no matter what. In past years, after students graduated, they would use such tactics as declaring bankruptcy to avoid having to repay the loans. This is no longer possible, and this course instructs you about options if repayment becomes a significant burden.

In some instances, your parents can also apply for low-interest student loans to assist in financing your education. They may also be obligated to complete the online course from your school. They too must complete a FAFSA.

The amount of the loans will be included in the award letter from your school's financial aid officer. If you feel you will need additional funds for costs beyond the officer's estimation, be sure to discuss the matter with the officer upon receipt of the award letter before signing it. The officer's job is to try to keep your obligations (especially loans) to a minimum, but he or she may make unrealistic estimates, especially in the area of transportation to and from school and those additional lab, uniform, and equipment fees. Unexpected financial obligations can undermine your efforts and cause significant stress. Plan ahead!

Some schools also offer tuition payment plans that can minimize the need for aid if you have significant savings or income. Whatever you can afford to pay as you go will offer you savings in the long term. Be sure to explore all your options with your financial officer.

Surviving School

Nursing school, no matter what level you're attempting, is going to be intense and time consuming. Your clinical classes will take place during any and all shifts to give you exposure to the real world as a nurse. Being bright-eyed and bushy tailed at 6:30 A.M. doesn't leave a lot of room for sleep, never mind partying until all hours. Your prerequisite courses, especially in math and sciences, will be comprehensive and exhausting. If you have work and family obligations, you will have an even greater challenge finding time to sleep.

Time Management

There are a number of online resources for time management tools, such as calendars and communication tools. Yahoo!'s groups and Google groups offer free sites for chats, calendars, message boards, study groups, posting information, sharing notes, etc. This can be set up by your instructor or a small group of students, or your nursing school may set up a group for your school. There are many generic groups for nursing students to share information or to vent frustrations with students from other schools.

Each individual can add information to his own portal for his own reminders or to share schedules with family members. Facebook and Twitter and other social networking tools offer opportunities to communicate with your group members and stay current with activities and events as well. These notifications can come to your phone and instantaneously update you.

ESSENTIAL

Time management skills and tools are essential to surviving nursing school even for the student who has no outside obligations. Learning to use a calendar and to schedule everything in your life, including meals and sleep, will become second nature to you.

Students with children or other family obligations often find themselves neglecting family and friends altogether, especially during peak periods such as midterms and finals. Using tools such as calendars can help your family and friends know your schedule and help you find a few precious moments to share together.

Study Groups

Finding and forming study groups with your fellow nursing students is one of the most important steps you can take. The sooner you do so, the better. No one is going to understand the challenges you face better than a fellow nursing student.

You will also begin to form the kinds of bonds that will teach you (and reinforce) the basics of teamwork. Some students will emerge as natural leaders and others will learn support skills. Of course, there will be one or two who don't keep up their responsibilities, and you will learn how this affects the team and how to deal with them.

FACT

Working in groups helps you learn to share tips for studying or remembering facts. Sometimes a fellow student's explanation of something will make much more sense than the textbook or the professor does.

Forming study groups also helps you learn to network, build friendships, and have an outlet for expressing fears and frustrations. You will encounter students from all walks of life. You will all share a common bond of wanting to be nurses. Working together and bonding will help each of you build a solid foundation to become the best nurse you can be.

Stress Management

Stress management is another vital tool for surviving the rigors of nursing school. It goes hand in hand with time management, but stress management goes further toward helping you to cope, especially when time gets away from you or it just cannot be managed. Nursing school is intense and if you cannot find some time to relax and relieve the stress, it will get the best of you, guaranteed.

Taking time to practice yoga or take a run or brisk walk might seem like time better spent studying, but the truth is, taking the time to de-stress and clear your mind can be better than hours of endless, intense studying. A balance is essential to a healthy mind and body. Learning to do this now can be a tremendous help later on during stressful times in your career.

Use Your Time Wisely

Take advantage of every spare minute you have. Study or do homework in between classes. Read your texts on the bus ride to and from school. Hang sticky notes with questions or important tidbits of information in such places as the mirror in your bathroom to review while brushing your teeth or on the refrigerator or other places you frequent in your dwelling to help you review as you go about your activities of daily living.

ESSENTIAL

Call or text message a study group member for a quick quiz on a troublesome subject a few minutes before that dreaded exam. Tape class lectures to review in the car or on the bus.

Try to minimize your outside responsibilities. If you need to work, try to work only as much as you absolutely have to in order to meet your very frugal budget. If you have a family, get family members to pitch in as much as they can to help around the house or hire some part-time help. Schedule some special time to be with your loved ones. You could even have them quiz you or be your patient as you practice making an occupied bed or giving a bed bath.

Your First Clinicals

When it comes to clinicals, be prepared. Read up on the patient's diagnosis and treatment modalities, including medications, and be prepared to describe the patient, his symptoms, and his response to care.

You will be nervous and scared the first time you have to do anything. The first thing the patient is going to ask is if you've done this before. On a rare occasion you might have to fib a little, but in most cases, being honest and telling them you're trained and prepared and that your instructor or preceptor is right there just in case will be just fine. Patients expect nurses to be honest and ethical. If you tell them what's going on, they're usually happy to cooperate. And if they're too scared to let you practice on them, then it's usually for the best if you don't. Be confident and mature. If you squeal and flinch, you're going to terrify the patient and your instructor won't be pleased!

Look for opportunities to observe and ask for a chance to perform and demonstrate your skills whenever possible. This is where you will learn. Understand if someone tells you no, particularly if your instructor is busy helping another student. Sometimes the nurses just don't have time to help you, and sometimes you'll encounter a nurse who has forgotten what it's like to be a student. Some of the floor nurses love students, some tolerate them, and some absolutely hate students! The reasons why are not always important.

ALERT

Some instructors love to intimidate their students and others tend to mother them to death. If you are mature and adult in your behavior, you should be able to handle any situation with tact and finesse.

Not all clinical instructors are created equal either. Some are current with their skills and some haven't touched a patient in ten years. Occasionally, you may encounter one who went straight for the PhD and has never done any real nursing. Some will be demanding and others entirely too laid back.

Your education is going to depend a lot on you and how assertive you are. Review the clinical objectives of your course and make your own checklist of skills you're expected to learn for that rotation. Long before the end of the term, you should be reminding your instructor of anything you haven't at least seen being performed. If you fade into the woodwork and hope never to be called on, don't be surprised if you find yourself moving from one rotation to another without amassing enough clinical skill to make you feel comfortable when you're out in the real world. Or if you have a professor who hides from the students and isn't around enough to help you obtain and refine your skills, you might be likewise ill prepared if you don't speak up.

Graduating and Preparing for the NCLEX

You made it. You survived your surgical rotation without fainting each time the surgeon made the first incision, you saw many births, and you held a few hands while patients faced death and even when one or two let go and left this world. You emptied a lifetime's share of bedpans and urinals, and now your favorite dream is anything that doesn't include hours of lung sounds and heart sounds and bowel sounds.

Celebrate! You passed and now it's on to the real world of nursing. You may receive your pin and/or diploma in a private ceremony. You might also attend the graduation exercises for your school, but you are done!

The Nursing Oath

One of the most common elements of nursing graduation programs is the Nightingale Pledge, often referred to as the Nursing Oath.

I solemnly pledge myself before God and in the presence of this assembly, to pass my life in purity and to practice my profession faithfully. I will abstain from whatever is deleterious and mischievous and will not take or administer any harmful drug. I will do all in my power to maintain and elevate the standard of my profession and will hold in confidence all personal matters committed to my keeping and all family affairs coming to my knowledge in the practice of my calling. With loyalty will I endeavor to aid the physician in his work and devote myself to the welfare of those committed to my care.

This pledge is an adaptation of the physician's Hippocratic Oath. It was written in 1893 by Lystra E. Gretter and a committee from the Farrand Training School for Nurses in Detroit, Michigan, in honor of Florence Nightingale and all that she had done to elevate the profession of nursing.

Preparing for the NCLEX

After graduation, many students experience a withdrawal syndrome. After spending such an intense time with their classmates, not seeing each other on a daily basis can be difficult. If you use this time wisely to gather your former classmates together for group study sessions for the NCLEX, it can be advantageous in many ways. Not only does group study relieve the withdrawal symptoms, but it also re-establishes effective study habits.

Many schools require students to take NCLEX preparation exams during their course of study and some require students to pass a mock test in order to graduate. Taking these tests as you go along in school not only helps to prepare you for the NCLEX by sharpening your test-taking skills but also serves to reinforce your knowledge and test-taking skills and to point out your weaknesses.

CHAPTER 4

Deciding Where to Work

Congratulations, you made it through school! Now it's time to find your first nursing job and get some experience under your belt. If you found yourself graduating with less experience than you had hoped to have, this is your opportunity to expand your skills and build your confidence. Even if you have a very specific idea of where you want to work and what you would like to specialize in, you will be well served to have a well-rounded background of med-surg (medical-surgical) experience to build on if possible.

It's Not Easy to Find a Job

The economic downturn that began in 2000 and became a recession by 2008 adversely affected the health care industry in many ways. Job losses and dissolving 401k and other retirement funds caused many older nurses to delay retirement or to return to the field from an inactive status or retirement. Employers grabbed up these experienced nurses in lieu of hiring new grad nurses.

Health care jobs were already becoming scarce because increasing unemployment decreased the numbers of people with health care insurance. In uncertain times, elective care is often put on hold. And even in the face of a pandemic from the H1N1 flu virus, Americans scrambled to do everything possible to stay well and avoid the high costs of health care. Consequently, there were far fewer hospitalizations from complications of the flu or other illnesses. In a majority of facilities, lower numbers of patients led to a decreased need for more and/or new nurses. This has created a false sense of security that the nursing shortage has ended when indeed it has not.

As the economy recovers, the Patient Protection and Affordable Care Act is implemented, and more people have access to health care coverage, the need for nurses will grow once again. This time it could possibly grow exponentially and almost overnight.

With 1 million more potential patients having access to health care, the need for more nurses will expand. And as older nurses have the opportunity to retire with financial stability, there may be a mass exodus.

Until that time, new grads may be hard pressed to find jobs. Hospitals have a renewed power to pick and choose who they want instead of a desperate need for just a warm body to provide nursing care. With new mandates to improve the quality of care or face huge fines, hospitals will continue to look for nurses with higher levels of education as well as experience.

If you're a new grad with less than a BSN-prepared education, this may be the perfect time to continue your education. The future of nursing is going to be about expanding roles in patient education and providing primary care. For example, the need for nurse practitioners will grow faster than most.

You may also have to consider looking for employment in less popular, less populated areas. Markets such as large metropolitan areas are saturated and are likely to remain so for quite some time despite the economy. Many small towns and rural areas are in great need of nurses. After gaining some experience in a year or two, you may find yourself much more valuable in the location you prefer.

You may also have to consider less popular non-hospital settings such as clinics, long-term care, community or public health, mental health, or rehabilitation. Some suggest working as a CNA or finding a non-nursing job in the setting you prefer so that you can become known.

Why Choose a Large Teaching Hospital?

If at all possible, one of the best places to train is a hospital associated with a medical school. By the same token, your first job as a nurse in one of these facilities can be one of the best experiences you may have in your career. Patients in a teaching hospital are primed for students, and these patients have a good understanding of the culture in a learning environment. These facilities often have more funds available to afford state-of-the-art equipment. The doctors are usually well versed on the latest in procedures and treatments. In addition, you will be exposed to patients with far more complex diseases and those having experimental treatments.

Start General—Then Specialize

Once you have gained a strong foundation of experience in basic nursing care for adults, you can branch out into more specialized care, giving you options to go anywhere in your career. You will always have the confidence that you have developed your skills and seen and done a wide variety of procedures successfully. If you don't have this opportunity, opt for the most general experience you can get in your area. No matter how much experience you may have gained in school, a good solid foundation as a generalist will give you the tools to build your career in any area of nursing.

This general background will give you both the experience and the credibility to be able to move laterally and to move upward. The additional advantage is that even after a long career in a highly specialized area, most nurses with a strong generalist foundation will find the courage to move into an entirely new realm much more often than those who headed straight to their specialty area after graduation and stayed there for ten years. These nurses tend to feel trapped because they have been pigeonholed and don't have a general background to fall back on.

ESSENTIAL

Not all new nurses will find jobs in general med-surg nursing, but if you have an opportunity to do it first, grab it. If not, try to float through as a per diem nurse. You won't regret it. Some nurses feel that it is not necessary to have a year's experience in med-surg nursing. However, if you want to eventually move into something like home health or another field in which you will have a lot of autonomy, you need a strong general background.

One of the reasons most nurses leave nursing is because of burnout and feeling trapped with nowhere to go because they are too specialized and making a change would take too much re-education. This seems to be especially true for those wishing to move from something like pediatrics into adult care. The nurse with the general med-surg background has many opportunities to move directly out of the hospital into such areas as clinics, home health, and case management. With some additional training or internship in a specialized area, they can move into a multitude of areas such as ICU, pediatrics, rehab, oncology, and women's health and clinical trials.

Broaden Your Horizons

As the economy recovers and the nursing shortage grows, things will change once again. The one advantage of a nursing shortage is that you can find a job almost anywhere. If this opportunity presents itself to you, take advantage of it and get the best experience you can in your first year. Then the whole world of nursing will be wide open to you. Look for an opportunity in a supportive environment. When the nursing shortage worsens, you might find yourself working in an area staffed primarily by new grads and nurses who have only one or two years of experience. This won't afford you the best scenario for finding help and guidance as a new nurse.

Think about some of the hospitals where you have done your clinical rotations. Which one might offer you the best opportunity to spend at least your first year gathering all the experience you can get?

ESSENTIAL

Some career counselors feel that nurses can move into any field with ease and succeed because of the nurses' training and their strong critical thinking skills. Nurses have a well-rounded education and are trained to think on their feet.

As the nursing shortage grows, look for renewed opportunities, such as externships or long-term orientation programs. Externship programs are usually offered to student nurses during the summer months. You work in a clinical environment under the supervision of a preceptor. This is an opportunity for private tutoring to learn procedures and to see firsthand the day-to-day functioning of the hospital. Unlike an assignment in school where you may only care for one or two patients on a very limited basis, in an externship program you will work with your preceptor as he performs his daily duties.

Working as a Graduate Nurse

Some states allow new graduates to work as a graduate nurse (GN), which gives them the privileges of working as an RN prior to taking and passing the NCLEX. Not all states allow this, so you need to check with your state's Board of Registered Nursing.

In addition to the rules set by each state for graduate nurses, hospitals may impose even stricter regulations for GNs. For instance, a GN might be granted full RN privileges in a particular state, with the exception that she must sign documents with her GN status instead of using the RN. In addition, there might be other restrictions: A GN might only be allowed to work on the day shift (whether eight- or twelve-hour shifts) and must have a preceptor assigned to her. She may not perform any procedure until her preceptor checks her, dispense any controlled substance medications, or take verbal orders from a doctor.

FACT

You can find a list of all State Boards of Nursing at *www.ncsbn.org*. This is the National Council on State Boards of Nursing. Website addresses and contact information are given for all fifty states. They will include information or links to the LVN/LPN boards as well.

For students who will not be able to work as GNs because their state law prohibits it, seek out other opportunities for employment in the health care field such as in an emergency department or EKG (electrocardiograph) tech. These positions are often available to students as well as graduate nurses in addition to nursing assistant roles. Any of these positions will provide you with a firsthand view of how a particular facility or hospital runs and whether it will offer you the experience that you will need once you get your license.

Passing the NCLEX

Don't despair, not every nurse will pass the first time. Some have even had to take it three or four times! Any number of factors can affect whether you pass. One of the most important reasons for taking practice tests throughout your nursing education and then again in final preparation for the NCLEX is that it helps you to know and understand your weaknesses and strengths. This allows you to spend more time brushing up on areas you don't know as well. But don't forget to take one last quick review of your strong areas.

As soon as you walk out of the test, you should have a good idea of what you nailed and what areas you struggled with. Write down the things that you immediately remember having had difficulty with. Whether or not you pass, you need to review these things to improve your knowledge base.

If you didn't pass, you know what you need to concentrate on for next time. Take a break and don't beat yourself up. Try to examine the outside factors that may have influenced your performance. Did you have something to eat before the test? What time of day did you take the test? Was that a peak performance time of the day for you? Did you have a fight with your significant other? Were you rushed to get to the test site? Did you get lost or have a hard time finding parking? All these things could have been enough to distract you even just a little so that you were not at your best.

QUESTION

If I don't pass, can I take the NCLEX again right away?
No, you will often have to wait as many as ninety days. Check with your testing center for the exact wait time and procedure to reregister and reschedule. Be sure to do this right away. Don't hesitate or wait.

Everyone is nervous, but were you especially so? What could you have done to help yourself relax a little more? Examine all these factors and see which ones you can better control next time. Make a mental note or write them down for yourself.

Learn from your mistakes. Take the opportunity to seek out patients and scenarios that were troublesome for you and understand why your answers were incorrect.

You won't receive a copy of your test, so you will have to rely on your memory of what was difficult for you. You should also double-check anything you felt you nailed to be sure you did.

ESSENTIAL

Check for practice tests online. Search for "NCLEX" and look at as many of the sites that come up as you can. Some are free and some require fees that can vary greatly. Start with the free ones, of course. Improve your knowledge, build your confidence, and go and take the test again.

In a few days, begin to study again. Go to the bookstores and look through all the preparation guide materials. Maybe a different source will pose questions or scenarios in a different way and help you to understand and remember them better.

If you have been working as a GN, you won't be able to continue at this status. Perhaps your hospital or facility will allow you to stay on as a nursing assistant. This would be valuable, as you can continue to observe procedures and scenarios that will help you learn and review for your next testing session. As you will have seen, the NCLEX tests your knowledge of facts, as well as the nursing process. If you struggled with the nursing process, then you really need to spend time in patient care to get a good foundation of how it works. Even if you have to take on another role, such as an EKG tech, you should be observing the nursing process from every angle and imagining what you would do and how you would proceed in the same situation.

Being a Hospital Nurse

You don't have to be a hospital nurse forever, but you do need to have a solid foundation of skills and the best place to get that is in a hospital. If you have worked as an aide for a year or more and have had the opportunity to observe procedures and treatments and have had a very strong clinical education, you might not need as much experience. However, nurses and even physicians don't learn everything they need to know in school.

If you had an externship in the hospital during your schooling, you might also be well prepared. And if you are going to have an internship in another facility or environment, you might be ready to move into another area of nursing. Of course, if you are an LPN who has completed an RN program, you should be able to move into another role more easily as well.

There are many different roles and career options for nurses beyond the hospital setting, and you may have had some exposure to them either from clinical rotations or through previous careers. In many of these options, you will most likely have more autonomy and are less likely to have many more nurses around to help when you encounter a situation you are unsure of. You need to have a solid foundation of skills, including assessment and critical thinking skills in order to provide the best quality care to your patients. A hospital experience can provide you with exposure to more than you may ever need to know, yet it can also help to ensure that you can face any situation with confidence and skill for at least basic care until more advanced help can be accessed.

FACT

In a hospital environment, you will work with several nurses at a time and be able to pick their brains for tricks and tips that will be invaluable to you throughout your career for handling situations and performing procedures. In another environment, you may not have as many colleagues immediately available to consult for help and to learn from.

Be aware, however, that many positions require, if not highly recommend, one year's recent acute hospital experience. This is true even for new RNs who were LPNs prior to continuing their education. The reason is that the RN role is more advanced, particularly in the areas of assessment, leadership, and critical thinking responsibilities.

Talk to the nurses who work in the field you are interested in and get their opinions on the best way to gain the skills and experience necessary for that role. This will be the beginning of a lifetime of networking. Be sure to thank them for their advice.

A year from now, you will look back and realize that what you learned in school is by comparison a mere grain of sand in your eye to what you have learned in the past 365 days. Make the most of it and you'll never regret it.

The Interview

This is a critical time in your first career option as a nurse. You might have been offered a job by one of the departments you did your training in. Try not to jump at the first opportunity even if it's exactly what you always wanted and you love the department and all the nurses in it. Investigate it and give it some thought before you say yes.

You don't want to find yourself working in that department on a different shift with all inexperienced nurses and short staffed to boot. Be flattered and enjoy the moment. Then sit down for a serious talk with the department head and ask questions:

- What shift would I be working on?
- How many nurses work that shift (what is the nurse-to-patient ratio) and who is in charge?
- How much experience do the nurses have whom I would be working with?
- Are there unlicensed assistive personnel (UAP) or patient care assistants (PCAs) on the unit? How many and who supervises them?
- What type of orientation would I have and for how long? Will it be on the shift I'm going to work?
- Who will be my preceptor or mentor? How long will I be able to, or be expected to, work with a preceptor?
- Are there unit educators and are they available on all shifts?

Then there are the basic questions you should ask any potential employer, such as:

- What type of equipment do I need to have? Do I have to purchase it?
- What style uniform or attire am I required to wear? Any specific shoes?
- Are there restrictions on jewelry, hair, makeup, nails, etc.?
- What are the rules about working weekends and holidays and who makes up the assignments? How do I request time off?
- What types of benefits are available and what do they cost? When do they start?
- How much malpractice insurance is provided and do I need my own policy? (This is always a good idea even if they say you don't need it.)
- Ask to see a copy of the job description.
- Will I have to be on call and what all does that entail?
- Will I have to float to other departments and how often might I have to work with floaters on my floor?
- How will my performance be evaluated, by whom, and how often?
- What is the probation period?
- Do they offer tuition reimbursement? Can I request time off to attend continuing education courses?

You should also have a professional interview with the director of nursing and most likely the human resources department. Be professional.

Dress appropriately. Smile, have a firm handshake, and make good eye contact. Be aware of your body language. Be attentive and honest with your answers. Have your questions written down so that you don't forget anything. Ask the same questions that you did in the more informal interview so that you are aware of any differences in the information, especially regarding policies about weekends, holidays, and floating.

ESSENTIAL

Before you make any decision, make sure you have an understanding of what is expected of you and the rules of the facility. The only dumb question is the one you don't ask. Be professional.

Remember that a job interview is a two-way conversation. You need to interview them as a potential employer as much as the employer needs to interview you as a potential employee to maximize the compatibility factors. Your questions will be as helpful to them as they are to you. The questions should be intelligent and well thought out.

CHAPTER 5

Surviving Your First Day

It's your first day of work as a new nurse. You're nervous and you probably didn't sleep well last night. Take a deep breath and relax; you're ready for this new experience. Eat something even if you think you can't; you won't function long without brain food. Give yourself plenty of time to arrive early without rushing.

Come to Work Prepared

Come prepared, arrive early, and take a moment to relax. Be sure to pack a lunch and a snack just in case you can't find anything in the cafeteria that you can eat. If you're not working in a hospital, you may not have an opportunity to go out for a meal, or perhaps everyone eats in.

Dress Appropriately

Dress the part. You'll never have an opportunity to make a first impression again, so make it a good one from the get-go. Your appearance will be graded by your coworkers, your employer, and your patients. If you look like a nurse, you'll gain respect from everyone. Your clothes should be clean and wrinkle free. You should be clean and impeccably groomed, without perfume or aftershave.

ESSENTIAL

Before your first day, you should know what time you need to be there, what you need to bring, and what type of orientation you'll have. You should have read your job description and your state's Nurse Practice Act. (A copy is available at your state's Board of Nursing website. See *www.ncsbn.org* to find your state board.)

Nursing is a more conservative field in the sense that flashy, fashionable dress is really not appropriate. This is true even in roles where nurses can wear street clothes as opposed to a uniform. If you think about it, would you really like to be cleaning up someone's vomit or incontinent stool in your best dress or in scrubs? On the other hand, would you be more confident in someone who is dressed in clean whites or in someone whose uniform looks like it hasn't been washed in a week and whose hair hasn't been combed since last Thursday? Spend your money on flashy clothes for after hours, and keep to the basics of clean, fresh uniforms and modest jewelry for work.

Bring Your Equipment

In most cases, your first day will only be an orientation. This should include a quick overview and tour of the facility and introduction to the members of the organization with whom you will associate and those you need to know for such things as payroll or parking permits.

Although this may be an all-day orientation, you should come prepared with your nursing equipment unless you were told otherwise. This should include your watch, stethoscope, bandage scissors, pocket flashlight and pen in a pocket holder, and a new edition drug book or a smartphone or mobile device with up-to-date pharmacology software or application. All items should be clearly labeled with your name and contact information. Doctors are notorious for walking off with items such as stethoscopes and bandage scissors.

FACT

You'll need to bring any paperwork you were given. This might include forms you need to return, an employee handbook, your job description, and anything else they asked you to bring when you were hired. Always carry your driver's license, nursing license (if you have it), CPR card, and copies of any certificates you have received. Unless you have already provided your Social Security card, you may need to have this with you as well.

As you meet people and tour the facility, try to get an idea of the culture. How are people addressed? Who is introduced with the most formality? Read the body language and get a sense for who's serious and who has a sense of humor. Listen to the comments and the tone. You can quickly pick up on who is well respected, whom you need to watch out for, and who will be a terrific resource. Remember to make a good first impression on those you meet. Smile, shake hands when possible, make eye contact, be friendly, and try to make an association of the name and face with what department they work in. You won't remember everyone, but at least you'll recognize a few people.

Get the Equipment You Need

If your stethoscope from school was cheap and is worn out, treat yourself to a new one. You deserve it. If you're going to be working in a specialty unit, you may need a more expensive and specialized model, but check with the other nurses on the unit for advice first. They may have information about discounts and opinions about one model over another.

A big must is some sort of drug book or software, and it needs to be an up-to-date edition. You must always use the most recent edition of a drug book, application, or software for your smartphone or mobile device. And you should always discard the old ones. Don't pass them off. Information may have changed significantly in the past few months, and you don't want to inadvertently give someone wrong data. New drugs won't be in your four-year-old edition.

Read your drug book or practice with your apps or software and become familiar with it so that it is easy for you to use quickly. Understand how drugs are cross-referenced, how to find side effects, and what the nursing implications are for each drug. Know how to find the tables that list sound-alike drugs. Keep this book (or device) with you at all times and use it. Never give a medication you are unfamiliar with under any circumstances. Never take a verbal order for a medication without repeating it back to the physician and verifying that it is indeed the drug she is prescribing. Then look it up. If you have questions, refer to the pharmacist for assistance or call the physician back for clarification.

ESSENTIAL

As always, your total image as a nurse depends on being clean and prepared. Keep your equipment clean and orderly. Remember, put your name and contact information on everything.

Make sure that your other equipment is clean and in good working condition. If your scissors are dull or rusty, be sure to clean and sharpen them or replace them. If your pocket flashlight doesn't have replaceable batteries, check it. If it's no longer bright, toss it out and replace it. Try to find one with replaceable batteries and lightbulbs and keep extras in your locker.

Be sure you always have a working pen in your pocket. Have a spare ink refill or extra pens in your locker as well. If you need a red or other color pen, consider a multicolor pen and be sure to have replacement ink refills as well.

A pocket holder for your pen, scissors, clamps, and flashlight is always handy. It usually has a place to attach your keys and to even carry a little money or your ID. If yours is dirty or worn out, buy a new one.

Invest in a Smartphone or Other Mobile Device

A smartphone or mobile device can be a lifesaver. It's smaller than a drug book and can contain a vast amount of important information that is available at the touch of a button. The software has search capabilities to provide quicker access. The initial investment can be less than $100 and has the option of adding on more memory and accessories as needed.

What Is a Smartphone?

Technology continues to advance, and in the future you can expect to have even smarter and better devices with apps and software to make your life safer and easier.

Smartphones come in a variety of choices from various manufacturers. They will also vary depending on the phone service carrier. Some of the more well-known smartphones today include the BlackBerry, the iPhone, the Android, and the Palm Pre. Many more will be developed until an entirely new technology takes over.

You might even use an iPad or other manufacturer's tablet-type computer device, but these are in a larger format and not as easy to carry in your pocket. They might, however, be used in such places as at the nurse's station or on med carts.

PDA stands for personal digital assistant. Smartphones, iPads (or other table devices), and PDAs are virtually hand-held computers. Most phones are about three inches by five inches and about one-half inch thick. The tablets are somewhat larger, ranging from about 4 inches by 6 inches to about 8 inches by 10 inches. They are a bit larger but still very portable.

The older model PDA comes with a small device called a stylus that acts like a pencil and a pointing device. Most new ones have touch-screen technology. These devises all have a keyboard, which is usually a full QWERTY style keyboard or touch screen, or a combination of both.

Types of Software

Many kinds of medical and nursing software or apps are available on the market. Every day, new apps and software become available. Some of the nursing apps and software that can be very useful include medical reference libraries, medical math calculators for drug dosages and IV drip rates, and medical dictionaries. A number of the most popular nursing drug books are available for these devices as well. Other items include patient tracking systems; medical eponyms; immunization schedules; laboratory values; medical rules such as trauma scores, Apgar scores, and pre-operative risk scores; and clinical guidelines for things such as cholesterol management and cardiac condition management.

The built-in note or memo pad can be useful for recording patient information, such as vital signs, in lieu of using small pieces of paper in your pocket. This information can be easily deleted once you have entered the information into the patient's chart or electronic file.

The software and apps are reasonably priced and, with registration, often comes with free or low-cost upgrades. The advantage the smartphone offers over a traditional paper drug book is that it can be updated more frequently so that access to the most accurate information is at your fingertips.

In some facilities, these devices are being used as adjuncts to computers for bedside access to a paperless medical records system, which can include up-to-the-minute information from lab results to the latest vital signs. Of course, they have to meet strict encryption and privacy restrictions. As technology improves and enhances the capabilities, the possibilities are endless for managing patient care with these devices. As society moves toward paperless systems, it is important for nurses to stay technologically savvy.

Buy Comfortable Shoes

As a student, you no doubt discovered the value of comfortable shoes. However, your budget may not have allowed for something better than a good supportive athletic shoe. Now that you are working as a nurse and may be working more than the one or two days a week you had clinicals, comfy shoes are a must!

In fact, your shoes may be the most important part of your uniform and equipment. You will be standing on your feet for hours. And you know how uncomfortable shoes can spoil your mood and make you cranky. When your feet hurt, your back and neck can hurt and you can even develop a headache and so on until you are miserable.

ESSENTIAL

You need shoes that will provide a strong, sturdy base for ensuring your own safety. You need to set your feet to bend your knees and get the leverage you need to lift and transfer patients and to move beds and equipment. You will have occasion to run and move quickly. You may need to climb onto a bed for CPR, and you'll need shoes that don't fall off or impede you.

Perhaps most important of all, you'll need a shoe with a non-slip sole. Your shoes can make or break your day. Invest wisely. You may have to experiment with several before you find one that's best for you, or you may find a terrific shoe the first time out. Again, this is something you can ask your new colleagues for advice about. They may have hints about a particular shoe and some of the peculiarities of your new unit.

Many nurses prefer a clog-type shoe made of soft PVC. These often have an ergonomic design to the sole that offers good foot and back support. You may also find it helpful to have two or three different shoe types and to trade them off. When they get worn down on the sides or heels, you'll need to replace them to maximize your comfort and support, as well as your safety.

Be comfortable: Nursing is hard work. Shoes are a very personal choice, and nursing shoes are not going to win any fashion awards. The key is support and comfort. You may have a very narrow foot and need a shoe with laces or straps and buckles. Your shoes are vital to job performance, so give them some careful consideration.

What to Expect as the New Nurse

As you transition out of orientation and into your regular assignment, expect to be treated as the new guy. You'll have to earn the respect of your new coworkers. You'll have to prove yourself to be accepted as one of the team.

ALERT

In some instances, you may encounter a nurse or two with a strong dislike for students and new graduate nurses. This is unfortunate, but not uncommon. Sometimes the dislike is well founded from a bad experience when a novice nurse presented a liability issue to another nurse, but even this is something that nurses need to take in stride.

In a setting where the staff is especially short-handed, it can be an added stress to the older staff members to have new nurses who need additional help and supervision. However, these nurses should also have a sense of relief that there is new blood flowing into the system and feel a sense of responsibility to nourish and protect the new grad. You may also encounter some issues of professional jealousy. Other situations can arise because, as a new grad, you may be much younger than some of the LPNs or nursing assistants you may be supervising.

Other Issues You'll Encounter

You will meet many new friends and allies. You will find a mentor and learn many tricks and tips to help you provide excellent patient care throughout your nursing career. You can help improve this situation if you pay close attention to where things are so that you don't have to ask more than once or twice.

However, you are the low man on the totem pole. You haven't been jaded by some of the "entitled" or "revolving door" or "frequent flier" patients who can drive nurses mad. They will be sure to share the wealth with you by giving you all the patients they have burned out on or need a break from. This isn't always a bad thing, but it can be challenging to you as a new nurse. You'll bring new interest and knowledge to the situation, and you may find a way to help the patient better than anyone has in a long time. Don't be surprised if not everyone applauds your success though. Someone just might take offense or claim that you're just showing off.

You may also find yourself with most of the grunt work assignments for maintaining the unit. And if there is a particular employee who isn't well liked, you can be sure you'll be partnered with that person as often as possible.

Working on Holidays

When it comes to staffing for holidays, expect to be working the main ones. Remember, sick people don't suddenly get well for the holidays. Those nurses with seniority have already paid their dues and will expect you to do so now. In fact, it may take several years before you might see Christmas Day with your family. Memorial Day, for example, may just become your favorite holiday and one of the few you might actually get off. Of course, you'll have an alternate day off during that week as your "paid holiday," which can have its advantages. If you love shopping the day after Christmas, for example, this just might be an acceptable alternative. Remember, someday you won't be the low man and you'll have your choice of holidays.

ESSENTIAL

Spending a holiday with your patients can be a warm and rewarding experience. This is especially true with those patients who are alone or who may have been recently widowed. Making a difference in someone's life every day takes on an even more special meaning at such times. New nurses usually find this especially rewarding.

Take these assignments as the challenges that they are and do your best to make the most of them. Sharpen your leadership skills. Learn diplomacy and how to delegate, as well as how to negotiate when necessary. Be positive. Use the opportunity to prove yourself as a true team player and to earn the respect of your coworkers. Most of all, learn to provide the best quality patient care despite all odds. Become the best nurse you can be.

CHAPTER 6

The New Kid on the Block

As the new employee on the unit, you're living under a microscope. Your new coworkers want to see how you react to different situations and whether they should accept you into their lives. How are you going to affect their work environment? Do you have a clue about how to be a nurse? Or will you be a burden and need someone to constantly supervise you? This is your moment to shine and make a good impression. Make the most of it.

Orientation

You may be in orientation for the facility for several weeks or months, and that may be split with time on your unit. In any case, you will also have an orientation to your own unit. Pay close attention to all orientations you have and take notes. Review your notes and any handouts you were given each day.

Use This Time to Your Advantage

Your orientation will most likely be during the day shift, whether or not that is the shift you were hired for. You may be mixed with new hires from all disciplines or separated into nurses only. This might even be just new grads or a mix with all newly hired nurses. You could possibly be the only person in orientation at this time.

Get to know as many of your fellow new hires as you can. The medical world is very small and you'll never know when and where you may be working with someone again in the future. You are all new and nervous, and a friendly gesture will be remembered and appreciated.

You will also be instructed in the documentation policies. If the facility uses a different format for charting than you have been exposed to, be sure you ask for additional help as you go along. Never assume that you'll catch on later. Documentation is too important to let slide. Depending on the extent that computers are used in your facility, you will be oriented to their use as well. Not all computer programs are created equal, so if you need additional instruction, be sure to ask for it now. Take notes for future reference.

Orientation is the time to work out as many kinks and bugs as you can. The nurse educators are there just for this purpose. If you wait and think you'll learn it later, you may regret it. When you're working on the floor, you should never do something you are unsure of without asking for help. However, if this was something you should have learned in orientation, your coworkers might not be too happy with you. If you just need a little reassurance, that's one thing, but if you fail to utilize orientation to learn all that you can, your coworkers will resent it.

Learn Where Everything Is

One of the most difficult aspects for nurses working with new staff is having to take time away from their own duties to show the new staff the ropes. In most instances, your preceptor will also have to care for her own patients, as well as supervise you and show you around the unit. You might get a quick tour from the nurse educator, so pay close attention, and when your preceptor needs you to get something, surprise him by knowing where to find it.

Make note of where things such as the crash cart, fire extinguishers, central supplies, and linens are located. Learn how your medication cart is laid out and how it works. Even if you aren't allowed to dispense medications or controlled substances, know how it is done. You should know how to access the meds if it's all computerized and how to get a newly prescribed medication from the pharmacy. You should also learn how to get STAT (from *statim*, a Latin term meaning "immediately") meds when the doctor is screaming for them *now*.

Know how to obtain procedure trays and central supplies. How do you charge the patient for the supplies you use? What happens if you or someone else contaminates a sterile tray and you need to get another one? Is there a charge-off procedure? How do you order the lab work, x-rays, or other tests the doctor has just requested for her patient? How do you access the lab and test results? What about IVs? Is there an IV team? Do the interns and residents start new IVs? Where are the IV sets kept?

Policies and Procedures

During orientation, you will be introduced to the policies and procedures for your facility. You will also be shown how to use the various pieces of equipment and pumps used within the facility. You will spend time on clinical issues and you may at this time begin being checked off on procedures. This is the time to ask lots of questions and to speak up if there is something you are not comfortable with or have not done before.

Some of the most important items you need to locate are your reference manuals. These will be your policy and procedure manual (often referred to as the P&P) and your standards of care manual. Learn the specific protocols your facility has regarding things such as central line care. And are there any doctors who have their own specific protocol that differs from facility protocols? Watch and learn. Ask questions. Don't ever assume. Use your time wisely. Make yourself an asset to your unit.

FACT

Sometimes the policy and procedure manual (P&P) will be a manual written by your facility, and other times it will be a standard nursing procedure book. In this case, the facility has designated this book as its standard of care manual. Know where the P&Ps are and refer to them every time you perform a new procedure or one you haven't performed in a while.

Expect to Annoy Someone

As the new kid on the block, you're going to annoy someone: Whether it's another nurse or the unit secretary, it doesn't make much difference. There will always be people who have little patience for someone new. Or perhaps they had a bad start to their day or aren't feeling up to par. Try to apologize for whatever you did to annoy them and come back later and try to work it out calmly. Sometimes, you just have to ignore it and learn not to take things personally.

Be Punctual

Come to work on time. That means you should arrive and be ready to work at your scheduled time, not just rushing to clock in at the exact moment. Give yourself about fifteen minutes to put away your belongings, get a cup of coffee, and greet your coworkers. If you plan on this extra time, then if you occasionally encounter heavier traffic or other unforeseen situations, you should still arrive on time.

Don't call in sick unless you really are. Nursing is not a job that can wait to be done until you get there tomorrow. If you're not there for your scheduled shift, everyone else is going to have to pick up some of your work, along with their own. Of course, if you are harboring germs, please keep them to yourself and don't share them with your coworkers and patients.

Be Prepared

Come to work prepared. Have all your equipment ready to go. If you have a locker, leave things at work so they aren't forgotten on the table at home or left in your car. If you don't have a place to leave them, utilize a backpack or other tote bag to keep them all organized. Start the day with a smile and a positive attitude. Greet your coworkers with a warm hello. But don't overdo it. Be sincere and use the person's name.

Work Well with Others

Ask for help when you need it. Offer to help if someone is in need and always say thank you. Understand your job description and learn what others' duties and roles are. Know who can do what so that you aren't asking someone to do something outside his scope of practice or job description.

Compliment coworkers on a job well done. If a patient tells you something nice about another nurse, pass the comment along to the nurse and even to your supervisor. All your coworkers are resources. Those who have been there the longest can be very valuable in educating you on the culture, history, and traditions of the facility and your particular unit.

ESSENTIAL

The best way to avoid being the "annoying new nurse" is to do your job right. Ask intelligent questions. Think before you ask—do you know the answer? And don't be a whiner.

Leave behind your attitude of "this is how we did it in school" and open your mind to different ways of doing things. However, you don't need to pick up the bad habits others may have either. Be diplomatic. You will find your way and gain the respect of your coworkers if you are warm and friendly, honest, open to suggestion and criticism, and you take responsibility for your actions.

Ask for Help

In most cases, you will be assigned a preceptor who will be in charge of showing you the ropes and supervising you as you perform procedures for the first time. She will not be your personal tutor or always available to you, as she will have her own assignment. Sometimes a preceptor has volunteered for the role and sometimes it has been assigned to her. Be sure you understand which way the situation is and how it can differ.

Dealing with Your Preceptor

In some instances, you may not like your preceptor and vice versa. Do look at the situation with an open mind and give it a genuine attempt before you go to your supervisor. If you do have to go to your supervisor, don't go in blaming and bad-mouthing the preceptor. Ask your supervisor for suggestions on how you might work it out first. Maybe she has some insight into your differences and can give you some guidance. If all attempts fail, then take the burden for the failure yourself. Rather than blaming him for the failure, realize that perhaps it's you who just can't seem to find a way to work with him. This goes a long way in showing diplomacy and teamwork. It also shows that you have respect for your coworkers and the maturity to handle an impossible situation. Ask for another preceptor and allow your supervisor to handle the change in a diplomatic manner.

Ask your supervisor and preceptor whom you should go to if you have questions and neither of them is available. If they say you can ask anyone else, just be sure to ask if there's someone they prefer you NOT ask. They may have very specific reasons for their answer.

In addition to your preceptor, you may find a mentor among your coworkers. This person differs from your preceptor because she isn't assigned to guide you, but she may have very similar philosophies about patient care or a natural way of calming patients, an ease in performing her duties, or procedures that you admire and wish to learn. You may have many mentors throughout your career. You should aspire to be a mentor to others as well.

Don't Be Afraid to Ask Questions

You need to take your work seriously. You need to complete your assignments and communicate clearly with your coworkers at all times. If you need to leave the floor, you report off to someone who will cover for you. If you have questions, you need to be sure to ask them. Don't be intimidated by the other nurses. They have more experience than you have right now, but you have worked just as hard to become a nurse. You will find that asking questions does not make you look stupid or ignorant but rather shows a desire to learn and a respect for your coworkers' knowledge and ability. In health care, learning is an ongoing process for everyone.

FACT

Pharmacists are great resources. If you can't find a drug in your drug book, software or app or in the *Physician's Desk Reference* (*PDR*) on the unit, call the pharmacist before you give a drug that's new to you. If you question a dosage, ask the pharmacist. Perhaps the physician made an error or has a reason for the dose and it should be clarified. The pharmacist will usually be happy to assist you in this.

If you haven't done something before or are uncomfortable with a procedure, ask for help. Be honest; don't try to bluff your way through something, even in the event that you find yourself alone with a physician who expects you to assist him.

Talk to the Whole Team

Look to the other resources around you for answers as well. Social workers and therapists (physical, occupational, respiratory, and speech) deal with the same patients. These other staff members may have an entirely different perspective on the care a patient needs. Sometimes patients respond to them in a different way, either positively or negatively, for various reasons. A patient may be combative with the nurse who is trying to administer medication or perform a procedure, but he may be totally cooperative with the physical therapist who's helping him to walk. The patient doesn't like the medicine or the procedure is invasive, but walking will get them out of there sooner. Maybe he doesn't understand the need for the medication or that it will help him just as much as the walking.

It is also helpful to learn the role that each discipline plays on the health care team. Nurses tend to believe that they have total responsibility for the patient and need to understand how and when to delegate. If you have a better understanding of the part each team member plays, you will also be less likely to overstep and interfere with the total plan of care.

When Patients Question Your Age

Unless you look seventy or older, you're going to be told over and over that you're too young to be a nurse. Some patients will mean it as a compliment and others will be frightened and worried that you don't know what you're doing. The patient might think that you haven't had enough experience and might ask you to please not touch her. You will need to reassure her that indeed you have graduated from an accredited school of nursing and that you have been trained to perform whatever it is you are doing.

If you need to do something that you haven't done before, be honest and let the patient know that your preceptor is right there. If you're just being checked off on the procedure, let her know you have performed this before but it's hospital policy that your preceptor check you off before you can do it alone—it's just standard procedure.

Don't let this bother you or destroy your confidence. You have completed your formal education to this point and you know how to be a nurse. You have to respect the patient's fears as well and do your best to prove your competence and gain her confidence. Explain any procedures carefully and encourage the patient to ask any questions. Take the time to understand what she knows and does not know about this illness and her health status in general.

ALERT

Your challenge is to gain the patient's confidence so that you can be effective in providing care. Sometimes, no matter how hard you try, you may not succeed. You may have to request a change of assignment with an older nurse for the benefit of the patient. After all, it's all about patient care and not your ego.

If you look young for your age, you might have patients telling you this for some years to come. It's like being carded when you buy alcohol: annoying, but enjoy the compliment, it won't last forever. While age has nothing to do with your ability, some people, particularly older people, seem to lack confidence in someone they feel is too young to have enough experience.

Gossip and Office Politics

The political climate and culture of your unit should be set by the management, but sometimes it is the "old guard" or long-timers who seem to have an upper hand in the way things get done. That isn't to say that the management isn't effective or is a pushover. It just usually means that there are one or two staff members who have a strong sense of entitlement because they have been there forever. They have paid their dues and get first choice at the perks, such as holidays and scheduled meal breaks. Sometimes they are RNs and sometimes they are nursing assistants, so it isn't always rank that gets or expects the privileges.

FACT

Your best option as the new kid on the block is to sit back, listen, and observe. Watch the dance. While sitting back can be frustrating, it can also be amusing to see who kisses up to whom and why. You will see who aligns with whom and who has more credibility. You'll learn whom you can trust and around whom you need to be very careful what you say.

Don't get caught up in the gossip, but pay attention to what is being said and who is saying it to avoid becoming a topic yourself. Understand the lay of the land. Gossip is an inherent part of almost every workplace. You may not be able to avoid it. Listen politely and move on. You won't have enough information as a new member of the staff to distinguish what is true and what isn't, so it's best to try not to make judgments based on what you hear. Give people the benefit of the doubt and form your own opinions based on firsthand experiences. Try to be fair and equal in your treatment of all your coworkers. Look for the good in everyone and avoid bad-mouthing anyone.

If you have a conflict, try to be direct and discuss it calmly and rationally in private with the person(s) involved. If you can't resolve it, see if you can at least agree to disagree and move on. If it is affecting your performance, you may have to speak to your supervisor, but again do this in private and in confidence. Ask for his advice on how to solve the problem rather than blaming or bad-mouthing the other person. Don't become emotional; stay calm and focused.

ALERT

Some of your coworkers are going to see you as a threat because you represent new blood and new ideas. Some people just don't like change. And others will be jealous if your ideas are considered while theirs are sidelined. Others will see you as a gosling to take under their wing and mold into a similar version of themselves. Some might smother you and others can be quite helpful.

The truth is, you will learn something from everyone you work with. Try to stay focused on your own beliefs and goals and try not to get swept up in the plan for making you a clone of another nurse.

Build relationships with your coworkers. Some of them will develop into lifelong friendships, as well as professional relationships. Don't be afraid to become friends with your boss, but remember that she is your boss and you need to maintain a professional relationship as well. Don't take advantage of personal friendships to gain professional stature or to promote unfair politics.

Always keep your head about you and follow your gut instincts and common sense. Some new nurses doubt their instincts, when in fact most of the time they shouldn't. Just because a colleague advises you to do something a certain way, if you aren't comfortable about it, chances are good that it may not be right. Don't readily assume that this person is correct or that he has some hidden agenda to discredit you, but tactfully seek a second opinion. And then tactfully explain why it was a wrong move for you if the person questions why you ignored his advice.

As you make friends and build relationships within your facility, you need to keep in mind that others will judge you by the friends you keep. You should be open and accepting of all your coworkers, but take care in choosing your close relationships.

Be a Team Player

Not everyone knows how to be a team player and support the team's work. You need to be a helper. Don't be above getting your hands dirty. Team players understand that the sum of the whole is always greater than the value of the individual.

The goal in health care is to improve the quality of life and outcomes for the patients. Some nurses may be better than others are at some aspects of care, while others may excel in another aspect. The expectation is not that everyone becomes a perfect nurse but rather that each contributes what she can to the whole to provide quality care. This might be only a small, supportive role for others in some instances. In other situations, the others might play a strong leadership role and you'll take the supportive role. Everyone pulls together to meet the goals for the unit and the patients.

FACT

Remember that there is no "I" in team. If a pitcher on a baseball team tried to play all nine positions at once, he'd get pretty worn out after a minute or two and would not be effective against a team of nine weaker players who all worked together with the same goal in mind. It takes a team to cover all the bases and to work together to reach the goal successfully.

Learn to accept your role as a team member. Support your coworkers where they fall short, and step up to the plate when needed to lead the group. United you will succeed. Separately you might not be effective. The goal is to enrich the life of the patient, not to promote your self-worth. The rewards you reap will come in the form of satisfaction, not for becoming a superstar, but for having played a part in making a difference in someone's life today.

No Brown Nosing

Just as you don't want someone taking your idea and running to your supervisor and claiming credit for it, neither should you try to take unfair advantage of a situation by brown nosing or kissing up to your supervisor or other superiors. There is a time and place for sharing ideas. Understand the chain of command and follow it for expressing new ideas, as well as for voicing concerns and complaints.

Just because you are the most recent grad on your unit does not mean you are the only one with new and creative ideas. Don't be a "know-it-all" either. All your nursing colleagues have been to nursing school and learned the same things you did. Some things have been updated, but they've continued their education too. As time goes by, you'll develop a sense of when it's appropriate to chime in with your suggestions, and as you earn the respect of your coworkers, they will begin to listen to your suggestions and appreciate them and might even ask for your input.

ESSENTIAL

Be open and willing to trade assignments and shifts as needed with your coworkers, and you'll help to foster an atmosphere of "you scratch my back and I'll scratch yours." Show that you are a team player.

Give and Take

Give genuinely of yourself and don't look for secondary gains. Try to get to know something about your coworkers outside of the workplace. Show an interest in who they are as a person and not just a nurse or other health care worker. This will provide you with tremendous insight into how they behave in the workplace.

You may not like every person you work with, but you should be able to respect the job they do or how they treat the patients. Some people don't have a great bedside manner or people skills, but they have great compassion and can give a shot or start an IV with the least amount of pain for the patient. Or perhaps they have a great sense of humor and bring a smile to the faces of the patients. Give credit where it is due.

You are going to spend a great portion of your life each day with these people. Try to find ways to build camaraderie and make the job fun and fulfilling for everyone.

CHAPTER 7

Your Scope of Practice

One of the most important aspects of your job as a nurse is to understand your scope of practice. Each member of the health care team is allowed to perform certain duties based on the content and level of education he or she has received, the license granted, and the specifics of the laws and regulations of the state where he or she practices.

"Do No Harm"

Although the physician's Hippocratic Oath does not actually contain these words, it is definitely implied that all members of the health care team should always strive to do no harm. What does this mean? Certainly, as human beings, no one is perfect. However, by virtue of the fact that nurses hold lives in their hands, they are expected to do all that they can to not harm anyone. Mistakes can happen and inevitably they will, but there are rules in place to help to alleviate the possibility of mistakes. It is the responsibility of all nurses and all other members of the health care team to follow those rules to ensure the safety of all.

ALERT

Many patient safety rules or goals are based on pure common sense. Some are more elaborate. Each institution will have variations of its own rules and goals based on mistakes others have made and their attempts to prevent a reoccurrence. Others will be based on preventing common errors based on data collected by organizations such as the Joint Commission on Accreditation of Healthcare Organizations (JCAHO), whose goal is to advocate for quality and safety for all.

One problem is that some nurses get very lax in performing all the double checks that help to prevent errors. You may know a patient personally or have spent significant time with her and feel a little too confident that you don't need to check the name band with each medication administration. The first time your confidence betrays you, however, will be a devastating mistake. It may not in any way be harmful to the patient, but your own self-confidence will take a dive.

Understanding Your Colleagues' Scope of Practice

Every day, your commitment to make a difference in someone's life should include doing all that you can to prevent mistakes. In addition, you need to have a good understanding not only of your scope of practice, but that of your coworkers as well. You want to have a clear idea of what others are capable of as well as what they are allowed to do so that you don't expect a level of understanding that is not there.

Harm can be done, for example, by expecting an aide to understand the correlation of the symptoms she is reporting to the untoward events of the day for that patient. Nurse's aides and LPNs do not assess. They collect data. Therefore, it is the RN's responsibility to obtain reports from the aides and LPNs as often as possible and to direct them in what other symptoms she expects to be reported immediately.

No matter what level of nursing you are functioning at, it is always in your own, as well as the patient's, best interest to understand each person's scope of practice. If you are the aide or the LVN/LPN, you aren't responsible for assessing and analyzing the data. However, it can be in everyone's best interest to have an understanding of what other symptoms might be important to report and why. This can be especially important and helpful in the event of short staffing. Concise communication is vital to quality patient care. If you are ever in doubt, it is always best to ask for assistance or another opinion. To err on the side of safety is always best.

If you are an aide or LVN/LPN, it is vital to remember that, first, nurses never diagnose, and, second, that your scope of practice says you don't assess, you only collect the data. Always work within these parameters.

Life Happens

If your significant other kept you up all night sitting in the ER because of an illness or injury, you aren't going to function at the optimum level in your practice of nursing. You cannot safely perform your duties as a nurse if you are impaired. If you have a fever and severe head cold, your judgment will be impaired (not to mention your illness is contagious). These are times when you need to call in sick.

On the other hand, you have a responsibility to be at work when you are assigned. Don't choose the night before to party all night. Don't decide to watch the entire twenty-four-hour marathon of your favorite old TV show. Be responsible. Plan your life around your job. Your first responsibility as a nurse is to your patients—to be the best nurse you can be. You cannot be your best if you are not prepared.

ESSENTIAL

"Do no harm" means coming to work prepared. Part of being prepared means not being impaired. That means you have had sufficient sleep and nutrition and that you are not under the influence of alcohol or drugs. It also means you are not hung over and not unwell. You are alert and ready to accept the responsibility to perform your duties as a nurse today.

Your State's Nurse Practice Act

When your license arrives, it will probably be accompanied by a copy of your state's Nurse Practice Act (NPA). If not, you can obtain a copy from your state board of nursing. You can find this information online either from the National Council of State Boards of Nursing (*www.ncsbn.org*) or by an Internet search for your state board of nursing. If you have not yet taken your NCLEX or received your license, be sure to obtain a copy of your state's Nurse Practice Act. Some states offer a downloadable copy from their website that you can print for reference.

FACT

The Nurse Practice Act (NPA) is the group of laws set by each state to protect the public. It defines the scope of practice for nurses in that state. The NPA includes the requirements for education and licensing of the nurse. It also includes disciplinary and punitive measures for unsafe practice.

It is the responsibility of each licensed nurse to read and to know the contents of his own state's Nurse Practice Act. The NPA will be different for RNs, LPNs, and APRNs (advance practice RNs). You will be held accountable for this information. If you make a mistake, your defense cannot include "I didn't know that I couldn't do that." As a licensed nurse, you are expected to know. Read the NPA and understand it. If you have questions, ask. Your board of nurses is there to answer your questions and to help you to understand your scope of practice.

In general, your NPA will describe what you are allowed to do based on your education and license. Most have some sort of scope of practice algorithm or decision tree built in that follows a commonsense approach. Some of the questions involved in this process may include:

- Is the act or procedure allowed by the NPA?
- Have you received the necessary training? Do you have the knowledge required?
- Are you competent to perform the procedure or act?
- Is the act or procedure considered an acceptable standard of care for a nurse to perform?
- Do you have a valid order from a licensed physician to perform this act or procedure?

If any of these questions can be answered "no," then it is not within your scope of practice to perform this act or procedure.

Be aware that the Nurse Practice Act will change. As technology changes, the act is periodically updated to reflect these changes. As health care is legislated, your NPA may change. What you need to understand is that you may find that you are suddenly allowed to do something that you have not been trained to do. That does *not* mean that you can perform it. Nurses are required to continue their education. If your position requires you to perform new duties as the technology changes, be sure you keep yourself up to date with education, in-services, and certifications. And ask for a preceptor when learning new procedures.

How will you know what is new with your NPA? Nurses need to stay informed. If you haven't read your NPA recently, get a new copy. Subscribe to journals. Join your state nurses' association, or at least subscribe to its e-mail alerts and be included on its mailing list. Read your local newspaper. Be informed of health care issues and how local and national legislation affects patient care, as well as the nursing profession. Become an advocate. Write to your legislators. Be an informed voter.

The Realm of Responsibility

It is important for you to have an understanding of the organizational chart for your facility. Where does the buck ultimately stop? Who is that person? In addition to the organization, it's vital for you to know who is in charge on your unit at any given time. Don't be surprised to find yourself in that role someday. It may happen sooner than you think or hope for. Be prepared and know who your organizational support members are.

When to Delegate

There may be a time to delegate and a time not to. It's important to understand the full situation and not to waste time and resources. The important thing to remember is who is responsible for what. Work your way backward from the person providing the direct care all the way to the physician who prescribed the care. The responsible parties also include everyone in the chain of command in the nursing realm. Where you fit into that realm, along with the extent of your personal responsibility, may differ for each of your assigned patients depending on who is assisting you in their care for that particular shift.

ALERT

Only RNs are allowed to delegate. Delegating is a diplomatic process. You must understand the scope of practice for all involved and understand how well each person functions in his role. It is also important to understand any personal shortcomings and how well you can trust those to whom you delegate responsibilities.

The goal is always to provide the best care possible for each patient. If some of your patients require more of your time and attention than others do, you may need to delegate. If you are an LPN, you cannot delegate, but perhaps you can discuss the situation with your supervisor and have some of the responsibilities reassigned. If you are an RN, you need to keep in mind that you are still ultimately responsible for those patients whose care you have delegated to others.

Know Your Staff

If you are in charge of the unit, you are further responsible for all the patients and the staff under you providing their care. In this situation, you really need to know your own capabilities, as well as those of your staff. You will need to implement a plan and allow yourself time to supervise all staff. In the event that you are shortstaffed, you will need to call upon all your leadership abilities to ensure that everyone is working together and knows her responsibilities.

Each person needs to understand his own scope of practice and when to ask for help. It is vital to the well-being of all involved that no one oversteps his bounds. This situation seems to arise when staff members are also nursing students.

For example, your best nursing assistant is in his last year of a BSN program. You're shortstaffed and a doctor wants you to assist with a procedure *now!* Another patient needs to have a Foley catheter inserted because of incontinence issues, and no one else can do it right now. The aide has inserted many catheters in the past month under the supervision of his instructor and feels confident. He volunteers to help you out. *Don't do it!* Ask the aide to explain to the patient that you have been delayed and to assist the patient by offering a bedpan or padding the bed with some waterproof pads until you can get there.

ESSENTIAL

Sometimes a staff member who is less frazzled may see a solution you haven't considered. Work together and listen to your coworkers. Remember, the safety and well-being of the patient are foremost. The goal is to provide quality patient care.

Perhaps the aide is a graduate nurse who hasn't taken boards yet—you still shouldn't take chances. An LPN may have been allowed to perform a procedure in a previous job and is willing to help out but isn't allowed to do it here. Again, delegate responsibilities that assist you in getting to your duties quicker but that don't exceed anyone's scope of practice. On the other hand, if you're being asked to do something outside of your scope, suggest something you can do to assist the situation but don't take on the responsibility for something you are not allowed to do.

Clarifying the Nurse's Role

As a member of the health care team, your responsibility includes informing patients and their families of your role and scope of practice on the team. If you are working as a CNA (while attending school or prior to becoming licensed), you are not a nurse. In keeping with your role and scope of practice, if the patient needs more complex assistance than you are able to provide, help them to understand who can provide that and get the help they need. Of course, if their need is urgent, all you have to say is, "Let me get the nurse for you." Later you may have an opportunity to explain the organization to them.

Sometimes patients refer to the aide as their nurse and the RN as the treatment or medication nurse. Everyone can help alleviate this situation with a simple correction to the patient and by referring to each other by the appropriate title. The intention is to inform the patient and not to mislead her. If the patient doesn't understand your role, she may be frustrated with the care she is receiving. A patient may also make demands that can jeopardize her care, as well as cause you professional issues as an employee. This can escalate if there are language and cultural barriers for the patient or the staff. Setting a tone and precedence for using appropriate titles can make an important difference in the quality of patient care.

Misunderstandings about a role or scope of practice can also affect the credibility of the health care worker in the eyes of the patient. This can happen frequently in a setting such as home care where different disciplines visit at different times and even different days. As an example, the patient may have a home health aide (HHA) three times a week, and the RN visits only monthly for catheter care. The patient is a diabetic and often has questions about something she read or heard on television. The HHA is also a diabetic and feels free to discuss what her physician told her about this. The patient sees her aide as "the nurse" and gives more credence to the information she has shared with the aide. When the RN visits, the patient doesn't voice her diabetic concerns because she feels that her needs have been met by "the nurse." The patient also doesn't understand exactly why someone else comes to change her Foley. No one suspects anything until a supervisory visit is made and the RN observes the discussion of the diabetic care during the bath. No harm was done, but the aide was overstepping her scope of practice.

It is not uncommon for a patient to confide more in his aide. The aide often spends more time with the patient and is involved in care that may be more intimate, such as bathing and toileting. If you have seen a patient's backside or cleaned up his mess, while helping to protect his dignity, then the patient often feels more comfortable in sharing his concerns and fears. This can be very beneficial as long as the whole team understands the situation and averts potential problems.

Nurse Wannabes

A nurse wannabe can be potentially more harmful than patients who consider the aide to be their nurse. The fact is that anyone working in the proximity of a medical environment is going to pick up on the lingo. Their curiosity is going to be piqued, and they are going to absorb a lot of medical knowledge. However, if they have not had the training of a nurse or physician, they often don't understand the bulk of what they have learned. More important, they may not understand the potential for harm. That can be the most deadly issue of all.

Nurses don't diagnose, but "want-to-be nurses" sometimes do. Patients may not understand that their best friend, who works in a doctor's office down the street, may not be their best source of medical care or advice.

There is far more to medical education than understanding anatomy and physiology. Just because the doctor's receptionist can tell where your bladder is and even how the E. coli may have been transferred from your rectum to your urethra on the toilet tissue doesn't mean she knows how to treat the urinary tract infection (UTI). Nor does she understand why you shouldn't take a particular medication because you have a history of allergy or maybe even poor renal or liver function.

This scenario could also be the result of a patient calling the doctor's office. The high costs of health care have driven many physicians to dispense with nursing staff in their offices. Instead, they may have lay personnel only, or they may have trained medical assistants or CNAs as any combination of their receptionist/front office/back office help. The trained medical help will have been instructed not to exceed the scope of their practice, but the culture of the environment may not support this.

Other situations exist where the lay personnel may indeed work in an office with nurses, as well as doctors. They see certain situations over and over again. The above example might be of a receptionist in a urologist's office. A UTI is a commonly treated disease, and she has learned a great deal about how certain infections can be introduced into the body and how they are commonly treated. But this doesn't make her a doctor or a nurse.

FACT

This well-intentioned employee should remind the person asking her advice that she is not a trained medical person. She could explain to the person that this is what she has learned in her experience as a matter of conversation. However, her only advice should be for the person to consult her own physician as soon as possible.

Her advice to her friend about proper hygiene measures to avoid future contamination would be well intentioned. But given the context of where she works, she shouldn't be giving advice that could be considered practicing medical care without a license.

All too often these days, doctors are overbooked and not readily available for questions. The Internet is a vast pool of easily accessible information. The media is full of advertising for medications to treat this complaint or that. The climate is ripe for self-diagnosing and self-medicating. As nurses, the challenge is to educate the public to take responsibility for their health but also to seek qualified medical care as needed.

As nurses it's important that we educate the public that nurses don't diagnose unless they have the advanced education that NPs have. For diagnosis, the person should be directed to seek medical advise from a physician, osteopath, NP, or PA (physician assistant).

Additionally it's important to make the public aware that many of the jobs nurses may have held in the past are now being staffed by lay people and medical assistants. These are not nurses and the public should be asking about credentials before they assume the person is a nurse. On the other hand, the medical assistants and lay people working in doctor's offices, clinics, and other facilities should be clear with their patients that they are not nurses.

Nurses Never Diagnose Disease

Nurses never diagnose a disease or illness unless they have been specifically trained to do so such as a nurse practitioner has. Nurses make nursing diagnoses only. They assess the patient, the situation, and the health care incident and its risks, and they determine an appropriate nursing intervention based on the nursing diagnosis. This is known as the nursing process. It will be discussed in more detail in a later chapter, but this is the premise of the RN's education. LPNs don't assess patients, and therefore they don't make nursing diagnoses either, although they may play an integral part in the health care delivery process of the nursing intervention by collecting data and reporting it to the RN.

Friends and Family

Just like your non-licensed medical personnel coworkers, your friends and family will bombard you with medical questions. Sometimes they may ask you to figure out what medication or treatment the doctor gave them in his office today. That might be easier if you knew exactly why they saw the doctor, but you may not be able to ascertain the answer to that question. Put on your thinking cap and pull out your trusty magnifying glass; it's time to draw out all the facts and investigate the situation thoroughly.

You can provide instruction in basic nursing care, but be careful not to prescribe over-the-counter (OTC) medications and treatments. Nurses don't prescribe either. (Nurse practitioners are allowed to prescribe medications if it is allowed in the NPA of the state in which they practice. The NPA will spell out the specifics for this.)

ALERT

Your responsibility as a nurse is to educate and to encourage your family members to seek the advice and counsel of their physician. You do not have a license to practice medicine, and indeed you have a license to protect your patients.

Refer Them to Their Physician

If friends or family members are asking you about a diagnosis or pre-scribed treatment they have received, be sure to ask them first what they have already been told by their physician. You can educate them in lay-men's terms, but always refer them back to their physician for medical advice, treatment, and diagnosis.

ESSENTIAL

Your scope of practice is as a nurse. Don't try to play doctor. Know whom you are discussing care with. If you don't really know the person, use your gut instinct that tells you to be very cautious. Encourage the person to seek qualified medical care. Remember to do no harm.

Suggest a list of questions or symptoms the person needs to bring to the attention of the physician. Give the person instruction in symptom management and what signs and symptoms to observe that could be cause for more immediate care.

If the person is really confused or perplexed with a situation, offer to discuss it with the physician. Have the person clear any Health Insurance Portability and Accountability Act (HIPAA) restrictions first. If this is not possible, don't second guess or make assumptions. Suggest questions he can ask to help clarify the situation and provide both of you with a better understanding of the situation. Have him let the physician know that his nurse friend or relative is trying to help him understand and the doctor may provide more information to you.

CHAPTER 8

Time Management

Give yourself some time to become efficient and at ease with your job. Much of this is not new, but the intensity will be markedly increased for a new nurse. Your coworkers have been at this for a while now. Soon you will be able to get through the day without feeling overwhelmed and out of control. Pull together your best time management and organizational tools, and you'll be on the right track.

Improving Quality of Care and Reducing Stress

Nursing has always been a demanding field. It's physically challenging, as well as emotionally. No matter where you work, be it in a hospital, long-term care facility, clinic, home health, or hospice, today's patients have a much higher acuity level. They are sicker and need more care, attention, and education. Their care will be much more technical as well. And they will spend less time in any given facility or with any health care agency.

Nurses have to keep up with the skills and knowledge base required and constantly strive to provide the very best quality care. Hospitals face huge fines and loss of reimbursement if they don't meet or exceed certain quality standards. Home health agencies must collect data on their Medicare patients. The analyzed data is published online to allow consumers to compare home health agencies in their geographic region.

The bottom line is that the pressure to succeed lies mostly on the nursing staff. Nurses have to work harder and smarter to reach these goals for their employer. Time management and organizational skills are more important than ever and will continue to be so in the future. Nurses must hit the ground running each and every shift and keep running until they can run out the door each day.

To keep up with this pace, nurses have to take care of themselves. Taking care of yourself so that you can take care of others has to become an integral part of your life. This includes good nutrition habits, good sleep habits, and making sure that you get some relaxation on a regular basis. Meeting the needs of family friends and maintaining the fast pace of life as a nurse can become very overwhelming in a hurry.

It's important to make a plan and stick to it as much as is humanly possible. Put your organizational skills to work and perfect them in your personal life. Buy nutritional foods so that you don't grab junk food because that's all you have. Set a schedule for sleep hours for you and your family and stick to it. Arrange care for your children if you're working swing or night shifts and need to sleep at other times than they do. Plan activities and time to share with your family and friends and put your job behind you.

Planning Out Your Day Means Prioritizing and Reprioritizing

Arrive early. Give yourself a few minutes to put your things away, get some coffee, and relax for a moment. Running late and rushing in to clock in just on time won't give you the best start to your day. Check out the tone of your workplace. Has it been chaotic? Or is it quiet and calm? This will give you a clue to at least how your shift will begin. Every day in nursing is a new adventure. No two days will be alike, and it's almost guaranteed that something will happen when you least expect it. Expect the unexpected and it won't be so troublesome. The best way to prepare for the unexpected is never to procrastinate. Whatever you have put off doing will almost always end up embroiled in chaos and even more of a chore to complete.

Report (when the nurses leaving report to the next shift about each of the patients, such as any symptoms, issues, etc.) will be more meaningful if you can find out what your assignment is before report and have a few minutes to gather some information about the patients. Then you can ask pertinent questions. If this isn't possible, pay close attention and take notes during report.

Plan your day by tasks and try to get the least appealing things done as soon as possible so they don't weigh you down. Of course, you will have to do tasks that are based on time factors; such as med rounds or wound care that's scheduled two to three times a day. Be ready for things to change as a new admission arrives, a doctor needs help with a procedure, or a patient falls. Then you'll have to stop and reprioritize. You may have to ask for help and delegate some of your work, and check up on it later.

First Things First

Ask your nurse manager to try to arrange for you to have as many of the same patients as possible for a few days so that you can get used to the lay of the land and learn more about how things work in this facility. Familiarity with the patients will also help you understand the report process and glean more from it. Once you're finished with report, examine your priorities again and make necessary adjustments. Plan for the possibility of a new admission or unexpected discharge. Even if you might not be assigned these responsibilities right away, you'll budget time for them. Then if someone else needs help, you'll be able to volunteer a little time. Helping out in this way will help make you part of the team.

Make lists of what needs to be done. These should be quick notes and not elaborate.

- What is urgent?
- What treatments, such as dressing changes, need to be done and how many times during your shift?
- Who is going for tests?
- Who is having other care, such as physical therapy?
- Who needs assistance with activities of daily living?
- When are your meds due? Do you have them all? Are any new to you? If so, plan time to look them up.
- Who was having pain issues or nausea, or was in need of many PRNs? Check to see when they had their last dose and make note of it. Write it down.

Some nurses carry a small notebook in their pocket, others use a clipboard, and others use a smartphone. Whatever your choice, always have something to write on. Don't rely on your memory.

Make Rounds

Even if an aide or tech is taking vital signs, look in on each patient. Introduce yourself as the person's nurse. Perhaps your facility has a white board in each room to write your name on. Ask how the patient feels and if he needs anything right now. Keep moving and don't linger. Write down any requests so you can get them done right away.

When you are done, look at your lists. Who needs what now? Is that pain medication due, or do you need to remind yourself to get it in an hour? Let the patient know if there is any delay.

Get to your urgent issues first. Next, decide what you really don't want to do and get it over with. The longer you put off doing the things you dislike or are uncomfortable with, the more troublesome they can be to your day. These duties will weigh on you, and, if you get behind, they will only make you feel that much more overwhelmed and out of control. Next, do any other treatments you need to complete and pass your meds. Make a quick check on everyone.

Then take inventory of what supplies you need to replenish in your pockets, as well as at the bedside. It's always helpful and a time saver if you have a few supplies in your pockets. This can include items such as gloves (lots of them), adhesive bandages, alcohol swabs, a small roll of adhesive tape, and a tape measure or other wound measuring device. Depending on your unit, there may be other small items you could include in your pocket inventory. Some facilities have gloves in every room, which can be quite helpful.

Use a Timer

One of the things that you will need to be very organized about is anything that needs to be delivered or administered at a specific time. This can be medications or treatments. This might be an IV medication or oral or injectable meds. It could be a dressing change that needs to be performed several times a day. Other things such as lab draws, breathing treatments, or whirlpools are usually handled by other staff, but if your facility is very small, these might be your responsibility, as well, or you may have to assist with transporting the patient.

You should always be aware of when your patients will be having any therapy or tests in order to coordinate care. Check them before they leave the floor and when they return. Freshen their beds while they are gone, or delegate this to an aide. Prioritize all your timed events and then make sure that all the supplies and meds you need are available. Order any missing pieces or ask your unit secretary to assist you in obtaining them.

If you have a mobile device, cell phone (if allowed to be on), or timer on your watch, set it for the timed events. If not, you will need to keep a mental note and frequently check your watch. You might also ask the unit secretary to remind you, but don't put all that responsibility on someone else. Anyone else should just be as a backup reminder.

In many instances, you should have the patient watching the clock as well. They can call for you if you're running late. This helps to involve them in their care and gives them some responsibility.

Check with your coworkers to see what and how they keep track of any timed events.

Chances are, you may have more than one thing to do at the same time. You will have to prioritize these as well. Try to do the quickest one first, perhaps a few minutes before the appointed time if that is okay. Anything that has to be more exact will have to be planned for. This could be an IV med or an insulin dose just prior to a meal.

Stay Organized and Focused

If you get delayed or have trouble meeting all the demands, don't forget to ask for help. Nurses are overachievers and this work is all new to you. Don't put anyone, especially the patients, at risk. Delegate what you can and focus to complete the rest. It is usually easiest to delegate simple, uncomplicated matters that will require the least amount of discussion. This will maximize the amount of time you afford yourself to complete a more complicated task.

Organize the task in your mind before you begin. Explain all procedures to the patient. Don't expect to be speedy. Take your time and observe. Make note of how this might be made easier next time and how the patient responds. If all goes well, pat yourself on the back and record this one for your mental journal of accomplishments for the day.

Move on to the next task. Whenever you have a relatively calm and quiet moment, take a deep breath, and reflect on the positives. Peek in on all your patients. Catch up with any of your aides or techs to find out how their day is going and if they have anything to report about your patients. Be sure to ask them questions. They are not trained to assess and may not put the same measure of importance on a symptom or complaint.

If you delegated anything, be sure to find the person and find out how it went and say thank you. Offer to reciprocate if you can or at least acknowledge that you will return the favor at some future point. Review your assignment and see what is left for the rest of the day. Cross off those things you have finished. Make any notes that you need to help you later. Prioritize again.

Document as You Go Along

After you have completed a few tasks, take a moment to chart. Be sure to include all pertinent data regarding complaints such as pain or nausea, how well someone tolerated a procedure, the size of the wound, color of any drainage, odors, and signs and symptoms of infection or healing. If you did any patient or family teaching, document the outcome and note what they need to do or learn next.

Remember you are discharge planning from the moment of admission, so you need to help the patient and family assume responsibility for the patient's care after release. The patient and his family might need help when they first get home, but you have begun the process toward making them independent. Whatever you can include about what the patient or family member learned or demonstrated will be most helpful to the discharge planner as well as the physician.

ESSENTIAL

Never rely on your memory. Write things down. Use your notebook, clipboard, or mobile device. Organize your notes. Have one sheet for each patient. You might think about a simple form you could devise for your notebook or for your device that could simplify your notes. Writing everything down also helps you to prioritize tasks and organize your day and skills.

If you document as you go along, you'll find yourself ready to go home at the end of the day without having to spend an extra hour doing paperwork. Things will be fresh in your mind and you'll be far less likely to forget some all-important information than if you let the day get away from you. If you do forget something, be sure that you know how to add an addendum to your notes and how to document an event out of order.

Find a System That Works

Some nurses use sticky notes to write things down that they need to relay to the physician or other team members, such as the discharge planner or perhaps a physical therapist. This way they can leave the note in the chart for that person and not have to rewrite it later. These notes can be very helpful and can save a lot of time.

One habit to avoid is using multitudes of small pieces of paper to write your notes on. Some nurses routinely grab paper towels to scribble on. This might work in an emergency, but is not a good habit to learn. Keep your notebook in your pocket or buy a smartphone. The less time you have to spend trying to piece together a multitude of small pieces of paper or to dig through the trash to find those wound measurements the doctor asked for, the more time you'll have for your regular work. And you'll once again reduce the opportunities for sabotaging your day and finding yourself out of control and overwhelmed.

Written Record and Legal Document

Always remember that the medical record is a legal document. It is your proof that you did something. You want the chart to reflect the quality care you have given and the patient's immediate outcome or response. You want to protect your nursing license at all times. Accuracy is a vital element. You are providing an annotation of the patient's experience for all other health care team members to refer to in analyzing the patient's progress and outcomes.

ESSENTIAL

Don't make charting a chore; it is vital to the continuum of care. Think of it as your chance to prove that you have provided excellent care and that you have made a difference in someone's life today.

Many people feel that the paperwork is an annoyance and insignificant to patient care. The truth is that documentation is one of the most effective means of interdisciplinary communication that the health care delivery system has to offer. In the absence of face-to-face opportunities, the written record affords you perhaps the only form of communication and evidence of the care delivered and the patient's response/outcome.

Documentation does not have to be a dissertation or a thesis, but it needs to include enough information to paint a clear portrait of the events of the shift. Any nurse following you should be able to read your documentation and have an understanding of the patient's condition, as well as the care you provided and how it affected the day's outcomes for that patient.

Avoid Leaving Projects for the Next Shift

Some days will flow smoothly and you'll sail through them. Others will be wildly chaotic and you'll feel like you're spinning out of control. Sometimes someone else will be the one having an impossible day. Sometimes everyone's day will be completely chaotic all at once. That is the life of a nurse.

Your job is to figure out how to get all those challenges under control, complete your assignment, and seemingly putting out a million fires all at once. The biggest challenge some days will be in getting it all done without killing yourself or someone else. Some days it will seem impossible to get all your work done. Life happens. There will always be unforeseen circumstances. However, you need to strive to complete your assignment and not leave something for the next person to do.

ALERT

You may have to frequently remind yourself of the reasons you became a nurse. Perhaps even why you gave up your boring desk job as an accountant or nixed that plan to be a pilot in the seventh grade. One thing is for sure, life as a nurse is never boring. Each day brings a whole new set of challenges.

On occasion, going home at the end of your shift may not be possible. In some instances, you will be expected to stay and finish the job, and, at other times it might be okay to leave it for the next shift to carry on. But in all instances, your supervisor needs to know. The more advance notice you can give her, the better she can deal with the situation. Sometimes it can be delegated to someone else and other times she can include it in the assignment for the next shift and the nurse need never know it was left over. The supervisor will also have to approve your overtime or assign you to complete it without any extra pay. Don't beat yourself up over it. If you gave it everything you had, then that's all you can do. If you procrastinated and wasted time or spent time goofing off, then you have no one else to blame.

Reflect back on your day each day. The first thing to consider is whose life is better because you were there today. Pat yourself on the back and make a mental note. You might even want to have a journal or a blog where you write about your accomplishments. (Be careful about privacy.) Patients may not have an opportunity to say thank you. Your rewards come from the knowledge that you made a difference. Your memories are your proof.

Next, you need to think about what worked well and why. Then you need to think about what could have gone better and how you can improve outcomes. Learn from your own experiences. This will help to build your confidence.

Be realistic and honest with yourself. If you need additional time or help, discuss it with your nurse manager. She's going to know it if you keep having days with incomplete assignments, so talk it over. Every nurse was new at some point. She may have some valuable suggestions and together you can work out solutions. Ask for feedback from your coworkers as well. At the least, you'll let them know you are acknowledging your shortcomings and trying to improve the situation.

Expect the Unexpected

Someday you will learn why you should never procrastinate! Everything is going smoothly after a bit of a bumpy start to the day. You have theater tickets for the best show in town, and you hope to get off right on time so that you can make it without rushing.

A Typical Story

Your last major task is to change the dressing on your least favorite patient. She is a cranky woman of about seventy, who was admitted a few days ago for a severely infected wound. She had her leg amputated mid-femur some months back, and she ignored the pressure sore that her prosthesis caused. She's still very angry about the amputation, which was caused by some sort of accident. No one has taken the time to talk to her about the accident or her feelings. She is too cranky and demanding. In fact, everyone avoids her room, and the door is kept partially closed so that nurses passing by aren't flagged down to assist her with a never-ending need to rearrange her pillows and admonishments for not knowing exactly how the pillows should be.

No one can blame you for making her dressing change your last priority. The wound is large and the odor is powerful. It makes you gag to see the flesh, and the smell is more than your already queasy stomach can handle today. If you make it the last thing to do today, you can slip in, do it, bring her a pain pill, rearrange her pillows one last time, and tell her you have to rush off for report now—document and report off, your shift is over.

You finally assemble everything you need and even have her pain med with you. (The patient refuses to take it before the dressing change.) You walk in and hear a thud. Your heart stops for a moment and then you realize that the patient in the next bed has apparently fallen in the bathroom.

Compound the problem with the fact that you work in an old facility that is just now being brought up to code. The bathroom door opens inwardly and the patient, who weighs about 200 pounds, has fallen so that she is blocking the door. Your patient is frantic and screaming at you to do something. (Can't she see that you are trying to get the door open?) The patient inside is not one of yours so you don't know very much about her situation. (Just one more complication.) Oh yes, her nurse is on a break, and you're covering because this one "is stable and shouldn't need anything for the next fifteen minutes."

It's only been a minute, but it seems like an hour has passed when you give up on the door. The patient is not answering you and you need to get some help. In what appears to be slow motion, you finally reach the hallway and flag down a coworker to go and get some help. Your coworker has panicked and called for the code team. The crash cart and all the bells and whistles will arrive any second, and you hope it's not all in vain. In fact, it turns out to be a good call because when they finally get the door open by some miracle, the patient is on the floor in full cardiac arrest.

Her nurse is still on a break, and so, by default, she is your patient now. The code team handles it, but you are required to remain present.

You will be responsible for accompanying her to the ICU if they can revive her. If not, you'll be doing postmortem care. Oh, and you still need to change that dressing. Now the cranky patient has been traumatized by this event.

All's Well

Long story short, the patient is revived, her nurse returns in the process and will accompany her to ICU after you give her a report on what you witnessed and document it all. Once you calm your own patient down, you do finally get the dressing changed. It's now way past time for you to be on your way to the theater, and your friends have given your ticket away. (Good thing, you're too exhausted to go to a show now.)

The one good thing in all this is that you have an opportunity to talk to your patient. She opens up about her own fears and how horrendous her accident was. She has had her own epiphany today—at least she lived through it. She thanks you for your extra-gentle touch today and expresses admiration for how calmly and professionally you handled the situation with her roommate just now. Hopefully now you will remember to do the things you dislike the most first. Don't procrastinate!

The Importance of Writing It Down

Never count on your memory for complete accuracy. Write things down. Don't keep information in your head. Communicate and share what you know. The possibility always exists that you could be called away from your unit, and if you haven't communicated with others, tasks could be mistakenly repeated or omitted.

The patient's safety, well-being, and positive outcomes are your prime objective. Your best proof of what you did and the patient's outcome is in your documentation. You may one day need your documentation to be detailed enough for you to testify without a shadow of your own doubt that everything written is exactly as it happened. You won't be given a chance to supplement or to add your own comments later on. The documentation has to stand on its own.

Documentation Technology

A PDA may afford you the best possible solution. You can set up a new screen for each of your patients in the most basic of notepad software that comes built-in with your PDA. Smartphones may have a great app just for this. Or you can choose from an elaborate number of other software or app choices that can include customizable forms to write your notes in.

Your facility may even have the capability of using software that can be synchronized with the main systems to upload from your device directly into the hospital's records. This is becoming more commonplace, especially where computerized record keeping has been utilized for some time.

FACT

Some wireless, paperless systems have the capability of documenting at the bedside, which affords you the opportunity to document immediately. Without this type of situation, your best means of presenting the most accurate documentation is by taking notes and then documenting from them as soon as you can.

The advantage of a PDA or smartphone is that you can protect your files with a password. Even if you misplace your device and someone picks it up, they won't have immediate access to confidential information.

Organizing Your Notes

New systems and electronic devices with software and apps will be developed over time to help make the nurse's life easier. Whatever system you choose, the more you can customize your work for yourself, the more time you can save on the other end. This will ensure that your documentation will be more accurate and timely as well. Don't reinvent the wheel; ask your coworkers if they have something similar that works for them. Perhaps you can brainstorm and come up with something that you could share and duplicate.

Other considerations for your note-taking system include a means to keep the information confidential. You don't want to drop scraps of paper from your pocket in the hospital cafeteria with identifying information on them, along with current vital signs or medication notes. You obviously don't want to lose them and you certainly don't need others finding them.

Another purpose for your notes includes making lists of the following:

- Information you need to share with other team members about a patient.
- Things you need to research on your own for your benefit, such as a new diagnosis.
- Meds that are new to you and you need to look up today.
- Resources you need to check on for patient teaching.
- Positive things that happened today.

Throughout your career, you should always be on the lookout for new ways to help you manage your time. Use it wisely, and you will appreciate having more time to spend with your patients.

CHAPTER 9

Utilizing Teamwork

Teamwork requires each member to have the ability to communicate, to problem solve, and to negotiate while working toward a common goal. Each team member shares that goal and takes ownership of their shared responsibility to achieve that goal. As a Japanese proverb states: "None of us is as smart as all of us."

What Is Teamwork?

Teamwork is defined as the collaborative effort of a group to achieve a common goal. In health care, the goal is to improve the quality of life and outcomes for the patient. This is achieved as all the team members involved in the patient's care work together to provide the highest possible quality of care.

Even in situations where the patient dies, if the team members have coordinated their efforts to provide the best of care and to ease the pain and suffering of the patient and his loved ones, then the effort is successful. This is an example of a situation where the goal may not always include the patient getting better. But it doesn't mean that even for a few seconds, the quality of the life wasn't improved just a little. Did the patient die with dignity and were you there by his side? Then you improved the quality of his life.

ESSENTIAL

Sometimes you have to dig a little deeper or look at the situation from a different angle or perspective to see the success. It won't change the fact that it always hurts to lose a patient, but it will help to give you the strength to carry on and to help others in the same situation.

Your Common Goal

Health care naturally lends itself to teamwork. There isn't a time when one individual is solely responsible for a patient's outcomes. There will always be at least the patient and one other health care team member. More often than not, there will be several team members. Together you will work toward one goal: improving the patient's quality of life and outcomes from a spell of illness or chronic disease by promoting wellness.

Take time to get to know your teammates. Sometimes you will have to make the first move and other times someone will take you under her wing. In either case, if you learn a little about each person, you'll gain some insight into who they are and how they work. You won't like everyone, but if everyone is a team player, you'll be working together for a common goal and liking or not liking won't matter much. Strive to keep up your end of the bargain and stay focused.

> As the new kid on the block, you're bound to feel a little out of place at first, but if you understand that you have a role as a team member and work toward this common team goal while providing the best possible care, you'll find your place.

Teamwork Give and Take

You can learn a lot from your coworkers through working on a team. Who is strong clinically? Who exhibits the best leadership and how? Who drives everyone crazy and why? Who is a weak team member or perhaps not a team player at all? How does management deal with them? Whether good, bad, or indifferent team members, you will take away valuable lessons for your own self-improvement.

Of course, teamwork always works best when everyone is a team player. If each person is working alone and for his or her individual stardom, you won't have a team. One person who is not a team player can spoil the effort for everyone else. This kind of person makes you want to avoid or work around him to virtually eliminate him. Sometimes that's just not possible and the spirit of the team is broken.

The team leader or unit manager sets the tone and is responsible for keeping the team intact. All team members have to be dedicated to the common goal as well. If someone isn't working out, the entire team needs to work toward pulling her in. But the team leader is ultimately responsible to support the team in doing this. Sometimes the team has to approach the team leader and bring its concerns about this member to her attention.

How to Delegate

Only an RN can delegate. To delegate is to entrust or transfer the power, authority, or responsibility to perform a task to someone else. In nursing, it is usually "per occurrence" and should be limited to care of patients who are stable or who have a predictable outcome. You should never delegate care for an unstable patient.

ESSENTIAL

In delegating care, it is essential for the RN to understand the scope of practice and/or job description of those to whom he is delegating. He must also have an understanding of the level of skills the person to whom he has delegated a responsibility possesses. The RN retains responsibility for any task that he delegates.

No one is expected to do it all. In fact, if you find yourself doing things that could or should be done by someone else, then you are wasting time and resources. However, if the other person is busy and the job needs to be done, then anyone available who can do the job should be helping out.

Delegation is an art that will take some time to learn. To some, it comes more naturally than to others. But for an RN, it is an essential part of the job. In addition to specific tasks, you may need help in aspects of a patient's care, including assessment, identifying problems and goals, planning and implementing a strategy for the patient's care, maintaining safety, dealing with emergencies, and evaluating the effectiveness of the care. These responsibilities would not be delegated away, but rather you would be looking for input from other staff in making decisions and implementing patient care.

Understanding the scope of practice or job description and skills of those to whom you delegate is essential to the quality of patient care. You don't want to put anyone at risk. That includes you, your coworker, the patient, your supervisor, and the facility, among others.

In the performance of your assignment, you may find tasks that you need assistance with; for example, an IV medication has not been dispensed from the pharmacy. You could ask the unit secretary to call and check on it for you and to pick it up if necessary. If a patient needs some assistance in eating and you have a dressing to change and an IV to start, you could ask an aide or tech to help feed the patient. You could ask the

LVN/LPN to dispense a PRN medication if you need to attend to a task and the patient is in need of the med right now.

FACT

Remember, unlicensed persons, such as nursing aides, UAPs, and techs, will not have a scope of practice as defined by law. Instead, they will function under a job description as written by the facility. Ask for a copy of each and know what they can and cannot do before delegating.

These are ways to begin to learn how to delegate. Start with small, uncomplicated tasks that you could certainly do yourself. If delegating these kinds of tasks frees you up to complete a larger, more difficult task and doesn't overburden someone else, then they can easily be delegated away. As you become more comfortable with delegating, when you have a more complicated task that you need to pass on in order to admit a new patient, then you can begin to delegate more. Always say thank you, and whenever possible do something to return the favor.

The RN Is Responsible for the Team

In the process of delegation, the RN remains responsible for the task that was delegated. You need to follow up and evaluate the procedure or task. If you asked the aide to feed your patient, it is your responsibility to follow up and see that it was done, and to see how much the patient ate and how well the patient tolerated the food. How much was the patient able to partici-pate? Did the LVN/LPN give the PRN medication? How long ago? And did it help with the symptoms?

As noted above, as an RN, you are responsible for your team. Perhaps you have an aide and an LVN/LPN working with you. You have your own assigned patients, but perhaps you are expected to oversee the patients assigned to these two as well. Or perhaps your job is to supervise the aide and the LVN/LPN and oversee the care for all the patients they are caring for without an additional specific assignment of patients yourself.

You could find yourself in charge of your unit for a shift sooner than you think possible as well. This is more likely to happen for the BSN-RN, but depending on the availability of staff, being placed in charge of a unit could happen to anyone. Be prepared.

Remember, the shortage of nurses is expected to worsen over the next fifteen to twenty years as older nurses retire and more patients have access to health care coverage. Sometimes facilities seemingly care more about making money and staying afloat than in protecting nurse's licenses or providing the best care to patients. One issue raised here is staffing ratios, which are being debated all across the country. You need to look out for your license and be sure to protect your patients' rights.

If you are an LPN, you most likely won't find yourself in charge unless you work somewhere other than a hospital, but you could be responsible for supervising an aide or two and reporting to the RN. The ultimate responsibility will fall to the RN, but your assignment in supervising should be clear to you. No matter what level you are on the nursing ladder, you are always responsible for your own actions. Your goal is always to provide the best care possible and to be mindful of your own scope of practice and job description.

No One Is above Emptying Bedpans

More than one nurse has gone into nursing confident that bedpans are not an issue because the nursing aide takes care of them. The truth is that no one should ever be above emptying a bedpan. Your goal in becoming a nurse was to help alleviate pain and suffering and to make a difference in someone's life every day.

When you answer a call light or if you are just walking down the hall and get flagged down to help someone on or off a bedpan, you need to help and not put it off saying, "I'll get your aide for you." Of course, if you're on your way to another patient to assist a doctor or were right in the middle of a new admission and cannot stop, a quick explanation and a call to the aide could be appropriate.

Don't overuse this excuse. Even the director of patient care services or director of nurses has probably been seen recently rolling up her sleeves and getting back to the basics of patient care.

FACT

Being seen as "too good" for the realities of patient care can be very harmful to your professional reputation and could be just cause for your coworkers to lose respect for you both as a nurse and as a team player.

The patient's dignity is at risk and should never be compromised by anyone involved in patient care. Elimination is a fact of life. It may not be one of the most pleasant aspects of patient care, but how you handle yourself and how you react may make a big difference. Do your best to make that difference a positive one.

Can You Make This More Fun?

The management in any organization will set the tone for the culture and atmosphere of the facility. Health care is a serious business and shouldn't be taken lightly. However, that in no way means that the staff should not enjoy their jobs and the company of those they work with.

You will spend a major portion of your life at work with your coworkers. It's important for you to get to know them in order to have a better understanding of who they are and what is important to them. Your coworkers will become like family in the best of situations. Like family, there will be your favorites and those you wish would just move out or grow up. Get to know a little about each one, and you'll have a better insight into who they are professionally.

Some Examples

You know that the cranky woman named Susan, who works as an aide, also cares for her bedridden elderly mother. She works full-time. While she is at work, her sister cares for her mom, and when she gets home, her sister goes to work and she assumes the care of her mother. Usually, it's bedtime for Mom, and Susan can get some rest; but some nights, Mom is up all night demanding attention. Susan tries to be cheerful, but her responsibilities at home are taking a toll on her. What energy she has is spent on the patients, and she is very short with her coworkers.

If you know that Steve, one of the LPNs, lost his five-year-old daughter to leukemia about three months ago, you'll have a better understanding of why he always begs to switch patients if he ends up with a cancer patient. It is unfortunate that the nurse making the assignments hasn't taken the time to understand this or apparently has no sensitivity to his issue.

If you know that Judy, one of the RNs, has two teenage latch-key sons, who report in when they leave for school and when they get back home, you'll understand why she takes a quick personal call almost as soon as she arrives in the morning. Her husband is in the army and has recently been deployed out of the country into a very dangerous situation. She and her sons have this pact to stay in touch to help reduce their stress levels. (Otherwise, non-emergency personal calls are really frowned upon.) But everyone seems to understand because they know about it. In fact, if the boys don't call, the unit secretary goes looking for Judy to find out why.

Having Fun at Work

In some facilities, the administration encourages a playful atmosphere to help reduce stress and to encourage a strong team effort. There are several approaches to this kind of work environment. One of these has come to be known as the Fish Philosophy. You can learn more about this at *www.fish philosophy.com*. It developed at Seattle's Fish Market Place and has evolved into a whole program of learning to have fun at work while improving performance.

ESSENTIAL

A major challenge in health care is to get the patient involved and to take responsibility for his own wellness and outcomes. If the invitation is enticing, the prospect for success is greatly improved. If the health care staff is having fun, the patients should be more interested in taking part.

The premise of most of these programs is to help individuals to focus on what they bring to the team, including attitude and the ability to focus each day, and encourages individuals to find ways to make work fun and to help each other.

Tension Between Shifts

Each shift has its own unique assignment depending on the time of day. For instance, the day shift will have to contend with the majority of the therapy sessions, x-rays, scans, and other tests that will usually take the patient away from the unit. They will have the majority of the discharges, as well as admissions. Bathing and linen changes are done in the morning. Coupled with the individual needs of each patient, every staff member has more than enough to accomplish. Everything should be done to avoid leaving anything extra for the next shift to handle.

Night Shift versus Day Shift

Sometimes a competition develops between shifts. For instance, in a situation where the facility runs on two twelve-hour shifts (7 A.M. to 7 P.M. and 7 P.M. to 7 A.M.), the P.M. or night shift is often the "stepchild" so to speak. It becomes the inferior shift. The nurses on the A.M. or day shift often feel superior because they are working the "chosen" shift, the shift everyone wants and has to pay her dues to get onto.

In this instance, every time the P.M. shift leaves something for the day shift to complete, another demerit is piled on to their already poor reputation. The day shift is often very put upon and cannot possibly understand why the night shift can't get things done while most of the patients are sleeping.

ALERT

When a team works well together, not completing assignments is usually avoided except under extreme circumstances. However, when staff members are not team players, the system tends to break down. This is exactly the situation that needs to be addressed with and by management.

Of course, if the day shift leaves something over, they're leaving it for the poor stepchildren because they were too busy. Never mind that half of the patients spent the day somewhere else. Everyone needs to do his or her part and to work with the system and not against it to ensure everything gets done each shift.

Solutions to Shift Rivalry

Some activities that can help build team spirit include a column in your facility newsletter to spotlight employees in a "get to know them" manner. Bulletin boards where employees are encouraged to post family photos should be encouraged on the units. These could include family pets or vacation photos or pictures of a coworker's latest remodeling project. Devote a few minutes at staff meetings or once a week at report to share information about your shift and your family of employees.

When planned for, a few minutes spent devoted to team building will benefit everyone. Team building is not necessarily something that should be allowed to be put off just because the shift is too busy. This should be especially true if your team isn't working well together and needs to get back on track.

ESSENTIAL

This rivalry seems to happen everywhere. How far it's allowed to go depends on the strength of the management. Utilizing events such as parties and picnics can help give all employees an opportunity to mix and mingle and get to know each other. Other activities throughout a facility or just in a particular unit can be utilized to promote team growth and well-being as well.

When a team is working well together, tasks usually won't be left undone. Team members will work together to help each other complete their assignments so that they can get out on time. A happy environment fosters improved productivity and less stress and can go a long way toward helping to retain the staff you have.

CHAPTER 10

Learn from Your Mistakes

Nurses don't make mistakes, do they? The truth is nurses are human and no one is perfect. You will make a mistake or two in your career. The object is to avoid the mistakes that are unnecessary and to keep anything beyond your control to a minimum. There are many safeguards that have been developed to help all health care workers avoid mistakes.

Slow Down and Take a Break

Wage and hour laws have been written to ensure job safety both for the worker and employer and for the product. In health care, the product is the patient. These laws will vary from one state to another, but the U.S. Department of Labor does have regulations that the health care industry must follow. These are set forth in the Fair Labor Standards Act. For further information, see *www.dol.gov/whd*. You can also access your state's labor laws from this site.

ESSENTIAL

It is not up to your employer to ensure that you take your breaks—it is up to you. Make sure you take your breaks. It's easy to get into the habit of skipping them and, in some units, to feel like you can't take a break because it's so busy and you are so shortstaffed. You may experience peer pressure to skip breaks.

For purposes of illustration, assume the following information fits with your state's laws. After four hours on the job, you are expected to take a fifteen-minute break. If you work over six hours, you are expected to have a meal break of at least thirty minutes. This time possibly grows to an hour if you work eight hours or more each day. In a twelve-hour shift, you should have a one-hour meal and two to three fifteen-minute breaks.

Find a Way to Take a Minute

Even if you can't take the full amount of time because you are so busy, try to take some time. You do need to eat and take bathroom breaks. Help each other be able to do so. This is where a strong team approach will be most helpful. Don't abuse the situation, but do help each other to get away from the unit.

Some facilities have breakers or float personnel who just cover for breaks and meals. A unit must have a licensed person on duty at all times. Unless your facility allows LPNs to be alone on a unit, an RN must be on duty at all times. If you are the only RN on your unit, someone must come and relieve you for your meal break. You must be able to take a meal break free from interruption, or your employer must pay you for the time. You could possibly take your other breaks in the nurse's lounge or break room. You would still technically be on duty and available. Breaks do not have to be uninterrupted.

Avoiding Burnout

While recent studies have not shown that nurses who don't get breaks make more errors than those who do, the studies have shown that among nurses who do take breaks, those who take longer ones are less prone to making mistakes. The findings also show that staff burnout and staff departure are major problems related to not getting breaks. What this most likely means is that nurses who aren't taking breaks are intensely aware of the potential for harm; they are making more of an effort to protect their patients as well as their licenses. This added stress will eventually lead to burnout and cause nurses to leave their position.

FACT

You really need to be able to walk away from the job for a few minutes and clear your head. This will help relieve stress and give you a new perspective on the tasks at hand. It affords you a moment to take in some nutrition and fluids and to visit the bathroom.

Burnout and staff retention are issues that severely affect the nursing shortage. They are issues that nurses have to contend with and must be addressed in solving this crisis. If you and your coworkers get into the habit of not taking your breaks or allow your employer to abuse the staff in this manner, your facility will continue to suffer. Work with your nurse manager and your facility to solve this problem and improve the working conditions. Having satisfied staff members will go a long way in recruitment and retention issues.

Learn to Say No

As the new member of your unit, you may be compelled to volunteer every time there is a new need. This will no doubt help you gain experience, but it can be very taxing as well. You need to know your own limitations. And you need to be mindful of what work you may be passing on to your coworkers in order to take on a new assignment. On the other hand, you don't want to pass up experiences or seem never to be willing to take on additional work.

Sometimes this involves serving on committees within your facility. This will afford you an opportunity to get to know others and to work toward solving issues that you and your coworkers have expressed. It may be something that you attend on your time off, or it might take you away from your unit for a scheduled period of time.

Sometimes you may just be adding on a patient or two or other duty on your unit when someone has called in sick and no replacement can be found. Handling the extra patient may make you a helpful team member. However, when taking on this responsibility causes you to have to ask for additional help to accomplish it, perhaps you and your coworkers would be best served if you don't take on the additional assignment. You could just volunteer to help the person who does accept it.

The most important time to say no is when you are being asked to do something you have never done before or are not competent in and you are expected to do the task without a preceptor or other assistance/supervision.

You will sometimes be asked to work an additional shift. This shift will be either a double shift, or portion thereof, or an additional day in your work week. You will be compensated at an overtime rate, but you should realize that overtime is taxed at a different rate and you won't be taking home a lot more money. Your primary consideration should be your ability to safely perform your duties under these circumstances, and you should be honest about it with your employer before you agree.

ALERT

You will likely be "guilted" into the extra hours, but you may have very good reasons for not being able to do it. You may have plans that can't be changed or a child to care for. You may not be feeling well. You may already be working on very little sleep and be too exhausted to continue. Be tactful but firm.

These situations unfortunately are a fact of life, especially in a hospital setting, and everyone will probably have to take a turn. If you can't do it this time, be sure to say that you would be willing to take your turn another time. This willingness to share responsibilities will help to ease any resentment from coworkers. If you can work some portion of the extra assignment, offer that to your supervisor as a possibility, and perhaps she can work something out so that no one is overburdened any more than necessary.

Using Your Policy and Procedure Manual

Each unit should have a copy of the facility's policy and procedure manual (P&P) as well as a standards of care manual. Some facilities write their own manuals, others buy standard versions. Some facilities have a combination of both and cross-reference them. Be sure you know where these manuals are located and use them frequently. Make copies of pages as you use them to take home and review. The P&P manuals are meant to help prevent errors and set a standard of care.

ESSENTIAL

These manuals describe how a procedure is expected to be performed in this facility. You are expected to know this and never assume that the way you learned to do something is the only way to do it and is acceptable everywhere. Locate your manuals and read them. Fill any free time you have familiarizing yourself with the contents.

Each time you perform a new procedure, you must refer to these manuals first. Even if the procedure is not new to you, but it is the first time you have performed it in this facility, you must refer to the manual. You will show your preceptor that you are eager to do things correctly if you have already reviewed the manual before consulting with him to check you off on a procedure. Whenever you change jobs or facilities, one of the first things you need to do is to review the P&P for that facility. These manuals will be very different and very similar at the same time.

If your facility uses a purchased P&P and you have used this P&P before during your schooling, don't assume you don't need to refer to it. This facility may have updated or changed portions of the manual, and the only way you're going to know for sure is to check. By the same token, if you're about to do something you haven't done in a while, always check the manual for possible updates.

If a particular doctor has his own way of doing something, he will usually bring it to the policy committee at a hospital, and they will review it and incorporate it into their P&P manual. Therefore, the information in the manual is never carved in stone.

For example, a physician might have a very specific procedure for central line care. This might involve swabbing the site six times instead of the standard three times each with alcohol and betadine (or perhaps another antiseptic). Some might want a 2 × 2 used routinely, while some only want a transparent dressing. And there might be a particular way you must curl the line and secure it with tape or risk having your head torn off.

Your facility might have specific tasks that can only be performed by RNs even though most anywhere else an LVN/LPN can perform them. Your facility may have implemented very specific procedures for patient identification that must be used at all times. If you aren't familiar with the manual, you could be omitting an important step.

In addition to knowing the scope of practice or job descriptions, you must follow procedure in your facility to ensure safe practice and safe care for the patient. You are responsible for knowing this information.

The P&P might also include organizational information, such as procedures for voicing a grievance, how often the manual is routinely updated and reviewed, what committees function in the organization, and how to contact them, and so on. Familiarize yourself with this and your standards of care manual. You may be able to answer many of your own questions or bring intelligent questions to your supervisor or staff meetings.

The Five Rights of Medications

There are "Five Rights" to accurate medication administration. Some have added to this list to make as many as Eight Rights. If all are observed, the potential for mistakes is drastically reduced. Nurses learn these rules in school. The tendency to skimp on them is a problem that often stems from factors such as overconfidence and staffing shortages. There is no excuse to skimp on rules; follow the rules and keep your patients safe.

These Five Rights are:

- Right Medication
- Right Dose
- Right Time
- Right Route
- Right Patient

The Right Medication

Check the label on the bottle, bubble pack, or other packaging; the doctor's order; and the medication administration record (MAR). If there are any discrepancies, ask. Check the chart and doctor's notes and ask the pharmacy. If doubt remains, call the physician for clarification.

The Right Dose

Check the doctor's order, the MAR, and the packaging label. If you are unfamiliar with this medication, check your drug book. Be sure you are using the most up-to-date source. If you are unsure of a dose, ask. Consult with the pharmacist or call the doctor.

The Right Time

Again, check the order, the MAR, and the medication label. Give the medication at the precise time. If you question the frequency, look it up, and if necessary, consult the pharmacist or doctor.

The Right Route

Again, always check the order, the MAR, and the medication label. Can this medication be given as ordered? Can the patient swallow it? Or can it be crushed? Is it available in a liquid form? If it's an IV med, is it compatible with the solutions and site? If it's injectable, what other parameters need to be considered?

The Right Patient

Most important of all, do you have the right patient? How do you know? Verify all the above steps and then verify the patient information. Check the wristband. Ask the patient to tell you his name and date of birth. If he can't tell you, does he know his physician's name? Is there a family member present to verify identification? Never assume that you know this patient or use the room and bed number as the sole means of identification.

The additional rights added by some nursing schools or boards of nursing include the Right Reason (why are you giving this medication?), the Right Documentation, and the Right Assessment. What assessment brings you to decide to administer this medication and what assessment says it was effective or not?

Double-Check and Document

When all these steps have been followed, check for any protocols from your facility, especially in regard to IV or injectable medications. Make sure the patient swallows any oral medications. Never leave a medication for the patient to take later. Observe the patient for a response and any possible reaction. Follow protocols for medications that require frequent monitoring and for any specific procedures or protocols required if this is the patient's first dose of a medication.

Document on the MAR and anywhere else appropriate whether additional information is needed or appropriate to the situation. Notify the doctor immediately in the event of any reaction or error.

Medication errors account for a major portion of errors in the health care industry and they are avoidable. Don't become a statistic. Don't take chances. Follow these Five (or Eight) Rights with every medication you dispense, including your own.

Patient Safety Rules

Patient safety rules were made for a reason. Patient safety is one of the primary issues facing the health care industry today. It is also one of the most studied areas. According to the Institute of Medicine, approximately 98,000 Americans die each year from avoidable medical errors. In an absurd comparison, a patient in a hospital is 40 percent more likely to be injured because of negligence than an airline passenger is to have his luggage lost.

One of the most prevalent reasons for medical errors results from the lack of adequate information. The inability to access information is the largest challenge. Doctors and nurses don't set out to make mistakes, but if they don't have the patient's medical history at their fingertips, errors can easily be made.

The credit cards in your wallet contain vital information about your identity that can be accessed just by passing its magnetic strip through a reader. But your medical records are often still maintained in large paper files held in hospital vaults and doctors' offices. In the event of an emergency, chances of accessing that information in a timely manner are very slim to none. We saw this become a huge issue after Hurricane Katrina. The move toward electronic medical records sparks great debate, but it can and will save lives.

The technology exists to solve this dilemma, but there needs to be an organization to oversee dissemination of information. Privacy laws recently enacted have both helped and hindered this process. One thing is for sure, these errors add to the high cost of medical care.

Errors in health care stem from several actions. These actions can be errors of execution, such as doing something incorrectly. They can be errors of omission, such as not doing something that needs to be done. And they can be errors of commission, as in doing the wrong thing.

Several nonprofit organizations have formed and stepped in to study the problem and to establish goals and interventions to help reduce and prevent medical errors. Accreditation agencies such as JCAHO have taken the issue seriously and have established standards that include patient safety goals. For additional information, see the JCAHO site at *www.jcaho.org*.

Each year, JCAHO implements mandatory safety standards throughout the industry for accredited facilities. For 2011, the rules include the following:

- **Correct patient identification.** Use two forms of identification, such as asking the patient to spell his name and tell you his date of birth. Some facilities use bar codes on patient wristbands.
- **Safe use of medications.** All medications must be labeled. For example, medications in syringes, basins, and cups must be labeled with the name of the medication, the dose, and who prepared it.
- **Infection prevention.** Follow CDC guidelines for hand washing. Take precautions with open wounds and surgical sites.
- **Medication oversight.** Find out all of the medications a patient is taking before adding any medications. Make sure there are not conflicts between the medications or contraindications. Ensure that the patient, caregivers, and all members of his medical team have a current and complete list of medications the patient is taking.

Following patient safety goals and rules will help to reduce the occurrence of medical errors. Staying informed about advances in medical treatments and procedures will help as well. And encouraging your facility and coworkers to become comfortable with technological advances will help health care move more quickly into a realm where medical information is stored electronically and immediately accessible.

When an Error Happens

If an error does occur, tell the truth right away. Don't make an error worse by trying to cover it up or sweep it under the rug. If you have done your best to follow patient safety rules and to avoid mistakes, chances are that it is a minimal mistake; but you must report it. Discuss it privately with your nurse manager or supervisor. Then notify the doctor and anyone else your supervisor says must be notified.

Remember the three types of errors: where you do something incorrectly; when you omit something; or when you do the wrong thing. Any one of them constitutes a reportable error. The damage done will tell you how dangerous it was, but other factors can be involved as well. These can include such things as whether you were preoccupied at the time, trying to do too many things at once, partied all night and didn't sleep well, or tried to do something by yourself and should have asked for help.

QUESTION

What should I do if I'm late passing the medications?
Perhaps you forgot to pass your medications before you took your break so you're a few minutes late in getting to them. You need to contend with this situation yourself so that it doesn't happen again, but it does not require notifying the world.

If you forgot to change an IV bag and now it has run dry and blood has backed up and the line is clotted, well, that's another story. At the very least, you need to pray that the patient has good veins and you can get the IV restarted easily. You will need to apologize to the patient and notify your supervisor.

Hopefully, your errors will be small and cause no real harm to the patient. However, if you have made a significant error, you need to own up to it and notify the doctor as soon as possible to begin to rectify the error. For instance, you were busy and gave the wrong patient a set of medications. You didn't take the time to check two forms of identification. The medications were for a patient who was away from his bed when you were passing these meds and you got confused. This was all the more reason to double check IDs, but you were sure you had the right patient because you have spent some additional time talking with him and his family.

In patients with his condition, one of the meds is contraindicated. You notify your supervisor and then call the doctor. The doctor is not happy, but says the patient has taken this medication before and had no ill effects from it. His orders are to keep a watchful eye on the patient, recheck his vitals in an hour, and call the doctor if the patient's blood pressure or heart rate changes. He further advises you not to tell the patient what happened because he'll worry needlessly at this point.

You will also most likely have to fill out an incident report that will be filed with the quality improvement/risk management office or with the director of patient care services. This report is a statement of the facts, a list of who was notified, and any untoward effects noted. It's kept on file in case the situation is investigated or any litigation proceedings are brought on by an incident for review by the facility. Incident reports should not be copied and placed in your personnel file and there should be no further mention of it unless something more serious develops.

Surviving Your First Mistake

Because you are human, you will make a mistake once in a while. As a new nurse, you will have spent countless hours feeling incompetent and stupid. You may even feel as if everything you learned in the last few years suddenly disappeared from your brain and is never coming back.

This is all perfectly normal. It's going to take time to feel confident and at ease in such situations. Every nurse before you has experienced this, and they are still nurses.

Slow down, ask questions, and remember that no nurse ever stops learning nor will he know it all at some point.

ESSENTIAL

If you make a mistake, tell your supervisor right away. Take ownership of it and learn from it. What can you do to avoid it and any similar mistakes in the future? Then move on. Don't dwell on it; there is nothing more you can do.

Hopefully, no one was seriously harmed. If you truly cannot figure out how it happened, you will have to let that go as well. You may understand it later.

An error is going to play havoc with your confidence. Expect this to happen and do all that you can to move on and prevent recurrence. If you have been keeping a journal of positive experiences, this may be the ideal time to review it and remind yourself that you have done many things in your short career to make life better for your patients. You did not intend to make this error and you will take better care never to repeat it.

Online discussion boards are full of comments from new nurses who have just made their first mistake or a colleague did and how they are dealing with it. Read them and pay attention to the responses from the experienced nurses. The experienced nurses share their own experiences, commiserate, and offer advice on how to learn from the error and put it behind you. Focus on the positive and the reasons you became a nurse. This too shall pass.

CHAPTER 11

What You Learned in School

School is behind you now, and your new "homework" each day consists of learning about policies and procedures and facility issues. You now spend a great deal of your "free" time looking up meds and diseases and treatment modalities. You haven't written a care plan or thought about a case study in weeks or months. You are simply overwhelmed with all that you have to do for your patients! How can you ever possibly apply anything you learned in school?

The Nursing Process

Ida Jean Orlando developed her theory of deliberative nursing process in the late 1950s based on her observations of "good" and "bad" nursing. The patient is the central theme of her theory, which is one of the most effective and practical of all nursing theories.

Basically stated, the nurse's primary role in the nursing process is to find out what the patient's most immediate need is and to provide assistance. This is accomplished in five steps: assessment, diagnosis, planning, implementation, and evaluation. The nursing process is an ongoing cycle of these steps that you will repeat over and over with your patients.

Ms. Orlando's original theory included the nursing diagnosis step in assessment and therefore had only four steps. In practice over the past few decades, the process has expanded to five steps.

Assessment

Whether you are aware of it, you adhere to the concepts of the nursing process every day. You assess patients constantly. If you are an LPN, your assessment is limited to data collection only, but you most likely report your findings to an RN and help her to plan and deliver the care needed. Assessment involves two steps: collecting data as you proceed with your assessment and analyzing the data to 1) determine the patient's health status, his coping mechanisms, and ability to use them and 2) to identify problems.

(Nursing) Diagnosis

These problems you have identified translate into nursing diagnoses. You might formally choose from the North American Nursing Diagnosis Association (NANDA) list, or you may only informally incorporate them into your daily routines. As you know, nurses don't diagnose illnesses except in the case of NPs, who have been specifically trained in this practice. Nurses make nursing diagnoses. Your diagnosis will provide the basis for selecting nursing interventions to help the patient deal with his current illness and health status. Nursing diagnoses are based on clinical judgment about how the patient, his family, and possibly even his community respond to his health status issues. These issues can be actual health problems, potential health problems, or any combination thereof.

Planning

The RN will develop a plan to prioritize the immediate needs of the patient that were discovered in the assessment and diagnosis phases. The LPN and nurse's aide, UAP, and other team members will be given directions about the plan. This plan may be a very formal written plan or may be just a verbal one made up on the fly utilizing your critical thinking skills. Your plan incorporates nursing interventions and goals to improve the patient's outcomes and the means to implement the plan.

FACT

The patient will always be the center of your plan when utilizing the nursing process. Plans and goals will be measurable and patient oriented, such as "the patient will demonstrate. . . ." Other measurable verbs include *verbalize, state, ambulate, describe, identify, perform, display, apply,* and *avoid.* Verbs that are too nonspecific and should be avoided include *learn, know,* and *understand.*

Implementation

Following all delegation rules, the RN will provide direct care, delegate as appropriate, and supervise the team in implementing the plan and interventions to meet the patient's immediate needs. The team members need to report to the RN any significant findings during this process. The RN needs to supervise the team and follow up to ensure that the delegated portions of the plan have been implemented.

Nursing interventions include treatments based on clinical judgments and medical knowledge and necessity that will enhance the patient's outcomes. These interventions may be initiated by the nurse, the physician, or other health care team member.

Evaluation

Based on findings reported from team members, including hers and the patient's, the RN will evaluate the effectiveness of the plan. She will make revisions as needed and discuss them with team members, including consulting with the physician for new orders. The RN will also evaluate for new requirements and begin the process again.

The evaluation process is a reassessment. It includes collection of subjective data, which is what the patient or team members tell you. You will also include your own objective data, which is what your senses tell you—what you see, smell, hear, and feel. The subjective data is the symptoms and the objective data is the signs.

ESSENTIAL

Even if you don't actually write out a formal care plan for each patient, you are still using the nursing process to direct your care. The care you give and delegate and the documentation of that care reflect the five stages of the nursing process: assessment, diagnosis, planning, implementation, and evaluation.

The nursing process is one of the most misunderstood concepts. Most students struggle with it, and for some, it takes a long time before it becomes clear. As you deliver your care each day, think about how you are applying this process to your patients.

NANDA

The North American Nursing Diagnosis Association is an international agency that works to develop, classify, and update nursing diagnoses to help direct the nursing process.

The term nursing diagnosis was first used in 1953 as a necessary step in completing a nursing care plan, but it wasn't until 1973 at the first meeting of the National Group for the Classification of Nursing Diagnosis that the term became widely used. This group evolved into NANDA in 1982.

The current NANDA list for 2009–2011 contains 206 approved nursing diagnoses. In the summer of 2011, the list will be reviewed and revised. Official NANDA publications are the only way to ensure you have the most current approved list. These are available for purchase from their website, *www.nanda.org*.

Using NANDA's system is another nemesis for many nursing students and often doesn't begin to make sense until you are actually using it on a regular basis to direct the care you are providing to your patients.

The diagnosis may be something that you use formally with written care plans and goals, or it may again be something you draw from informally. On any given day, your patients will exhibit more than one problem requiring nursing interventions. These can range from issues with their own well-being, such as acute pain, to psychosocial issues of powerlessness and anxiety. The problems can also involve issues with their family or with caregivers who exhibit their own inability to deal with the patient and his pain and anxiety.

Your assessment and interventions will involve determining the signs and symptoms that contribute to the pain and measures that help to reduce the pain and to provide measures to both increase the patient's tolerance as well as reduce the pain.

Your goals will be measurable and realistic, such as "The patient will state that his pain level is reduced from 9/10 to 4/10 with the use of relaxation techniques, therapeutic massage, and medication regime by day three of the current admission."

Using Care Plans

Some institutions forgo formal written care plans because of staff shortages and time constraints—until time for surveys. Others use them in varied forms, from simple and barely complete, to something your professors would hail as an "A" paper.

The fact is that whether you have a formal written plan, as you use the nursing process to deliver your care, you will formulate a care plan for each of your patients. Each time you perform a nursing intervention you will have goals for your patient's outcomes and will assess the response to the intervention.

Some regard care plans as a waste of time, but actually, if used properly, they can be a time saver. Each shift doesn't have to reinvent the wheel. Perhaps issues have been reprioritized because of some changes; the care plan disseminates this information to the team. Without some form of formal plan, the continuity of care is compromised, and the quality of care and outcomes are no longer optimal.

ESSENTIAL

Care plans provide a road map for the entire team to follow in providing care. These plans also provide evidence of where you have been and what worked and what didn't. If a problem has been resolved, it is crucial for the team to know it and move on. Valuable time can be lost continuing to focus on an issue that is no longer important.

Care plans are an important part of the health care delivery process and should be utilized. This is more important now as the delivery system shifts away from primary care back to a system used in the 1970s and early 1980s where RNs were team leaders and LPNs and aides provided most of the hands-on care. Today, as more and more unlicensed personnel are used, the level of responsibility placed on the RN is compounded, and a road map for care is even more essential to keeping everyone on the same page.

Cultural Differences That Affect Health Care

The United States is a melting pot of ethnic and cultural diversity. In a health care setting, this can cause a nightmare for the patient and the health care team. Imagine a young woman being brought in by paramedics from an automobile accident. She is bleeding from somewhere under her clothing, and the first thoughts of the emergency workers is to cut away her clothing so that they can examine her. She speaks very little English and is extremely distraught that a male nurse and EMT are in the room as she is being exposed.

This could describe almost any young woman who is vitally concerned with her own modesty, but suppose it is a young Muslim woman who has recently emigrated here. That changes the situation, and it becomes more apparent that her cultural values can adversely affect her health care situation as she struggles to remain covered and delays diagnosis and treatment.

Or perhaps a young child of Jehovah's Witness faith is critically injured in an accident and has lost a significant amount of blood. His religious beliefs prohibit transfusion of any form of blood products.

e! ALERT

Just as you wouldn't classify all diabetics into one category and expect that they will all react to a specific diabetic regimen in the same manner, you cannot lump all people of one culture, race, or religious belief into one category. Health care needs to be individualized for each patient, and in doing so, you need to take into account all aspects of who this person is.

Transcultural health care models have emerged over the past thirty years, but as far as nursing care is concerned, the nursing process still drives how the care is provided. You need to assess all patients, diagnose their nursing health care needs, plan for their care, and implement and evaluate the care. In implementing the care plan, you always need to consider who this person is, what they believe, and what their background is.

Cultural differences affect how people react to illness, respond to symptoms, seek medical care, and perceive the health care team members. All this affects how they will react to and respond to treatment and must be considered to effect the best possible outcomes.

You will also encounter cultural differences in your health care team. The team members will have varied beliefs and strategies for handling situations and patient care issues. Nurses need to listen and be tolerant. Being understanding of differences will not only broaden your own horizons but also will help you to become a better nurse. Ask questions, listen to the answers, be sensitive, show respect, and build trust.

Another emerging aspect of providing culturally competent care is that of ethnopharmocology. Research has shown that ethnic makeup can affect the response and effectiveness of drugs. For instance, African-Americans have a greater risk for developing delirium from tricyclic medications than whites. Asians have different reactions to some medications than other races. This opens an entirely new realm to understanding drugs.

One approach being emphasized by these researchers is to ask two important questions and listen carefully to the answers in order to better understand the cultural diversity issues in health care that affect your patient. These two questions are "What do you think caused your illness?" and "What do you think will help you the most?"

This approach not only helps to cut through the layers of diversity but also adheres to the premise of putting the patient at the center of the health care delivery model. It also emphasizes the patient's role in promoting his wellness and in his responsibility for his own care.

Clinical Pathways

Clinical pathways evolved in the early 1990s as a means to standardize care for particular medical diagnoses. Over the past two decades, they have changed to meet the needs of patients and will continue to do so. Today you might know these by another term such as care maps. These pathways or maps are multidisciplinary plans of care and can incorporate the possible nursing diagnoses that are most commonly found with a particular medical condition. When used appropriately, these pathways can drive the nursing process and contribute to the nursing care plan.

FACT

Clinical pathways, or care maps, provide a blueprint for multiple disciplines to coordinate care and achieve desired outcomes within a specified time frame. They include four main components: a timeline, a treatment plan of interventions, outcome criteria (measurable long- and short-term goals), and a variance record to allow for deviations to be recorded and analyzed.

Pathways are designed to standardize care and improve the quality of care and outcomes. The concept was designed to help ensure that a patient entering hospital ABC with congestive heart failure (CHF) would receive the same level and quality of care as if he went to hospital XYZ. Or that patients being seen by a home health agency in New Hampshire would receive the same care as patients being seen by a home health agency in Texas.

The downside is that many physicians and other health care team members feel that pathways condone a cookbook style of medical care and that not all patients fit neatly into the pigeonholes that pathways expect.

Clinical pathways are set plans for the care of a patient with a specific diagnosis, and as such, they are not easily individualized. It is important to select a pathway that fits the most pertinent needs of the patient.

These pathways allow for expected variances, but cannot possibly anticipate all combinations of factors. For example, a diabetic pathway would most likely include possible complications of neuropathy, retinopathy, and foot ulcers. It would not anticipate that the patient might also have co-morbidities of cancer or HIV that would certainly skew the care and interventions this patient would need. In the same manner, clinical pathways often don't adapt well to unexpected changes in the patient's condition.

On the positive side, clinical pathways support continuity of care and coordinate care across the clinical disciplines by providing clinical guidelines for care. They help reduce risks and contain costs. Outcomes and documentation are usually improved significantly by the use of pathways.

One of the most beneficial aspects of clinical pathways is that they include the whole team in planning and implementing care. This includes the patient, who is a major partner and player in the entire process.

Your facility may or may not use clinical pathways. Some physicians may have their own pathways or variations of standard ones. Some refuse to subscribe to the cookbook nature of pathways. You may see any combination of issues with pathways. Be sure to acquaint yourself with the expectations in your particular situation, and if you float to another area, don't assume the same rules apply.

Best Practices

This is a buzzword that really came to light in about the mid-2000s and continues to be used today. It's a great term, but it implies that the best practice is the final answer or the be all end all of whatever the experience is. In fact, the true best practice is one that continues to seek to improve methods as well as outcomes.

A best practice is a technique, a method, or a process that is believed to be the most effective means of delivering a particular outcome than any other for that particular situation or circumstance.

Best practices are practical techniques that are gained through experiences that are then used to improve a process or outcome.

In nursing, you use best practices to educate patients and other nurses or health staff in techniques and methods to achieve the best possible goals and outcomes. The best practice process becomes an integral part of the quality assurance and performance improvement processes in our patient care delivery.

Best practices most frequently take the form of short stories about an actual experience used to demonstrate the ways in which the best possible outcomes were achieved with a specific patient in a particular scenario.

The Idealistic Graduate

Most nurses leave school and enter the workforce feeling incompetent and scared to death that they don't know everything they need to know. The truth is you'll never know everything and you'll continue to learn something new each day. However, there will also be things you feel very sure of.

You may feel that your goal as a nurse is to spend as much time with each patient as he needs and to ensure that he leaves your facility or care with a full understanding of his health status and his role in promoting wellness. Your patients will never go home feeling as inadequate as you did when your grandmother had her stroke last year. Those nurses were just incompetent and you will never be that way.

This is a terrific goal, but you'll quickly learn that it's one that isn't always possible to meet. You should always strive for it, but you can't beat yourself up when someone calls in sick and a patient codes just as you were preparing to try to cram in extra teaching with your discharge instructions and the patient gets discharged before you can get there.

You may have learned a specific technique for a procedure in school or learned that this technique replaces one commonly used for years. When you observe a nurse using a different or possibly an obsolete technique, please don't rush in with an attitude of "this is the way it should be done!" The "this is the way we did it in school" attitude is not always welcome. Neither is "this is how we did it at XYZ," when you move from one area to another or change jobs.

Of course you need to advocate for the patient if someone is doing something you know to be harmful or risky, but you must use discretion and tact in doing so. You also don't want to alarm the patient or cause her to lose confidence or trust in your coworker.

ESSENTIAL

One of the things that usually hits new nurses is the lack of time they have to spend with each patient. Suddenly you are responsible for more than just the two or three you had at one time as a student. Now you're expected to provide or oversee all their care, not just a few hours of a shift or a few tasks to enhance your skills.

This is where your P&P manual comes into play. Perhaps your facility has guidelines for a procedure that are different from the way you learned something. Maybe these guidelines are outdated. Bring this to the attention of your supervisor for clarification or revision. Remember, never bring anything to the attention of your supervisor in an accusatory manner!

You can also use this opportunity to discuss the guidelines with your coworker by saying something like, "that's a different approach; would you please teach it to me? I learned it another way." This gives your coworker a mentoring opportunity and helps you to learn new tips and tricks.

If you know that the guidelines for the procedure have been changed, you can tactfully bring this up privately. You can say that you learned a new way to do that and ask if you could demonstrate it next time. Nurses should all be aware that health care advances occur all the time and should be willing to learn something new, but don't make accusations and comments in front of patients.

As long as there are several acceptable ways of doing something, none of which pose risks for the patient, your way is what you are comfortable with and someone else's may be very different. If the patient asks, you should always explain that there are different methods to accomplish the same thing. If the patient expresses a preference, don't take offense if he doesn't choose your way, and don't make a big deal about it if he likes yours better. Respect your coworkers for their diversity.

CHAPTER 12

The Patients

Patients are at the center of all health care. They are why you became a nurse. Making a difference in their lives is your primary goal. Focus on the patients and you will find success and fulfillment in your role. Some facilities choose to call them clients or consumers, but whatever the terminology used, they are in need of your expertise and assistance. All the things you learned in school will make more sense now as you put them to use.

Sick People Are Not at Their Best

With rare exceptions, most of the patients you work with will not be in a perfect state of wellness. They may have arrived at your doorstep critically injured, acutely ill, or maybe just with a few new signs and symptoms that need to be taken care of. Whatever the case, you need to always remember that your patients have a life beyond the present realm. They are mothers and fathers, sisters, brothers, grandparents, children, coworkers, and friends and family to many others you may never have reason to encounter.

They have jobs and responsibilities; they pay taxes and bills. They eat, drink, and eliminate waste from their bodies.

Put Yourself in Their Shoes

Think about how you are if you have just a simple nagging headache. Your concentration is disrupted. You might be cranky and short with others around you. You don't function at your optimal level. Someone meeting you for the first time might have a distorted view of who you are.

Compound that and place yourself in the role of the patients in your workplace environment. Would you become "the headache in 402 who's cranky and short with everyone"? Or are you Ms. Jones, RN, a new grad who is usually a bright, energetic young woman who loves her job and her patients. You're getting married in a few months and have a wonderful fiancé. You have two Labrador retrievers and like to camp and hike. The headache is interfering with your job. You're cranky because, when you get home, you have so many wedding plans to work on you don't have time for a headache!

No one is ever at her best when she doesn't feel well. Pain, nausea, diarrhea, itching, burning, and fever all take a toll on nerves and patience. The fears of the unknown, fear of dying, and fear of pain all create a tremendous sense of discomfort. Your role as a nurse is to help the patient retain her self-respect and dignity and to see beyond who the patient is today to who she is as a person.

Your patients' lives make up whom they are. Their agendas that are being disrupted right now are major concerns to them. The patients may even be grieving a loss of some sort as represented by this present illness.

They are also usually acutely aware of the fact that they are "not them-selves" at the present moment and may not be able to cope with that either.

How you cope with their behavior and issues and react to them affects the health care delivery process. You need to allow them to vent. Validate their feelings. Help them focus on learning how to cope and feel confident that you will assist them to gain at least some measure of control over this situation.

The Stages of Grief

Anyone facing a change in day-to-day life will experience a grief pro-cess. Illness presents a change. How dramatic that change is depends on the intensity of the illness. Your patient will run through the stages of grief as he deals with the onset of symptoms, receives the diagnosis, and learns to cope with the treatment and gets back to a new point of wellness.

Remember the stages of grief as described by Elisabeth Kübler-Ross, MD:

- Denial
- Anger
- Bargaining
- Depression
- Acceptance

The intensity and duration of each stage will depend largely on the sig-nificance of the change or loss. And remember, these stages are not always experienced in order and some may be skipped altogether. Anger, depres-sion, and denial are usually the most obvious behaviors demonstrated and should be your most obvious clues to issues with coping.

Coping with Difficult Family Members

A patient's family members come in all shapes and sizes and tempera-ments. The most important thing you need to remember is that they will have their own set of issues and coping mechanisms related to the patient's illness as well. They could also be the major focus of your nursing care plan if they present the problem with the highest priority.

Where Their Anger Comes From

Many times, family members will be your best allies in dealing with and helping the patient. They are often the primary caregivers. They know the patient best and can interpret and translate why the patient is having a certain reaction or isn't coping with a situation.

However, there will always be those who have no coping skills at all, cannot fathom that their loved one has this disease or illness, and wants everything (usually the most impossible things) done right now! They are never present when the physician is there or decisions are made but appear at the most inopportune moments demanding a full explanation of everything that has been said or done in their absence.

FACT

One of the most useful and effective aspects of communication is listening. Communication is a two-way process: listening and speaking. However, communication is not effective unless both aspects are given an equal opportunity. This opportunity does not necessarily have to be equal in time or quantity, but rather in quality. Many times the person just wants someone to listen—not even to respond, just to listen.

This difficult person will flex his muscles, make multiple unreasonable demands, and threaten to have your head on a platter. All this is usually based in fear, misunderstanding, and feelings of inadequacy. Peel away the layers and you will discover the basis for his outbursts and anger.

Listen to Them

Communication does not always have to be verbal. When you listen to what someone else has to say you show respect and you validate their right to have those feelings. Sometimes they just need to hear themselves say something out loud in order to better understand it themselves.

Sometimes they just want someone to listen to them vent. And sometimes they need you to listen and help them sort out their feelings and find solutions.

What they don't need is for you to take the situation personally and react. If they are accusing or blaming you for a situation, they don't need or want excuses or reaction from you. They probably don't want an apology. You are not the problem, you are just the messenger. They just want it fixed. They want to know how to cope, how to make it better, how to accept it, how to regain control over this feeling of helplessness.

Listen and then ask what you can do to help them, and be sure to enlist their help in fixing the situation.

Keep Them Informed

Anticipating needs and keeping patients and family members informed can avoid many problems. Give them an approximate schedule of the day's events. If a family member wants to speak with the physician, let the person know what time the doctors typically make rounds. This is usually in the early morning and could be well worth the family member missing a few hours of work to get some important information. If this isn't possible, encourage the person to speak to the doctor's nurse and find out when he typically returns phone calls. Many times, physicians return non-emergency calls after hours. Usually family members have left work by then, are on their way to the hospital, and are at the boiling point!

Have the family member leave a note for the doctor with the patient, or you can place the note on the chart for the doctor. Of course, you'll need to understand your facility's rules about HIPAA and other privacy issues and have any necessary authorizations available as well.

In most cases, you'll defuse many explosive situations just by listening and validating the person's right to be upset or afraid. Let him know that you are there to help and that you are on his side. Empower him by making him part of the team and giving him some responsibility.

When It's Okay to Cry with Your Patient

When events evoke an emotional response, it's okay to share the moment with your patients and cry. Many things can trigger emotional reactions; most of them are sad, but happy moments can elicit tears as well.

ESSENTIAL

You may encounter coworkers who don't show their emotions as part of their cultural background and personal makeup. You need to be open and accepting of cultural diversity and expect that they will be of your culture in return.

Some people see showing emotions as weak and will push their feelings down and remain controlled at all times. Sometimes, as the nurse, you may need to control your emotions to maintain control over a situation and to function normally. You may need to be the strong one for your patient or her loved ones. It is recommended that you allow yourself to break down and release these emotions at a later time. Like stress, emotions that are stifled for too long can be harmful both physically and mentally.

FACT

Tears are healing. This seemingly poetic thought has some scientific basis because the chemical makeup of tears is closely related to normal saline. Saline is widely used as one of the most effective antiseptic cleansers and moisteners to promote healing in wound care.

There is something to be said for being strong for your family and friends and that will be true at times for your patients. The fact is that your patients are an important part of your life. There will be some who touch your life more than others do. You will play an important role in their lives. It is only natural that you will develop attachments and share their feelings of elation when things work out and go well. So too you will share in their disappointment and sadness when things go wrong.

Losing Your First Patient

Perhaps you lost a patient or two during your clinical rotations. Or maybe you skirted the issue altogether and now, depending on where you work, you may or may not be likely to experience this soon. Almost everyone has experienced the death of a loved one or a pet. If not, they have experienced a deep sense of loss of some sort and have an understanding of the hurt and pain.

Whatever your prior experience, losing a patient is never easy and takes on many different possibilities for conjuring up emotions. Was it a sudden and unexpected event in a young patient, such as an arrest? Or was it a teenager who entered the ER via ambulance from a horrible traffic accident? After working on him for nearly an hour, your team had stabilized him, and then he suddenly arrested. Or was it the little old man with CHF who's been a frequent flier since his wife died a year ago? You just met him, but he reminded you of your grandfather, and you often found yourself sitting with him on your breaks. Perhaps it's an elderly woman you'd only just met yesterday, but whom you bonded with quickly.

Each of these scenarios evokes images and emotions that represent different levels of loss and can include your feeling inadequate or questioning your faith, the same as you would if the loss had been a loved one of your own. Your patients and your profession are all part of who you are. Death will always take a personal toll.

The first time will probably surprise you for two reasons: because it hurts so much and because of how long you will remember this day and the events. Expect it to hurt, and you'll be better prepared to face it and help the patient slip peacefully from this world and help his loved ones cope with his death and celebrate his life.

When Families Argue about Patient Care

You'll find yourself from time to time in an uncomfortable place—in the middle of family arguments and disagreements about a patient's care. There may be very good, sound, even reasonable reasons for not telling the patient something, but it may not be the best thing for the patient. Remember that you are not alone in this situation. Nurses enjoy a lot of autonomy and independence in their roles, but this is not the ideal situation for that.

To Inform the Patient?

When the family doesn't want the patient to know about her prognosis, you need to listen to the family members and gather as much information about why they think this is a good idea. Perhaps they will convince you, or perhaps you can gently persuade them to consider the fact that the patient has a right to know. At least until the doctor is involved, you need to respect their wishes.

Next, you need to gather information from the patient about what she understands to be her diagnosis and what she understands about the things the doctor has told her. This might be difficult to do if the family hovers constantly, but you need to try. Sometimes the patient is very much aware and knows that her family doesn't want her to know, so she plays along with it. If that's the case, you just need to be sure to let the rest of the team know what's going on.

When you have gathered your information, go to your supervisor for advice and help. She will want you to notify the doctor, and perhaps he'll okay social services to intervene. Perhaps the physician agrees that not telling the patient her prognosis is the best way to handle this situation. If you disagree, then you need to consult again with your supervisor about how to proceed. Sometimes the situation calls for more action and perhaps an ethics committee needs to be convened, but sometimes you just have to go along with the decision.

To Inform the Family?

When the patient doesn't want the family to know about his illness, this can also be an uncomfortable situation, but patients have a right to privacy. In fact, with HIPAA rules, you pretty much have to act as if the patient has made this request unless you have his authorization to do otherwise.

As with any portion of the patient's care, if his privacy issues are adversely affecting his care or condition, you need to discuss this with the patient and the rest of the team. Discharge planning begins at admission. If his safety is going to be compromised because of secrecy, then the situation needs to be discussed as a component to his care.

For example, cancer has always been the big "don't tell" issue. Your patient, Mr. Johnson, doesn't want to burden his daughter with the news. She has three small children, a full time job, and just can't handle another thing right now. Mr. Johnson lives alone and will drive himself to his daily radiation treatments. He assures you he'll be okay, but he's having severe diarrhea and nausea with the first two treatments he's had in the hospital. How will he safely drive himself to and from the treatments and maintain his nutrition and hydration at home alone? He's stubborn and strong. He's taken care of himself for many years since his wife died. Mr. Johnson stresses that he doesn't want to burden his daughter. After the treatments are done and he's in remission, he'll tell her about the cancer, but not until then!

Does the doctor know all this? Don't assume he does. Is this his long-time primary care physician or an oncologist new to Mr. Johnson? Is he aware that Mr. Johnson is having this reaction? Is he aware that he lives alone and has these intentions?

If Mr. Johnson is going to drive himself to and from these treatments, he won't meet the homebound criteria for home health. You need to be sure the discharge planner involves social services so that they can provide him a list of resources. And you need to impress upon him the need for an emergency contact person who *is* aware of what he's going through. Mr. Johnson is an accident waiting to happen, and while he's under your care, you and your facility have the responsibility to help him plan for his future care and to prepare him to go home and be safe.

ALERT

Patients who live alone should always have a designated emergency contact person who knows their health care conditions and any ongoing treatments. This may not always be a family member, but the designated person should be someone with whom the patient checks in regularly. This person should be aware of and take responsibility for this role.

You have the responsibility to honor his requests for privacy, but you also have the responsibility to ensure that he understands the possible consequences. You have to make him responsible for his own health status and to advocate for his wellness. Just because he's being stubborn does not relieve you of the responsibility of educating him about his choices and possible outcomes.

Patient Teaching

So many nurses complain that they never have time to do any patient teaching. While it's true that you may never have enough time or never feel that you can give someone your undivided attention for a significant time, you need to take full advantage of every moment to instruct your patients. There is really no excuse for not doing any teaching or for feeling that you have done none. Use every encounter with your patient to instruct or test his knowledge.

Patient education is an area where nurses will resume more and more responsibility. It is essential to helping patients assume responsibility for their own health status and achieving improved outcomes.

Each time you encounter your patient, you're assessing her and the situation. You're also carrying out the planned care and evaluating its necessity and success or failure. The data you gather is both subjective and objective. Listen to what your patient tells you. What has she learned about her experience? What does she understand about her signs and symptoms? What does she know about how to control them?

ESSENTIAL

As the health care model shifts from a sick care model to a wellness model, patient education becomes even more important. Nurses will assume a much larger role in patient education, especially under the Affordable Care Act of 2010. Patients need to assume responsibility for preventing illness and strive to achieve wellness.

Each time you give a medication to your patients, you should tell them what it is and what it's for. If they already know this, then ask them something about the medication or the diagnosis for which they are taking the medication.

Ask them about their discharge plans and what changes in their lifestyle this episode will cause them to make. If you are performing a task or treatment, explain all the steps and demonstrate them simply. If the task or treatment is something they'll need to learn, start immediately to teach them, and use each opportunity to have them participate more and more. If you use each opportunity to build upon the last one, the cumulative effect will provide a basis for you to expand on when you do find a few minutes to spend specifically on patient teaching.

- **Remind them of each lesson.** "Remember what I told you about your medications and the reactions to expect? Does it seem to be having this effect? Can you recognize a difference in the way you feel?"
- **Build on what you've been teaching them.** "Now that I've shown you how I do this dressing change, I want you to tell me the steps as we go along."
- **Have them demonstrate and participate.** "This time I want you to fill the insulin syringe and tell me why you're doing each step. Then I will do the injection, and next time you can do it."

It might add a minute or two to your procedures, but it accomplishes the most vital step toward making the patient independent in his own care and responsible for his own outcomes and health status. It also alleviates the need to carve out twenty or thirty minutes of rushed time just before you discharge your patient.

Explain to the patient that you have five minutes to spend with him now and what you expect to accomplish in that time frame. This will help to keep things focused and not get off track. Later you can talk about fun stuff.

As you spend your day teaching your patients and seeing the results, you'll reap the rewards of knowing that you have made a difference and not feel so much like all you did was push pills and fill out paperwork.

Empowering Patients

Teaching your patients about their health status—how to cope, what to expect, and what to do in certain situations—empowers them. It involves them in their care and gives them responsibilities for their own outcomes. It makes them self-reliant and independent, even if they need assistance to do it. You can help patients understand their role and responsibility in their own health status. They are the directors. They are responsible for the preventive care and outcomes.

ALERT

Television and other advertising media instruct patients with certain symptoms to contact their doctor about the specific medication being advertised. Patients self-diagnose, run to the doctor, demand this medication, and all too often the doctor obliges, continuing the sick care model.

Too many people believe that when they have an ailment and the doctor gives them a pill, they get better. They don't always understand the correlation of their lifestyle and other risk factors. Physicians don't have time to explain, and when they do, does the patient really understand?

Often, no one tells the patient that if he loses some weight, exercises regularly, and uses some commonsense pain relief measures, he may not need this medication at all. Advertisements in the media are paid for by the drug manufacturers. The doctor doesn't have the time to educate her patients or to respond to their repeated phone calls with complaints, and the patient falls prey to the quick fix.

Health education falls on the nurse. As health care costs rise and the health care model shifts to a wellness model, nurses are finding they need to be the primary health educators. If health care costs are ever going to be contained, consumers must take responsibility to understand their health status and become accountable for improving their health status using all measures possible.

Your role as the nurse is to help your patients see the whole picture: to help them understand their diagnosis, treatment, risk factors, contributing factors, and how to prevent complications and improve their outcomes.

For example, obesity is an epidemic in this country. It increases risk factors for many co-morbidities and affects the outcomes of any given treatment modality. There is no quick fix, and many times the co-morbidities make it harder to control and lose the weight. It is a prime example, however, of how the patient is the one who must take the responsibility for his own status. He is the one who has ultimate control over what he consumes and how much effort he puts into burning those calories.

The Learning Process

One of the most common ways to teach someone about something is to first give them some literature to read and then ask them to formulate questions for later discussion. Unfortunately, that isn't always the most effective means of educating most people. It may be an effective means of supplementing or reinforcing information, but not of initially learning something new.

Encountering Illiteracy

There are many education theories, but in plain English, learning styles will affect how well your patient interprets and utilizes the information you provide. One of the primary barriers to learning is illiteracy. You'd probably be quite surprised to find that your very bright, seemingly well-educated middle-aged patient is unable to read. He's probably very good at covering it up, and despite his inability to read and write, he has educated himself through other forms of media.

According to the U.S. Department of Education, more than 40 million adults in this country are functionally illiterate. Another 10 million can barely read and write. According to health literacy experts, almost 90 million Americans will have some degree of difficulty understanding written and verbal information and forms provided to them by their health care system.

Given this information, the next time you give a patient a handout or other form of literature, be sure he understands the information it contains. Don't expect him to learn from it, but rather it should serve to reinforce your verbal and hands-on teaching methods. Ask him what he read or heard and what he thinks it all means.

Try Different Methods

Some people will learn best from your verbal explanation, while others require a demonstration or pictures. Some can follow step-by-step instructions well, while others need to see the finished product before they can learn the steps. Some learn best by doing it themselves, while others retain the information better by watching several times first. Ask your patient what works best for him. How does he learn how to do things at work, at home, or with hobbies? By the same token, some nurses are better at teaching by telling and others by showing. Think about what your strengths are, and if your patient needs something different, ask a coworker to try another approach.

Return demonstration is a vital part of patient teaching. Never assume that a patient understands and is competent without having him demonstrate it to you. And always document what has been taught, verbalized back, and return demonstrated, as well as what needs to be reviewed. Ask leading questions, such as "What does this mean to you?" or "Tell me what you think I just said." This way you have an understanding of what the patient interprets. Don't just ask if he understands. Most people will say yes because they think that's what you want to hear. Build on what they do understand. And always use plain English, not nursing jargon.

Looking at the Whole Patient

Look at the whole patient, not just the disease. How many times was this drummed into your head in school? By now, you should have a good understanding of this concept. In order to individualize the care plan and maximize the outcomes for each patient, you have to look at the whole patient.

For instance, the patient in 204B has had a transient ischemic attack, which is how the hypertension was discovered. The hypertension is severe, and there is tremendous risk for cerebral vascular accident (CVA). Medication, a low-sodium diet, and stress management are the physician's directions. Typical drill, no problem, you can deal with this one in your sleep.

You understand that your job is to help your patients and their families and caregivers understand that all the patient's personal habits and lifestyle choices will need to be incorporated into long-term plans for coping with his health status. The patient's family, job, hobbies, culture, diet, and habits all contribute to his illness and risk factors.

Okay, so you enter the room of Mr. Hashimoto. He's fifty years old, alert, oriented, and sitting up in bed. He's yelling into his Bluetooth earpiece, flipping through information on his laptop with one hand, and is eating sushi, which he has just drenched in soy sauce, with the other hand. Another phone is ringing somewhere in the room. He's wildly directing you to find that phone for him.

Mr. Hashimoto is the owner of a very popular sushi restaurant and has just opened a new one across town that is struggling. He's yelling at the manager of that new restaurant and is threatening to fire him. As he's yelling, he's pouring more soy sauce on his sushi and frantically looking for his cigarettes. Your work is cut out for you!

Enlist the patient and his family and caregivers to see beyond the diagnosis as well. Convincing Mr. Hashimoto to look at the big picture is going to be a challenge. He thinks a pill will make him better and fix it all. Why should he have to do anything to help himself get better, the medication will do it for him. If his behavior had been calm and demure, and you had not witnessed his job-related stress, smoking habit, and dietary issues with the soy sauce, you might have missed out on all the clues that increase his risks.

You may not always have an opportunity to have an open window that provides you with as many clues as Mr. Hashimoto did. Some patients won't share these with you, and you will need to help them understand that they need to examine them for themselves in order to promote wellness and improve their outcomes.

A Little Knowledge Can Be Dangerous

One of the dangers of the prevalence of television and other advertising media pushing drugs is the public's lack of information. The information is usually there but too cumbersome for the patient to read through, listen to, or understand. "If you have these symptoms, you could have ABC disease, and you should talk to your doctor about XYZ drug." It is one thing if the drug is a prescription and quite another if it's an over-the-counter (OTC) remedy. However, it can sometimes be quite easy to get a physician to write that prescription without a thorough diagnostic process.

So many people believe that if they read something in a reputable periodical or see it on TV, that it's true. While these advertisements are generally truthful, the general public doesn't hold medical or pharmacological degrees. They might have a couple of the vague symptoms and think this new medicine will cure what ails them. If one brand name cold medicine didn't work, they'll try another (which most likely contains the same ingredients). Worse yet, if one dose didn't work, then they think that maybe a double dose will. Unknowingly, they may be overdosing on medications, such as acetaminophen.

Another issue is the casual conversations between patients about how they use their medications and patients who don't understand what their meds are and why they're taking them. For instance, the little eighty-year-old woman who tells you she is taking lasix and lanoxin. She knows the names, but she thinks they are "vitamins" the doctor gave her and has no idea that she has a cardiac condition and what signs and symptoms she should look for.

Another little eighty-year-old, Mrs. Giles, was admitted through the emergency room with a pulse of 35 and blood pressure of barely 80/50. She had been experiencing some angina earlier in the day, and her friend gave her one of her "heart pills" (a nitroglycerine). This helped, and the friend told her the doctor told her to take her "heart pills" whenever she had any chest pain. Mrs. Giles knew she took "heart pills" too, but her doctor told her to take one a day to prevent the "spells" she was having. Maybe he forgot to tell her she could take them if she had chest pain too. After all, she hadn't had these pains before, so they wouldn't have discussed this aspect of the pills. So she took her digoxin again because of the chest pain. It helped a little, so when she had pain again an hour later she took another one. A couple of hours later, her daughter came by and found her on the floor barely breathing. Mrs. Giles didn't want to trouble the doctor on a Saturday; she'd just try taking the "heart pills" first.

CHAPTER 13

The Doctors

You will hear horror stories about some physicians, while others earn rave reviews. The plain truth is doctors are human and, like anyone else, have their good and bad qualities, as well as good and bad days. Some have egos the size of the universe, and others are very down-to-earth. You will find that it is best to be open-minded and form your own opinions based on your own experiences.

Communicating with Doctors

In all instances, the physician must be kept apprised of the patient's condition. Any changes need to be communicated. Negative changes or worsening conditions need to be communicated immediately. Some instances of improvement, such as someone awakening from a coma, would necessitate immediate notification as well. Other changes, by common sense, can wait for a convenient time unless the physician has requested otherwise.

The one thing to keep in mind in communicating with physicians is that they are busy and usually just want the facts. They will want a specific picture of the situation. Never call the doctor when you don't have a recent set of vital signs and an assessment to provide. Always have your facts in front of you and not where you have to dig to find them. Make notes and compose your thoughts. Listen to her orders, read them back, and ask for verification of what you read back. Be concise, accurate, honest, and up front. If you are unfamiliar with something, say so and ask for a simple explanation or clarification. Identify yourself and state your credentials (RN or LVN/LPN). Clearly identify where you are calling from and which patient it is about.

Expect Respect

There was a time when nurses were considered to be handmaidens or just simply assistants to physicians. Nurses have evolved as professionals and have firmly established their own essential roles in health care. They complement the physician's care, but both are vital, primary members of the health care team. The nurse–doctor relationship has evolved along with nursing roles. Respect physicians and expect them to respect you.

Doctors and nurses have very different jobs, and each of them is equally important to the patient's health care issues. One is not superior or inferior to the other. You are both people and deserve to be treated with respect and dignity.

As gender becomes less of an issue for both nurses as well as doctors, both professions have grown in respect for each other. Realizing that each is a profession and not a gender has opened many avenues of communication and respect. New doctors and nurses have brought to their respective professions a sense of teamwork and camaraderie that has broken down a number of barriers and achieved a more equal relationship.

Earning Their Trust

As a new nurse, introduce yourself to the physicians. As with any of your team members, smile, use direct eye contact, and shake hands. Make a positive first impression. Let them know that you look forward to working with them. Take the time to get to know them and to build a rapport. Ask appropriate questions, and let them teach you. Most doctors love to teach.

Show them that they can trust you and that you will provide the care they expect for their patients. This will go a long way in the event that you have a question about an order or when there has been an error. They will usually go that extra little bit to explain, teach, or clarify something without an attitude of indignation. And if there is an error, although they may be angry or disappointed, they will have an understanding that you are human and will do the right thing to correct it.

If you question an order, remember that doctors are human and could have made a mistake. They could also have good reason for something. If you use an approach such as, "I've never seen that dose for that medication; can you tell me why you're ordering such a high dose for this patient?" you're more likely to get a nice answer than if you put them on the spot and say, "That's not the normal dose."

Coping with the Old-Boy Attitude

Physicians have tremendous responsibilities for the well-being of their patients. Time constraints and financial issues contribute to these responsibilities as well. For far too long, the general public has viewed doctors as being god-like or having powers to perform miracles. Physicians fostered this by allowing their egos to expand to enormous levels. This created a monster that has grown to be a malpractice nightmare. Slowly, as the wellness model of health care replaces the sick model, some of this will subside.

As the wellness trend toward focusing more of the responsibility on the patients for their health status grows, the legal issues are ebbing somewhat. Malpractice insurance rates have caused health care costs to become prohibitive for far too many people. The cost of malpractice insurance alone has put many doctors out of business. Congress has considered legislation limiting punitive damages in an effort to curb litigation, and some of this is contained in the Patient Protection and Affordable Care Act signed into law in 2010. Hopefully, those who seek to repeal this law will understand the merits of this provision.

For the most part, this malpractice explosion has been a somewhat humbling experience for physicians. In the past, physicians had an attitude of superiority unequaled by almost any other profession. The physician's bedside manner was atrocious, and his treatment of other health care professionals was unacceptable. When he couldn't cure someone or save a life, his "God complex" was suddenly under attack and his ability to produce the miracles he promised in question.

Changes in Health Care Affect Doctors' Attitudes

Health care is more of a consumer-driven field these days with all the managed care efforts, and physicians have had to learn to play the game. Patients have been forced to change physicians because of insurance coverage changes, so a new feeling of empowerment has emerged as patients realize that if they don't like their doctor, they can change. People used to be afraid of hurting the doctor's feelings. Others never knew that doctors could be caring souls. Now if they don't like their doctor's attitude, they move on.

As nurses demand respect and refuse to be doormats, physicians have had to evolve as well. The Good Old Boys have learned to behave for the most part. Nurses used to coin phrases about a physician's behavior, such as "He got an 'A' in How to Be a Jerk 101 and an 'F' in How to Care." Now there seems to be more of a sense that perhaps "How to Be a Jerk 101" is no longer a required course, but some still seem to take it as an elective.

There still are and will continue to be some who have the "God complex" and demand that everyone kiss their feet. The number of these types of doctors will be fewer and fewer as time goes on. In general, nurses avoid these doctors as much as possible; they learn how to stay out of their way, and word spreads throughout the ranks. Just do your job and lay low.

Facilities have found that they have the right to make choices, and, for instance, some home health agencies refuse to take patients from physicians who are abusive. In all honesty, they don't have a staff member willing and able to take on that case. The agencies are standing behind their staff and not exposing them to this abuse any more than they would to any other unsafe situation.

Your Responsibility to Your Patients

Nurses do need to advocate for their patients, but they also need to be professional and careful not to influence them. If you have a patient whose physician is a jerk, you need to follow his orders and care for his patient the same as any other. You can't express your opinion to the patient or family members. You need to be professional and keep it to yourself. If they bring it up, the only comment you could make is to remind them that they have choices and leave it at that. On the other hand, if it's an ethical issue or the care is substandard, you need to consult with your supervisor and your facility to advocate for the patient's well-being.

Patients may ask you to recommend a physician, but you should not do that. You can provide them with the names of several to choose from, but you need to remain unbiased. Your facility may have rules that even forbid this, and in that case, you must tell the patients to call a physician referral service or other resource.

With some of the obnoxious physicians, if you just stroke their egos a little bit, you can have them eating out of your hand and have control over the situation. As long as they get their attention and feel superior, they'll be nice. Anticipate what they want from you. Get their patients' needs attended to and send them off to their office as soon as possible.

Standing Up for Yourself

Some doctors are notorious for having tempers and throwing tantrums. You will most likely be witness to or the subject of one of these sooner or later. If you were wrong, say so. Be honest and up front at all times. If you say something like, "You have every right to be angry. I would be furious too," you'll defuse the situation somewhat. Let them vent. If you weren't in error, say so. Stand up for yourself, but don't let them get you caught up in their theatrics. Responding is different from reacting.

Never make a scene in front of the patient. If the physician chooses to demonstrate her unprofessional behavior in such a manner, let her. You should have more respect for yourself and your patients than that. Ask to speak to her privately later and let her know that she was rude or inappropriate. You don't appreciate being spoken to in that manner. You would not treat her this way, and you expect her to show the same level of respect for you. Even if you were wrong, she has no right to reprimand you in front of the patients and your peers. You are entitled to privacy for this kind of conversation.

FACT

> Many hospitals have instituted policies and rules that require physicians to attend classes on how to treat nurses and other health care staff and professionals. The airlines instituted this for pilots several years ago after a number of work-related lawsuits were brought by flight attendants against the pilots for similar behaviors.

Issues of violence in the workplace include verbal abuse and threats. Employers can be liable for not protecting employees from this kind of behavior. Nurses for far too long were subservient to doctors, and it is something not to be tolerated any longer. Health care facilities often placed a greater value on the revenue these physicians brought in than on the value of their employees. Those facilities that still adhere to this practice not only open themselves to liability issues but also to tremendous problems with retention of staff.

Physicians can also be intimidating just because of their vast knowledge and education. New nurses especially can fall prey to this. What you always need to remember is to put the respective roles into perspective. Your role is just as vital to the patient but in a different way. Respect the physician's knowledge and tap into it as often as you can. But know that it doesn't make him a better person or more of a professional than you.

Finding Mentors

Almost every physician has a love for teaching. Some are better at it than others, but take advantage of every opportunity you can to broaden your knowledge base. Establish a rapport with the physicians, and they will respect you and even seek you out to teach you. Be a good student. Be prepared and ask appropriate questions. You also need to be astute and understand when the physician is rushed or the time is not right. These are informal mentoring situations. Don't push and don't take it personally that the doctors are not welcoming the opportunity at this moment.

ESSENTIAL

Do your homework. When a physician has instructed you on a topic, do a little research to expand on what she has taught you. If you work in a teaching hospital, try to make occasional rounds with the interns, especially if this physician is teaching. If not, ask to accompany the physician as she makes her rounds of your unit. Share your knowledge with your coworkers so that they will be happy to cover your patients for a few minutes.

If you find information about a subject you have discussed with your mentors, share it with them and ask for their input. Perhaps it's something new that they haven't read yet, or maybe it's just additional information and they can fill in the gaps for you. Remember that not all physicians are cold blooded and uncaring. Most of them are very compassionate and helpful. They may appear to be aloof sometimes in order to set limits and be able to attend to all their patients. But usually they want to help you be better able to help their patients.

Patient and Family Education

No matter what the setting, physicians do not have the time to spend with patients and do an adequate job of patient teaching. Their time is more involved in the assessment and evaluation process. Any instructions are usually brief and to the point. Nurses have to pick up where they leave off and make sure that patients and family members understand the treatment modalities, any necessary lifestyle changes, and expected outcomes.

To do this, your best option is to be present to hear exactly what the physician has told the patient. However, this is not usually possible. Therefore, you will need to rely on asking the patient what he has been told, and hopefully the physician's notes can give you clues.

It is always an effective teaching option to ask what the patient knows or what he has understood to be said. You may get some great clues to his whole understanding of anatomy and physiology, as well as disease and treatment modalities and options. A diagnosis of cancer often comes with big misconceptions. To some, it is a death sentence no matter what type and site. Many men also have strange misconceptions, such as that having a vasectomy will leave them impotent or at the very least cause some erectile dysfunction.

ALERT

Never assume that just because the patient is bright and well educated that he understands anything about how his body works! Some people have very strange misconceptions and can make all sorts of erroneous assumptions based on misinformation.

You need to know where the gaps are and what information the patient needs to fill them in. With family members, as long as you are authorized to discuss the care, you again need to understand their knowledge base and deficits, what they have learned from the doctor and the patient, and what else they need to know.

People are resourceful, and the Internet and media offer vast amounts of information. There are support groups for almost any disease known to man these days. Again, nurses have to help patients and family members sort out the information, weed out misinformation, and understand the facts. It is important to keep the physician in the loop as much as possible so that she is acutely aware of what the patient understands and especially if the patient has a tendency toward great misconceptions about his body, his health status, and his treatment.

Learning by Observation

You will undoubtedly hear some wild tales and sometimes even horror stories about some of the physicians. They can range from abusive outbursts to demands for assistance or even comments with sexual overtones. Some prefer a dressing to be done a certain way, some don't want faxes sent to their offices, and some want a head-to-toe assessment with every phone call you make to them. Some expect all their ordered labs to be done STAT and reported to them within the hour.

Doctors' quirks and demands are part of the unwritten rules of the game, and in many cases, learning these as quickly as possible will behoove you. You need to remain open-minded and form your own opinions. You also need to heed the unwritten rule of being discreet when discussing individuals.

To some, Dr. Heart may seem to be an angry old woman who hates nurses and makes unreasonable demands. Even the nurses who hang out at the nurses' station instead of spending more time with their patients suddenly rush to give their patients care when she comes in. Perhaps she reminds you of your favorite great aunt who is a little crotchety and demanding. You recognize the same odd sense of humor and understand that this woman sets the bar high. She demands excellence and wants her patients' needs met without asking. She's quick and to the point, wastes no time, and expects that nurses be prepared and anticipate her needs. Your coworkers will marvel that you get along with this woman!

Others may think that Dr. Jones is a terrific doctor because he's charming and so good-looking. He's always warm and friendly and woos the little old ladies. His bedside manner is great, but you've seen better doctors. He is too concerned with making everyone like him to set limits and to expect his patients to do a little more for themselves. The nurses all seem to dote on his every request, but you see through his façade.

Listen to your coworkers and heed their advice, but learn to keep your opinions to yourself and always be professional. Show respect for others, and they will respect you.

To Date or Not to Date?

The first rule about dating coworkers is to be sure to understand the rules of your facility regarding this matter, including the unwritten ones, before you get involved with anyone. Discretion is the key and must be used at all times. The stereotype of young women becoming nurses to catch handsome young doctors will long haunt the nursing profession, but there is still some truth to it today. Some nurses do enter the profession intending to marry doctors, and for others it just happened that way—they didn't set out to marry a doctor.

Dating any coworker can be a precarious situation in any profession or workplace. For some, these relationships work out, and many marry and live long, happy lives together; for others these relationships can be short-lived and messy. Some employers forbid any type of fraternization with coworkers other than group social gatherings to avoid these kinds of situations.

If your facility doesn't forbid dating coworkers, proceed with great caution. If it doesn't work out, you may need to change jobs in order to avoid the uncomfortable place you have made for yourself. When people break up, their friends often have to choose whose side to be on. When you all have to work together, this may be a big challenge.

If you are dating a doctor or someone else in a more powerful position within the facility, you will most likely be seen to be brown nosing. Any advancement or promotions you might receive will probably be seen as special favors and not something that you earned. Keep that in mind.

Dating a coworker can create distractions as well. You might find yourself spending a great deal of time trying to steal moments to be together and alone or to discuss plans that could wait for after hours. If you are fighting or unhappy with each other, you can find yourselves being inappropriate to each other. Dating coworkers can also put you in a competition with others who may have shared a relationship with this person before or someone who is jealous of your relationship. If you're going to date a physician or other coworker, keep these points in mind:

- Understand your facility's rules first.
- Be discreet at all times and avoid public displays of affection.
- Never disclose private or intimate details of your relationship or about your partner to your coworkers.
- Don't spend all your free time at work (breaks and meals) with your partner.
- Don't take your problems to work with you. Leave your disagreements at home. Be professional.

Never get caught up in gossip and rumors about coworkers. Be discreet and stay out of other people's business. For instance, imagine that a doctor and your nursing supervisor were seen having dinner one night in an intimate restaurant. The rumors began flying early the next morning. People had suspected something for a while, but now there had been an actual sighting. The doctor is married. He's also angling for a position on the hospital board. A public affair could spell real trouble for him. Now imagine how embarrassed everyone was to find out your nursing supervisor is his sister-in-law, and they were planning a surprise party for his wife's fortieth birthday!

Utilizing Preceptors Effectively

Every new nurse will be assigned a preceptor in some fashion or another. Sometimes you will spend a great deal of time working with this person. Other times he will be the person you go to with questions or call to supervise your doing a new procedure, but otherwise you're expected to work fairly independently.

Some preceptors are micromanagers and would rather do it for you than wait while you figure something out or accomplish a task. Everyone is overworked and underpaid. Taxing someone by making them a preceptor is sometimes over the top for that person, especially if there is no additional pay.

New nurses who come prepared to work, eager to learn, and able to apply good common sense, along with critical thinking skills, to a situation will have the best experiences.

A preceptor's time is valuable; don't waste it. Be helpful and prepared. If you have to be checked off on a task, be organized and have all of your supplies ready to go and the patient informed of what's going to take place. Get in and do it and then thank your preceptor for her assistance. If you learned something from her, be sure to comment on how helpful that was.

If at all possible, try to help your preceptor out by answering a call light or two or assisting her with a difficult patient. Try to get to know a little something about her as a person. This may go a long way in explaining attitudes and issues.

If you have difficulties with your preceptor, try to work them out. Accept responsibility for the problems instead of pointing fingers, and ask what would be helpful. If all else fails, approach your nurse manager and ask for help with the situation, again not pointing fingers or placing blame.

Making the most of a preceptor situation can be a very valuable experience and in some cases, you may learn more from that person in a few short weeks than perhaps you did in several years of school.

CHAPTER 14

The Nursing Shortage in Action

There have been many cycles of nursing shortages in recent history, a trend that will likely continue for many years to come. The current nursing shortage is very real, although it appears to be stalled and camouflaged. The economy has been depressed and unemployment high. This results in elective and even some urgent health care being placed on the back burner. Hospital censuses have been low and job opportunities in many areas scarce. Retired and semi-retired nurses returned to the workforce and snapped up many job opportunities new grad nurses were hoping for. What's the real story?

Pulling Together to Survive a Shift

Nurses have always been overworked and underpaid. Throughout early nursing history, nurses were volunteers and clergy. There are old posters from the 1800s that speak about nurses' duties as those including swabbing floors and toilets and performing all sorts of janitorial tasks in addition to caring for their patients—all for wages that were a mere pittance. These stories were all true, and they set the stage for nurses to continue in this role for centuries.

In the past decade, however, nurses have been able to demand respect as a profession, with improved salaries and work conditions. As hospitals, a leading employer of nurses, experienced tremendous shortages, nurses took the upper hand and began making demands. Hospitals and other health care facilities began begging for nurses and created a variety of sign-on bonuses and enticements to lure what nurses there were into other positions.

Today, with a depressed economy, high levels of unemployment, and soaring costs for health care, the demand for nurses has decreased. In some part this is due to older nurses delaying retirement or coming out of retirement because of financial strains. It is also due in part to cutbacks.

As the economy recovers, you could see a sudden surge of retirement for aging nurses and a renewed demand for health care from an aging population led by the baby boom generation. Combining this with a decline in interest and enrollment in nursing programs because of a job shortage, we could face one of the most critical shortages of nurses yet.

Despite low censuses and a diminished demand for health care, the fact remains that you will find yourself working in situations that can be less than ideal. Cost-savings plans instituted because of the restrictions that managed care forced on the industry have changed some of the game plans and the players. Unlicensed personnel (UAPs, nursing techs, medical assistants, and a variety of other creative terms) still replace many nurses all across this country.

The challenge is to pull together and survive one shift at a time. This puts teamwork to the ultimate test. How well can you and your coworkers get along and help each other out? Everyone has to buy into it and be willing to help, or the effort can fail.

While a warm body capable of performing a few non-technical tasks can be welcome in desperate times, this also presents liability issues for the nurses in charge of the units and facilities under whose licenses these non-nurses are working.

The drill sergeant has to emerge and bark out orders. If each person takes a portion of the responsibilities and focuses on the goal of providing the best care possible under the circumstances, the situation can work and work well. But if someone wants to whine and fuss about having too much to do, then the energy is deflected to damage control and the outcomes will not be optimal.

When Someone Calls in Sick

When someone calls in sick, it is an unexpected event over which the facility has no control. Nor do they have any control over how many people may call in sick at the same time. Nurses are not immune to illness, and recent pandemic threats have raised the question of what might happen if the health care workers all got sick too. Calling in sick creates a situation where all available staff need to be reorganized to fit the acuity needs of the facility to provide adequate care to the patients. It is never ideal and can be very stressful to all staff, and especially new nurses who might be expected to float or to work with float nurses who might need more assistance or supervision than they do.

The Effect on Patients

In situations where mandatory staffing ratios that are dictated by law must be met, even one or two people in a facility calling in sick can create a crisis situation. Units may need to be closed and patients transferred. The facility may need to close its doors to any new admissions, leaving emergency departments filled with patients and emergency services diverting patients to other facilities.

All this takes the highest toll on the patients. Precious time can be lost in emergency situations if patients need to be diverted to other facilities, and short-handed situations offer less than ideal situations for delivery of health care.

This is why it is critical for all nurses to take their jobs seriously and be professional. If you need time off, arrange for it ahead of time, and if you're not really sick, go to work. Of course, there will be times when you are ill, and you must stay home and not share your germs with patients and other staff.

Using Floaters in Your Unit

When someone calls in sick, management will have to reorganize staff. Often they will ask for volunteers to float to another area and, if necessary, make an assignment. This creates a situation where you will have help. Float nurses can be very unfamiliar with your unit. Not only will they not know the layout, they won't necessarily know the staff and any particular nuances of how you function as a team.

How you accept and incorporate float help into your unit affects how well the situation can be managed. How willingly they accept the challenge plays a big role in the success as well. If the new person comes in with a chip on her shoulder and demanding to have her own needs met without regard to the game plan, then this situation can be a huge challenge.

Watch and learn how your management handles each situation. Are they timid, allowing the float staff to run all over them, grateful for the warm body, and forgiving of all the other issues? Or do they dictate and make the situation uncomfortable for the floater? Hopefully, the managers are good at being grateful and diplomatic about compromising so they can make everyone at least a little bit happy about assignments and breaks so no one is completely miserable. A strong team leader can pull it together and make all the difference.

When You Get Left in Charge

The day you have feared and avoided will eventually come to pass. For some, it will come sooner than later. It will always be sooner than you think you're ready for. Your supervisor calls in sick, and you are suddenly the senior person on the unit. Panic inside, but hold your composure. You can do this. And remember there's always someone you can call if you need help.

Take a deep breath, and call your team together. Let them know that you are capable of handling this and that you expect their full coopera-tion. If you all work together, you can get through this. Be confident, but not cocky. Make a plan together. Listen to everyone's needs and try your best to meet as many as possible. Enlist their help. This is the first big test of how much they trust and respect you. Always thank them for their loyalty and help. Recognize sacrifices and those who go the extra mile. Find a way to nudge the slackers as well.

ESSENTIAL

If things get really tense, call your team together for a moment to re-group. Break the tension with a funny story or have them all close their eyes, shrug their shoulders, and take a few slow, deep breaths. If this group enjoys singing a quick silly song or making a silly group cheer, then do it just to break the tension and make them laugh. Then see who needs help and who can help out. Begin again, renewed.

Sometimes the best approach is to work together. Try double-teaming a group of patients for a change. One person gets them all fresh water and gets them set up for the shift by fluffing pillows and fixing linens, etc. The other person takes the vital signs and attends to any requests for PRN meds. Work together to get procedures and treatments done. Take patients who need to walk for a stroll down the hallway together. Or one nurse walks the patients while the other straightens up the beds and prepares the medica-tions. Start at one end and get everyone else up to chairs for a short stay and then go back and fix linens and pass the meds. As you do, take the patients to the bathroom and then back to bed. Next, turn your attention to all your bed-bound patients and turn them together and check carefully for any skin breakdown or risky areas. In two hours, you can work together and repeat this process.

Just a simple change of pace and a sense of camaraderie can make the time seem to go by more quickly while helping staff to meet the needs of the patients. Sometimes the RN will do all the vitals while the aides and LPNs work together to double-team the rest of the bedside tasks. Working together keeps everyone involved and feeling a sense of accomplishment. It also gives you a chance to double-team the patients when providing instructions. If your approach isn't working, perhaps someone else's input will turn on the lightbulb and vice versa.

When staff works together, everyone has a sense of ownership, and no one feels more overburdened than the rest. It gives each person a chance to learn from his peers and to earn their respect as well. Use opportunities that can otherwise be less than ideal to build your team and to make the most of a bad situation. Learn that together you are strong and that staying focused will help all of you enjoy your job.

When Someone Quits or Gets Fired

As much as you may be dying to know the circumstances about why a coworker is no longer employed at your facility, this information is not going to be divulged. It is confidential information, and you know that if it were you, you would not want anyone else to know all the details.

If the former employee wishes to share the information with you, it is up to her, but you should not share it with anyone. You also need to remember that there are two sides to every story and that you're only hearing one. You might be privy to other details, but again that is not yours to share with anyone, including the ex-employee.

When someone quits, he may have shared with you his reasons why, or he may choose to keep the reason to himself. Your obligation is to honor his right to privacy. There may be other circumstances surrounding his choices in addition to what he chooses to share. These are private issues, and the rumor mills will always be running at full speed. Don't get caught up in the gossip. And don't let the negative energy that most of these situations are usually associated with get you down. Just because someone else chooses to leave or is fired doesn't need to put a damper on your enthusiasm as a new nurse.

There will always be negative things to dwell on; some will grow old, and you may eventually become weary of them. For right now, you need to enjoy your new position and make your own strides to help improve things. It is always sad to see a colleague leave, but you have to wish them well in their new endeavors and go on with your own. Don't ever feel guilty for choosing to stay in a job that is no longer right for someone else. March to your own drummer.

Why Nurses Leave Hospitals

One key element that researchers have found by studying the nursing shortage is that while hospital-based nurses love their work, they hate their jobs. This seems to hold true in many other countries as well, including Canada and England. Working conditions—not just being short-staffed—seem to be the dominant factor.

Nurses Leave Managers, Not Jobs

All too often nurse managers can be incompetent in the role. With growing shortages, sometimes people are promoted into positions for which they are not qualified just to keep the position filled. Strong, fair leadership is an asset and can be difficult to find. Even competent managers who show favoritism weaken the system. They build resentment in those who strive to do a good job and who are criticized or reprimanded out of proportion to the level of their mistakes, while others get away with all kinds of poor nursing behaviors. Eventually, this resentment causes good nurses to leave.

FACT

According to facts released in 2010 from a 2008 national sampling of nurses, the average age of nurses has risen to forty-six from 45.2 in 2000. By 2012, the average age will decrease to 44.5, but more than 25 percent of nurses will be in their fifties and will represent the largest segment of nurses in the workforce.

The workforce of new nurses is predominantly older as well. Many entering the nursing field today are in their thirties, with nursing as their second or even third career. Hospital work is physically demanding, and many new nurses are not staying in hospital-based jobs past their second or third year.

Nurses are professionals, and they set the bar high. They expect their peers to be held to the same standards and expect management to hold to these standards. If management allows a select few to not meet the standards over and over, good nurses will eventually take their strong work ethic and move on. Making everyone a team member with ownership of the successes, as well as failures, is vital. Letting everyone know that you are willing to accept occasional exceptional circumstances is important, but not allowing those exceptions to become the norm for a select few is an absolute. When team members feel that they have a fair and equal opportunity and that their contributions are valued, they will do anything for a manager. But when team members feel that some have advantages all the time, resentment abounds.

Managers who regard their workforce as individuals and human beings don't have to fall prey to favoritism. They don't have to be drill sergeants who show no compassion either. Management is a fine art. Setting the bar high and commanding respect is essential.

As you move through your nursing career, pay attention and learn from managers who are understanding and fair. Learn from their accomplishments and incorporate them into your game plan as you become a leader, or suggest them to new managers as they struggle to become good leaders.

A Problem and a Solution

Susan is an aide who has a bad back. She is always assigned patients who require little to no assistance with mobility. The others on the unit have the same number of patients assigned, but their needs are always greater than Susan's patients. Susan is always done first and never offers to help the others with tasks that she could perform without risking injury to her back. Management makes no effort to equalize the situation and offers no recognition to the staff who always picks up the slack.

A new manager comes in and sees the situation brewing. She calls a staff meeting and recognizes that Susan has special needs but asks that she take on some additional responsibilities to help out her team members. She will be partnered with a different team member each time she works and will be expected to be available to help with specific tasks. She will also be given a few extra duties on the unit, such as keeping the break area clean and stocked. Staff members seem skeptical that it will work since Susan has never been receptive to their requests for help. However, this is being mandated by the manager, so it might work.

After a few weeks, staff reconvenes with the new manager, and everyone is pleased with the results. Even Susan feels like she has become a valued team member and that her peers respect her and understand her limitations instead of snubbing her and resenting her.

Everyone needs to feel valued and respected and to feel that there are no double standards. As mentioned before, there is no "I" in *team*. Susan was not a superstar, but she was always being given special treatment. The old manager never saw the resentment brewing and never considered her style to be unfair and partial. She also couldn't fathom why she was losing the respect of her team.

What Nurses Need to Be Happy

Hospital and other health care administrators need to think outside the box and develop plans to assist nurses to continue to work and to have reduced physical demands, more flexibility, and career options, as well as better pay and benefits. They need to listen to their employees and the reasons why they hate their jobs. They also need to participate in the educational opportunities and training of new nurses, as well as enticing young people to enter the field.

The nursing shortage of the past decade was not solved with higher salaries and recruiting nurses from other countries, and as the economy recovers and older nurses begin to retire *en masse*, it still won't be a solution.

Women make up the majority of the workforce in nursing. Thirty to forty years ago when many of today's nurses were considering career options, they had few choices. Women became teachers, secretaries, or nurses. Today, women are not limited in their career choices. It is not uncommon for anyone to change careers several times in their lifetime now. Most nurses' skills transfer well to other fields, and because nurses are highly skilled critical thinkers, most employers will be thrilled to hire and train a former nurse to fill their positions.

FACT

Longevity in employment is something hospitals have barely begun to reward. Previously, only when a staff member reached a huge milestone such as twenty-five or thirty years did they even make any sort of recognition. Now some hospitals are honoring even first anniversaries and making monetary bonuses or other benefit increases at lesser milestones, such as five- and ten-year marks.

To recruit and retain nurses, hospitals, as well as all other health care venues, need to consider working conditions. With mandatory overtime and on-call issues, nursing could be considered the sweatshop of the new millennium. Patients are more acutely ill, and because of managed care and other cost-saving efforts, they leave the hospital sicker than ever before. This places a tremendous burden for patient education on the nurses, especially at a time when quality of care is being scrutinized and penalties for poor care will affect the bottom line for many institutions. The continued use of unlicensed staff places more responsibility on licensed nurses who have to delegate to and supervise these staff members.

Health care doesn't fit neatly into a nine-to-five job. Acutely ill people require care twenty-four hours a day. Others require access to their health care providers around the clock. Does that always mean that shifts need to be eight, ten, or twelve hours? Hospitals changed to twelve-hour shifts, offering nurses opportunities to work three days a week instead of five. This was great, and then nurses found that they could work for two hospitals and make far more money. And if they work for a travel agency and "travel" to a hospital fifty or more miles from home, they can earn tremendous salaries. So are salaries really not an issue?

Do nurses want more prestige? Do they want power lunches? Do they want to work shorter shifts, such as six hours a day, and maybe more short shifts? Do they just want someone to let them go to the bathroom and eat a meal? Do nurses want to be able to rotate shifts, especially shorter ones, so that they have opportunities to participate in their family's lives? Do they need to be thanked and recognized more often? Do they need new challenges and opportunities, such as changing units or trying out a new specialty without penalties? Other industries have had to rethink their work conditions in order to recruit and retain staff; perhaps it's time the health care industry did the same. Nurses need to be included in the decision-making processes and willing to make their voices heard.

Float Staff and Travel Nurses

The trend toward flexibility is a growing one. Per diem status and travel opportunities are still a big draw. These are costly to facilities and don't always cover all the bases. No one wants to work weekends and holidays, and finding loyalty to an employer is a challenge. Float staffs are usually per diem staff, but some hospitals and other facilities hire them as full-time employees who have the flexibility of working in different areas. Some facilities have great success with float pools and others do not. Again, the issues of mandatory overtime and being on call can be the problems that drive nurses away from some employers. With an unpredictable economy playing havoc with the health care industry, it can be difficult at best to set schedules.

The pros and cons of utilizing temporary staff of any sort can vary tremendously depending on the unit and the competency of the entire staff. Where float staffing is usually for a much shorter duration (perhaps only one shift), travel nursing assignments are usually longer-term arrangements, such as thirteen weeks.

While you will always be grateful for the warm body, someone new to your unit can be a liability or, at the very least, time consuming. The success depends on the acceptance by the staff, as well as the adaptability of the newbie. Unit educators can be a terrific help in orienting any new staff, but they don't always work all shifts. Float pools and long-term travel nurses are usually oriented to the units they may be used on. However, when this isn't the case, nurses who may be new to your unit can arrive totally unfamiliar with the unit.

Take a few minutes to bond with the new nurse and show him the ropes. Even if he has had some orientation to your unit, you know that there are nuances and peculiarities he needs to be aware of. Thank him for his help and be available for questions. Make his experience as pleasant as possible, and you'll improve the situation for today. You'll also avail yourself of the opportunity to learn from him.

CHAPTER 15

Expect to Get Sick

You work in health care, and you are exposed to all sorts of germs and chemicals every day. You should expect to get sick at some point. Like a teacher who spends eight hours a day with small children, you will be exposed to all sorts of nasty things. Many safeguards and infection control practices can help you stay well, but they aren't always foolproof.

You're Bound to Catch Something

Hospitals are notorious for harboring and transmitting germs. Other health care settings can be just as dangerous to your health. Your day-to-day exposure to patients with a variety of airborne bacteria and germs makes you susceptible. Even with the best hand washing and infection control habits, you are bound to catch something.

If you have underlying conditions, these can become worse. If you have any autoimmune diseases, such as diabetes or multiple sclerosis, you may find them out of control or out of remission. You may need to take steps to ensure that you eat properly and get enough rest. If you have a history of respiratory problems, such as asthma, you may be prone to catching a cold every time someone is admitted with a full-blown respiratory illness or even has a simple case of the sniffles.

ALERT

Health care is a stressful job and is not always conducive to the best of nutrition, elimination, and rest and relaxation habits. Are you taking your breaks and meals, or are you routinely skipping them? Do you get to the bathroom regularly, or are you holding it for hours at a time? All these factors can affect your own health issues.

Some of the commonsense things you can do to ward off problems include talking to your physician (or other qualified person such as a nutritionist) about vitamins and minerals that may help to boost your immunity. You need to drink plenty of fluids and eat well-balanced meals at regular intervals. You also need to make sure you get plenty of rest. This may seem impossible with your new work schedule, but you need to do what you can to maximize the effort.

In many instances, in time, you will adjust to the new environment and find that you are not as prone to catching things as you once were. You will build up an immunity to the germs that reside in or frequent your facility.

Infection Control

It's normal to get caught up in the efforts to protect patients from nosocomial infections and other hospital- or facility-borne illness, but it is equally as important to remember that you are also protecting yourself from the spread of disease.

Hand washing is the most effective form of infection control and a standard precaution. You need to wash your hands before and after contact with each patient. You also need to wash your hands between the dirty and clean aspects of procedures, such as dressing changes. If you touch your mouth or your hair, you need to wash again. If you handle equipment or trash, you need to wash your hands.

Every door handle and bed rail you touch will harbor germs. And, of course, after you visit the bathroom, you must wash your hands. This not only helps to stop the spread of infections and bacteria between patients, it helps to eliminate you as the middle man from becoming contaminated and getting sick. If you contaminate a surface, you need to follow your facility's protocols for cleaning it. This is often done with a diluted bleach solution.

FACT

Personal protective equipment (PPE) is worn to protect you from splashes or other exposure to bodily fluids that may be infected with such diseases as HIV, AIDS, or hepatitis. This equipment can be worn any time exposure to a patient's illness could cause you undue risk.

Don't forget to teach your patients proper hygiene habits, such as covering their mouths and noses when they cough or sneeze and by coughing or sneezing into their bent elbow. Teach them to place their tissues in a bedside trash bag instead of leaving them all over the bed. Teach them to wash their hands when they cough, sneeze, or handle the tissues.

Encourage them to have a bedside waterless hand sanitizer available if they can't get out of bed easily or if they cough or sneeze frequently. Instruct them to follow this at home as well to avoid infecting family members or re-infecting themselves. If you work diligently to eliminate the germs that you can be exposed to, you will reduce your own chances of catching something.

Stress Management

Nursing is a stressful job. Managing your stress is vital to your own health and sanity. Nurses are very good at teaching others how to handle stress and illness but are often terrible at taking care of themselves. Nurses are also very hard on themselves. Most nurses are overachievers and never slow down. That adrenalin rush is addicting, and it can increase the wear and tear on your body and soul. Nurses, especially those working in intensive care units and emergency rooms, get into a very bad habit of thriving on the adrenalin rush that accompanies an urgent situation. This habit can be carried over into the nurses' personal lives where they seem not to be able to function unless everything is whirring at a wild, frenetic pace.

ALERT

Stress can cause headaches and lead to migraines, backaches, and digestive problems, such as constipation and diarrhea. Stress causes ulcers and can lead to heart attacks and strokes. Stress will exacerbate any underlying disease you might have, such as diabetes or hypertension.

In the course of having to take control of situations all day long at work, nurses often turn into "control freaks" who want to have the last say in everything. The truth is that no one can be in charge of every situation, and the trick is to figure out how to not stress over everything that you cannot control. You need to learn to act or respond and not to react to situations. The first step is to accept that you are not in control of every situation. Some situations you can contribute to and others you will just have to leave up to others to control.

Keeping Sane

When your life is always running full-speed ahead, it can be difficult to ascertain what is significant and what isn't—everything seems to be dramatic. Slow down, and let life come into perspective. Take control of your life, and manage your stress. Sleep, nutrition, and exercise are key elements to controlling your stress. You need to balance them in your life. And you need to learn to relax. You should take some time each day to unwind. Your body needs to rest and recover. Set aside time and make it a priority in your life to just shut down for a few minutes. Close your eyes and transcend to your secret place for ten minutes.

ESSENTIAL

Is the problem that you're obsessing over something that you won't even remember tomorrow or next week? Or is it something that will impact your life until you fix it? You need to remember not to sweat the insignificant things. Take a deep breath and consider whether this is a big enough issue to worry about. If not, let go of it. If it is a significant issue, then calming down will help you find appropriate solutions.

Learn to Relax

Relaxation may not come naturally to you, especially if you're on a constant adrenalin high. Start with deep breathing. Sit in a comfortable position. Inhale through your nose and exhale through your mouth. Do this slowly and rhythmically. Close your eyes and imagine you are in your favorite place all warm, snug, and secure. Tense your whole body, and as you continue breathing, slowly relax your toes, then your lower legs, then your lower torso, then your upper torso, then your neck, and finally your facial muscles and your entire head. Continue breathing slowly. If you aren't completely relaxed, repeat the tensing and releasing. You can isolate areas, such as your shoulders, neck, and head, to relax if you need to.

Devote ten to fifteen minutes to this every day, and you will begin to see results within a week or two, if not immediately. Some people do this while they wait for dinner to cook, and others do these relaxation exercises to fall asleep at night. There are many programs for stress management. You may need to experiment to find something that works well for you, but you must control the stress. It will help you to do a better job, avoid burnout, and promote your own wellness. This may seem overly simplistic, but learning to relax and take control of your life in small ways can actually prove to be of huge benefit in the long term. By utilizing simple techniques, they can easily become routine so that when a very stressful situation arises, your body automatically goes into relaxation mode to protect you.

Proper Body Mechanics

Nursing has the highest risk for back injuries of any profession. You must do everything possible to protect your back. Most of these injuries are preventable. Stop and think before you do something that may injure yourself. Assess the situation and get help! Never try to move a patient by yourself. You could end your hands-on nursing career with one wrong move.

Back injuries among health care workers account for approximately $1.7 billion annually in medical care and lost days. Many employers have instituted mandatory back safety programs in an effort to decrease their premiums and prevent back injuries to their employees. Some hospitals have trained lift teams to perform any lifting duties throughout the hospital.

Proper body mechanics are essential in transferring and moving patients to sitting positions in bed. Hospital beds and tables are usually on wheels, but they have safety locks. Make sure to lock and unlock them securely and appropriately. Also, consider the additional weight of the patient to the weight of the bed before attempting to move it. Never skip any steps even if the patient is a small child. One wrong move can cost you your job and your back. Use gait belts and draw sheets whenever possible. And always get help from another team member.

Follow these rules when lifting or transferring patients to protect your back:

- Keep your lower back in its normal curved or arched position at all times.
- Move as close to the bed or patient as you can.

- Never twist; always pivot or side step.
- When lifting, set your feet in a position to give yourself a solid, wide base of support.
- Keep your stomach muscles tight, bow slightly at the hips, and then squat.
- Keep your head up and hold your shoulders upright. If you held a yardstick along your back, it would be perfectly straight.
- Push up from your knees and use your own momentum to help you lift.

If you do get hurt, report it right away and seek medical treatment. Early intervention is the key to successful treatment and prevention of permanent dysfunction. The trend now is to combine anti-inflammatory medications with physical therapy and as much normal activity as can be tolerated. Cumulative damage to your back can result in a very minor injury becoming the final straw that triggers a serious situation. Take care and seek treatment even for minor injuries.

ESSENTIAL

It is essential to assess the situation before you move a patient. Is the patient alert and oriented or confused and combative? How much can the patient do for himself? Compare the patient's size to yours. What do you need to do with this patient?

Be aware of your rights and consult an attorney if you are injured on the job. Keep a journal of all events and conversations. Be proactive and protect your body. Report dangerous situations and remind your coworkers if you see one of them using poor body mechanics. The nursing shortage is bad enough without nurses unnecessarily injuring themselves. Twelve percent of nurses leave the profession because of back injuries. If even half of the injuries can be prevented, it will go a long way toward helping to ease this crisis.

Avoiding Needle Sticks

Research has shown that approximately 93 percent of all needle sticks are IV related. These usually occur when piggybacking through a "Y" site on the IV line or with intermittent IVs through the access port. Other instances occur when lines are left dangling after being disconnected. As we move to entirely needleless systems and systems that incorporate fail-safe features, these statistics will dramatically diminish. However, nurses have to understand how to use these systems correctly in order to not cause other injury. Never assume one system works the same as another. Investigate and learn how to safely use each system.

The next most common occurrence for needle sticks is from needles protruding through a sharps container. There are two ways that this seems to happen. One is when the sharps container is over-filled and needles fall out. The other is when they are crammed into a crowded container and poke out through the side or top. Sharps containers should never be filled more than two-thirds full and then the container should be sealed and properly disposed of according to your facility's protocol. Safety caps should always be employed to prevent needles from protruding in the first place.

FACT

Needleless systems for IV administration have been mandated by Occupational Safety & Health Administration (OSHA) agencies in many states for years. Other states have voluntarily adopted these systems to protect health care workers and patients alike. Some states, however, have been reluctant to push for this move, and health care workers may still be working with IV sets that employ needles.

The needleless system virtually eliminates the needle stick problem from IVs. You simply cannot get stuck with something that is not there. Other forms of needle safety for hypodermic needles have been adopted across the country as well. These include needle guards that automatically or manually fold over the needle and syringes that allow the needle to be retracted after use. These systems help to reduce needle sticks from sharps containers by adding another barrier, but the sharps container should never be over-filled. Technology will bring new and better systems all the time. Be sure you know how to safely use each system, and don't take short cuts or ignore the safety mechanisms in place.

If your facility does not employ these systems, you should encourage the administrators to investigate their use and safety. Until then, you must continue to employ safeguards to protect yourself from a needle stick. Never recap and always have a sharps container within reach to dispose of the syringe and needle immediately after injection.

In the unlikely event of a needle stick, you must report it immediately. You need to be tested for exposure to such diseases as HIV and hepatitis B and C. Precautions need to be taken and possible future care needs to be ensured. Don't put yourself and your rights at risk by hiding the event.

When You Get Sick

If you are truly sick, stay home. Don't bring your germs to work; your coworkers and your patients really don't want to share your germs. See your doctor if necessary. Get rest and drink fluids so that you can get well as soon as possible. In an already short-staffed environment, they need you back at work.

Colds and flu will make their rounds. Be sure to get a flu shot when available. A pneumonia vaccine may also be advisable, especially if you work on a medical floor where you can find yourself exposed more often than other nurses or if you have chronic diseases. Discuss this with your physician. Do your best to avoid exposure and to keep yourself healthy. Reduce your stress, improve your nutritional habits, and get plenty of fluids and sleep. Don't let yourself get run down.

You also need to use your time off wisely. Don't call off and play hooky. Show up for work as scheduled, and when you have paid time off available to you, request time off in advance for recreational activities and relaxation. Once in a while, you will really need a mental health day, and this can be a legitimate reason to stay home, but again request the time off and try to use your time wisely. Use your days off to provide yourself with a mental and physical break from health care. Try to schedule your household duties before or after work. If you are organized, these duties shouldn't pile up on you so that you have to spend your entire day off doing laundry.

Don't try to overextend yourself. Some nurses work three twelve-hour shifts a week at one hospital and two or three shifts more at another. This may make you a lot of money, but it can wear you down and burn you out quickly. Be reasonable and realistic. Sooner or later, those who overextend themselves hit a brick wall. That's when mistakes and injuries are more likely to happen. Take care of yourself, and if you are sick, keep your germs at home.

CHAPTER 16

Working with Technology

The health care industry has begun to understand the need to come up to speed in adopting technology, but it has been a very slow process in many ways. Privacy issues are among the biggest concerns in moving forward, and it seems everyone has an opinion on the subject. Studies have shown that technological advances can help to prevent errors and provide for safer patient care. Electronic patient health care records can provide access to valuable information and can save time and lives. The technology to encode even the most complex patient's medical history on a magnetic strip such as those on credit cards, exists today, as well as the magnetic strip reader to encode and access the information.

Using Computers, PDAs, and Smartphones

Undoubtedly, if you just recently graduated from nursing school, you will have had some exposure to computers. Typically, you will have done some research using the Internet and even had some level of exposure to electronic records and charting. If not, please take the opportunity now to familiarize yourself with computers and electronic information devices. Technology is rapidly coming to the forefront in order to improve patients' safety and access to health care and outcomes, as well as to contain costs. In some areas, this will happen much faster than in others.

ESSENTIAL

The Internet can provide you with all sorts of information, such as the latest news on recent discoveries about diagnoses, treatments, and outcomes. You can access information about support groups and organizations that support research. You can find information about health care legislation being proposed and voted on. You can join listservs and receive updates and discussions via e-mail and RSS feeds.

If you need the latest information about a drug, there are multiple sites to choose from, including an online version of the *PDR*. Some require a subscription to access, but many times facilities subscribe, and you can access these from your facility library, your nurse's station, the laptop on your med cart, or your own PDA or smartphone.

Although some may still be using PDAs, smartphones have become the device of choice today. Applications for all of these devices include drug and medical reference books and tools. These phones and some PDAs also have Wi-Fi Internet access. More applications are currently available for the Android and iPhone formats than other smartphones, but mergers and acquisitions are in the works to expand the capabilities of the BlackBerry to have a programmable platform as well. Others will probably follow suit to remain competitive in this market.

Imagine having instant access to information about the new drug your patient is taking or an app to help you calculate pain medication equivalents or pediatric doses from adult doses without having to carry around sixty pounds of books or dig through a pile of books in the nurses' station.

For patient education purposes, you will be able to access medical references at the bedside to provide the latest information on a disease or treatment and use the device to record voice or text notes to remind you as you chart.

New nurses may not find this amazing, but their older colleagues will if they can get beyond the fear of using new technology. This is one way in which new nurses may be able to reach out to some of the older staff members and help them learn to effectively utilize these tools.

Technology Is Your Friend

As technology advances, there will come a time that even technological wizards will have to stop and learn to use new devices. With anything new, there will be a learning curve. You have to give yourself time to learn and perfect your skills. Some people will learn certain tasks more quickly than others will. Anything programmable or of a technological nature sends some people straight into a tizzy. Perhaps they never did learn how to record a message on their answering machine or how to program their VCR, let alone their DVR. Computers, PDAs, and smartphones send chills up and down their spine and can cause them to freeze in fear.

In the general workforce today, if you don't have at least some basic computer skills, your options are very limited. In your day-to-day life, you will encounter many variations of technology at home, in the community, and at work. Embrace them and allow yourself the time necessary to learn how to use them effectively. Help your colleagues learn to further the technology movement in health care. In the health care setting, aside from computer devices and smartphones, you will encounter lots of technology with devices such as various generations of IV pumps, tube feeding pumps, suction devices, ventilators, cardiac monitors, and so on.

Point-of-care testing (POCT) has become commonplace in hospitals throughout the country. In many instances, lab techs still perform the tests, but with special training and institution of protocols and regulations, nurses are part of this team now, especially in specialty-care units.

Every day you will likely encounter some form of new technology as more advances are incorporated into the health care setting. Help to embrace them. There are many options that can help to make situations safer, as well as more efficient. Take the time to learn how to use devices and software safely and correctly. You'll make it work for you and ease some of the burdens you face each day.

The Totally Paperless Hospital

A small ninety-two-bed community hospital in Jacksonville, Florida, has become an all-electronic health care setting. The completely wireless, digital facility opened in February 2005 and was built with the vision to be state-of-the-art. Tremendous challenges were undertaken in order to make this system work.

Baptist Medical Center South was built from the ground up to be a completely wireless, digital facility. All physicians and clinicians hired to be on staff signed an agreement prior to its opening that they would be committed to learning and using the technology throughout the hospital. They were provided extensive training in all aspects of the technology prior to the facility's opening; the staff will have ongoing training as the technology is upgraded in the future.

ESSENTIAL

Computerizing medical records is one information technology advance and many hospitals around the world have successfully implemented these systems. But completely automating departments throughout the hospital, including each bedside station, is quite another. Several large hospitals have tried and failed but continue to find ways to accomplish this.

It was a challenge for the nurses and doctors involved in designing the program to give up thinking about how they had always done things. The staff had to rethink how accessing information could be done much better and more efficiently through available technology. But the program is still succeeding. Having immediate access to medical records, x-rays, and laboratory results via a digital device at the bedside helps physicians provide timely information to their patients, and now the doctors have the ability to write new orders right there. They also have wireless access to the

Internet for additional evidence-based medical information. For the emergency department, having immediate access to prior medical records for previous history, lab results, and treatments is both a life-saving, as well as time-saving, improvement.

Physicians can customize care sets to design a set of standing orders to access and modify as needed, without having to constantly rewrite sets of orders for their patients. Nurses can do the same in care planning, and all bedside care can be charted from the patient's room. Supplies used can easily be reordered and charged to the patient without several intervening steps.

Today, hospitals all over the United States have paperless systems in use, and a 2009 study showed that patients' lives are saved and health care costs cut by using technology. The study was done with forty-one hospitals in Texas that used four different computer programs. Overall, patients seeking care in these hospitals were 15 percent less likely to die.

Increasing Your Knowledge Base

Just about the time you thought you were finished with school, you will find that learning in the health care field never ends. Every day you're likely to encounter something that you didn't know or that has changed drastically because of some new revelation. You will spend a significant portion of your "free" time researching and learning many more things than you learned in school. You will never know everything you need to know. The more you learn, the better prepared you will be to help your patients and to expand the knowledge base of your colleagues. Always try to share new information with your coworkers and encourage them to do the same with you.

Any of the major search engines, such as Google, Bing, and Yahoo!, have what is referred to as a "search" bar. In this blank area, you can type in the information you are looking for. The more specific you can be, the better your search will work. Use keywords, which are one or two words that best describe what you're looking for. You can also search using a phrase or question, but your results won't always be as refined. Keep trying, and as you get results, sometimes you'll find even better keywords to use. The Internet is a vast reference tool, but be sure to carefully check the accuracy of any information not derived from well-respected sources. You can do this by continuing and refining your search.

If you want to know something about multiple sclerosis, type in the words *multiple sclerosis*, and you'll find many thousands of sites listed in order of how that search engine ranks them. If you want treatment modalities, type in *multiple sclerosis treatments* or *treatment for multiple sclerosis*. You'll get slightly different sites, again based on rankings. You'll also get slightly different sites if you search more than one search engine, such as Google versus MSN's Bing.

If you want a very specific topic or person, use quotation marks around the information you enter, such as *"Florence Nightingale."* Otherwise, you'll find sites about Ms. Nightingale listed first, and then you'll see sites with information about other Florences and other Nightingales. If you use Google to search, you'll see "see similar pages" underneath each listing. You can click this to see more sites like the one listed. These can often lead to even more information or a more refined choice.

If one set of keywords doesn't work, try others. Think about what or whom the subject is, does, is famous for, etc. Keywords are used by web designers to get search engines to find their sites and rank them. They also utilize these keywords when they register or submit their site to a search engine themselves.

Using Your Facility's Equipment

During orientation, you should have been instructed in how to use the equipment available on your unit, but you may not have had the opportunity to really understand how all things work or may not have encountered an opportunity to use something since that day and now you need to or would like to know how. Ask for help.

ALERT

Some devices may be very sensitive and can be easily broken or significantly altered if you don't know what you're doing. This is true for those who may be technologically savvy as well. Sometimes devices are set up slightly differently than you may be used to or customized for your unit or specific users in your facility.

Sometimes software has certain features turned off or eliminated altogether that another facility or user may have access to. For example, the Windows operating system comes with certain games built in, but perhaps your system administrator eliminated them from the facility's computers so that users aren't playing solitaire instead of attending to patients.

Health care software can have multiple uses, including documentation, scheduling, and billing. This software may have many options for tracking physicians' orders, lab tests, and results. It can also keep an inventory of supplies, charge them out as used, and reorder them. Each additional option may tack on an added charge to purchase and use. Perhaps your facility only needs to use the software for documentation and billing purposes. Therefore, the inventory portions would be turned off, as well as the reordering option by the software seller. If you had used this same software at another facility previously, you might be quite confused as to why it doesn't allow you to access lab results. Or perhaps the situation is reversed, and now you have capabilities you are unfamiliar with.

ESSENTIAL

Default settings on certain devices may vary from one unit to another or one facility to another. Perhaps alarms have been turned off or set to low volume. This may be because of the personal preference of the unit manager or because of interference with other devices on your unit.

A fear of ruining or messing up the controls or defaults on devices is a prime reason that some people avoid technological devices altogether or fight using them. However, if you are careful and ask for help if you are unsure or don't know how to use something at all, then this shouldn't be a problem. Technology can be your best friend and a tremendous time saver if you give yourself time to learn how to use it correctly.

How Technology Will Help Reduce Errors

One advance in electronic technology for patient care is the use of bar codes on patient ID bands that are also encoded on the patient's chart, medications, and labels for laboratory tests, x-rays, and so on. When double-checking the patient's identity, the bar codes must match. These devices have been shown to improve patient safety, primarily by reducing medication errors.

Another device used is a microchip that allows a patient's whereabouts to be tracked throughout a facility. You can always find your patient. Perhaps he needs his IV bag changed, and you're on your way to change it when you discover that someone snatched him for a test without notifying you. Or perhaps the other person apparently forgot to check whether the patient needed the bag changed soon. By activating his homing device, you can locate your patient quickly and notify the department without having to make several unnecessary phone calls. The IV bag can be changed, and you will have avoided having to restart because of a clotted line.

Utilizing the drug reference guide on your smartphone, you see that a new contraindication has been noted for a particular drug you are about to administer. (This is an update that was made just a couple of days ago, and you received an e-mail to update your reference last night.) This medication should not be given to patients with end stage renal disease, and your patient is on dialysis. You call the doctor and inform him of the updated information, and he changes the order. The *PDR* and other printed versions of drug books won't have this information until the next printing. You may have received the information in advance of or concurrently with the pharmacy, and your quick action saves the patient harm.

There are multiple point-of-care (POC) devices and programs available for physician use. These allow physicians to use their own smartphones, PDAs, and bedside PC tablets, notebooks, laptops, etc., to write prescriptions and other orders. The tremendous advantage that these systems offer to both physicians and other health care workers is that they eliminate the physician's handwriting issues.

FACT

Patient safety and reducing medical errors have been a primary focus of the health care industry for years, but they have come under major scrutiny in the last decade. Organizations, such as JCAHO, have made these issues a priority and have set specific patient safety goals and standards each year for accredited facilities to meet.

Many times, these POC systems for prescriptions also include valuable databases, such as formularies for Medicaid and even specific insurances. They can include general pricing information and comparisons of brand name drugs to generic alternatives. The POC systems can include lists of sound-alike drugs, as well as other drug information. They can be synchronized and updated as needed and the physician alerted by e-mail or onscreen if the doctors are connected to the Internet via Wi-Fi or an in-house intranet system.

Additionally, there are many information technology systems emerging that will compare a patient's medical history to a database and provide clinical-decision support information. This may result in a change of regimen or treatment to meet present evidence-based medical care standards. This kind of comparison can reduce the need to reinvent the wheel with expensive tests, invasive procedures, and trial and error methodology for patients whose background and medical history match others in the database. These information technology systems can also serve to bring an out-of-touch physician up to speed on treatments and procedures and eliminate possible errors she might make by using outdated and even dangerous modalities that produce less than optimal outcomes.

CHAPTER 17

Discharge Planning

Discharge planning begins at the moment of admission. Years ago, patients would stay in the hospital for days and days, sometimes even weeks or months, but that doesn't happen today. Patients come in sicker and go home quickly and sicker than ever before. They need to go home well prepared. Families and patients have to be ready to take responsibility for care and custodial issues. Nurses need to educate them on how to promote their own wellness and prevent complications.

Beginning with Admission

The moment a patient is admitted, the clock starts ticking down the time that the payer allots for this spell of illness. Patients and families may have no idea that the patient won't remain in that bed until he is completely well or even able to care for himself again. They need to be educated, and they need to understand that the patient's stay will be short.

You will learn the patterns of how long certain payers will allow a patient to stay, and you will always be begged by some patients or their loved ones to do what you can to help them stay just a little longer. There will be little to nothing that you can do except to instruct them to discuss it with the physician and discharge planner.

Some people will have an attitude with a strong sense of entitlement. After all, they have paid for this insurance (or into Medicare) for many years, and they should get their money's worth. Health insurance premiums aren't meant to be a savings plan to be spent on the insured's health care, but some patients are unclear on the facts.

The fact is that medical costs are skyrocketing, and one of the ways this is being dealt with is the paradigm shift from a sick care model of health care to a wellness and prevention model where the patient assumes responsibility for his health status.

Simple math will demonstrate that even if this is the way insurance worked, their theory of having paid in so much doesn't really hold water. Say they have paid in $500 per month for premiums for twenty years. That totals $120,000. Subtract out all the money the insurance has paid out over those twenty years, and that won't leave much. To be generous, we could say it leaves $60,000. That can be gone in a very short hospital stay! Wait until they see their hospital bills.

Beyond this issue, there is the patient's shock that she will still be sick when she is asked to leave or to pay out of her own pocket to stay. And the three to seven days goes by very quickly. Remind her that today's admission date counts as day one no matter what time she was admitted.

When discussing this matter, put the expected stay into terms, such as "By Wednesday, the 4th, you will be discharged, so please plan accordingly."

There's not a lot of time, and you will be overwhelmed with all your patients and everything that they need to learn to take over their own care. Maximize your quality time. In every encounter with your patients and their family, you need to be doing some teaching about each and every task you are performing, from fluffing pillows to dispensing medications. Perhaps they will have home health services, but you need to start the education process on day one.

Mandated Reporting

You will have occasion to see many different situations. If you have reason to suspect any form of abuse or neglect, you must report it. It isn't up to you to make judgments, or to try to figure out why it's happening. You just have to report it. There is a team of professionals who will take it from there to determine how and why it's happening and what can or must be done.

Everyone worries about retribution for reporting, but not reporting can actually get you into more trouble! The laws protect mandated reporters. The reporter cannot be identified. Sometimes it's obvious, but you have every right to protect yourself and to suggest that any number of others may have seen or suspected something. By reporting suspected neglect or abuse, you help to establish a path for the situation to be improved and hopefully resolved for the patient.

ALERT

Mandated reporting laws vary from state to state. Be sure to understand what your facility expects you to do. Also, be sure that they are in compliance with state laws and not just trying to avoid trouble for themselves. If you have a question about reporting a situation, consult with your supervisor and ask for social services to be consulted.

Perhaps your patient is a stubborn elderly woman who lives alone and refuses to accept any help. She isn't safe at home alone, and that's why she fell. Her family is at their wits' end trying to force her to accept some help, but she fights them every step of the way. If social services has to become involved, they may be able to help resolve the situation by "enforcing the rules" that she must accept some help or be placed in a facility. Sometimes, there is really little that can actually be forced on a patient, but an outside official telling her she has to get some help may make a difference. This practice can at least give the family some leverage with her and raise everyone's awareness of the seriousness of the situation. Each time a report is made gives the protective agencies more power to eventually take action if necessary.

The physician needs to be kept abreast of the situation, and the discharge planner needs to know so that arrangements can be made for follow-up from community resources, such as home health and outside protective services. Reporting suspicious neglect and abuse is always an uncomfortable thing, but as a health care worker, it is your duty to do so. You are the advocate for the patient. Your job is to protect others and promote wellness. Be sure to understand your state laws and to stay informed.

Understanding Insurance and the UR Process

Each insurance payer will have some unique characteristics, but in general, they work in much the same way. Medicare has both an indemnity-type plan and several varieties of managed care plans known now as advantage plans. Medicaid is similar in each state, but each state can have different rules for qualification and administration.

The common factor is that medical costs are exorbitant and all forms of insurance are working to contain costs. Managed care organizations made a strong effort to continue to dominate in some areas, but the administrative costs involved have caused the downfall of many of these organizations, and many have actually gone bankrupt. This left patients out in the cold and physicians with huge unpaid accounts receivable. The trend is swinging back more in favor of allowing physicians to make decisions and to order a reasonable number of procedures and tests, while reserving preauthorization for only select items.

The process of selecting health care options from a network of providers with similar mindsets and goals has also released some of the strangleholds HMOs have had on the health care field. These issues have caused financial strains on physicians and facilities and have played a major role in producing the nursing shortage. The uninsured population is growing, which is a major concern for all. Health care issues are going to dominate the political arena for years to come, particularly since the baby boom generation is reaching retirement age.

ESSENTIAL

The Patient Protection and Affordable Care Act was signed into law in March 2010 but is under threat of repeal. There will no doubt be modifications to the act over the next years, but hopefully some of the main issues, such as not being denied coverage for pre-existing diseases, will prevail.

Medication coverage has changed dramatically, and the high cost of medications dictates many issues for patients. Recent surveys of the elderly have shown that as many as 20 percent have restricted the use of their medications because of prohibitive costs. This can be extremely destructive, especially when patients don't understand the dangers associated with adjusting dosages. Under Medicare Part D coverage for medications, hopefully, elderly Americans can receive affordable medication coverage.

Nurses need to understand insurance issues in order to help patients understand them and prioritize their medical issues. Most insurance companies have set standards that govern time allowances for hospital and extended-care stays. These are based on years of studies of standards of patient care and diagnosis-related issues. They are general guidelines, but unless specific instances and circumstances can prove to be detrimental to the patient's health, they will be followed.

In the event that complications develop, the utilization review (UR) department will be called upon to review the case and to determine if the condition warrants a longer stay. The UR department may also be called upon to review the case in the event that procedures or treatments are being denied by the insurance company to determine their medical necessity. The UR department also reviews cases for quality and performance issues and in the event that any unusual or nonstandard treatment is being provided. Their role is to advocate for quality of care and patient safety.

Patients need to take responsibility for their own health issues. They need to do all they can to promote wellness. Health care workers need to do all that they can to prevent medical errors and to alleviate cause for litigation. All these efforts will help to reduce medical costs.

The focus of health care under the prevention and wellness model will be on the patient learning to care for himself. He may not have the luxury of aftercare or home care visits. You may need to instruct him in how to care for his complicated surgical wound at home. You won't want to begin instructing thirty minutes before he leaves the hospital. That is why it is important to begin your discharge planning at admission. The patient will be well versed and more confident in his own care if you do.

Discussion of aseptic technique and standard precautions should accompany every dressing change, along with signs and symptoms of infection, such as odor, redness, or fever. You could say something along the lines of "I'm glad to see that your wound is healing nicely and without any odor or redness. You don't have any fever, which is also a good sign."

Involving Family Members in Your Teaching

Since the advent of shorter hospital stays, patients are being discharged much sicker than may be ideal and in need of much more complex and technologically challenging care. They may or may not qualify for, or have coverage for, home health services. Family members and other caregivers may be expected to assume full and immediate responsibility for assisting patients with this care.

Daily procedures may need to be switched to a later time frame in order to accommodate family members and to facilitate their instruction in the care. One reason home care nurses complain about poor teaching in the hospital is that daily procedures may be routinely done in the early morning and not during visiting hours or times when family members can be present. Consequently, patients are discharged with inadequate preparation.

ESSENTIAL

To maximize patient/family/caregiver education and improve discharge planning, routines may need to be reconsidered. Options for ensuring family members/caregivers are present need to be explored. These include having the caregiver come in early or delaying the procedure until the family member can be present. It also requires coordination of care with several parties, including staff, the patient, and the family members.

If you are dispensing a new medication, instruct the patient in its name, action, dose, and any side effects or other implications. For instance, if your patient has just started taking an anticoagulant medication, instruct him in bleeding precautions and measures to reduce injuries. Discuss the reason for this medication, such as a recent thrombosis or CVA or as a prophylactic measure following joint replacement surgery.

If the patient needs assistance to get out of bed to go to the bathroom and back, instruct the caregiver in proper body mechanics and transfer techniques. Encourage the caregiver to participate in the lessons to learn how to safely manage the patient. Demonstrate the use of a gait belt or other measures to assist with safe ambulation. Correct any bad habits, and work to instill confidence in both the patient and his caregiver that they can do this.

Encourage other staff to instruct the patients in their responsibilities for care as well. If the patient is going to need assistance with activities of daily living (ADLs) at home, have the family member present for meals, bathing, bed making, etc., to learn tips and tricks to help make their job easier once the patient is home.

ALERT

Mandated reporting laws vary from state to state. Be sure to understand what your facility expects you to do. Also, be sure that they are in compliance with state laws and not just trying to avoid trouble for themselves. If you have a question about reporting a situation, consult with your supervisor and ask for social services to be consulted.

You need to consider HIPAA and other privacy situations unique to your patient and get permission to instruct family members in his care. Then, similar to using every opportunity to include patient teaching in your care, whenever possible, you also need to take advantage of the fact that family members are present.

Understanding Home Health Care

If your patient is going home and not into extended care, she may benefit from home health care. The discharge planner will have explored this option with her and her family. Sometimes patients refuse home health care, often because they don't understand its purpose or role in their recovery.

What Home Health Care Is

Home health care provides a continuum of care from the acute hospitalization to help the patient adjust at home. Patient teaching is a primary function in the home. Home care is provided on an intermittent basis, meaning the nurse or therapist makes a visit to perform the care. This is not the same as private duty home care where a nurse or other caregiver is hired for shift work. A nurse may also be required to make a few follow-up visits for such things as assessment and teaching for post-op care or for assessing respiratory status after a bout of pneumonia.

Physical, occupational, and speech therapy can be provided in the home if there is a documented need and potential for recovery. Nursing tasks can include such things as IVs, tube feedings, wound and ostomy care, diabetic instruction, and general assessment of systems until symptoms, such as hypertension or congestive heart failure, are stabilized. Home health aide visits may also be included, as indicated, for personal care, as long as there is a skilled nursing or therapy need as well. A medical social worker could also be indicated to assist with short- and long-term planning arrangements and referrals to community resources.

What Home Health Care Is Not

Home health visits are intermittent and not intended to be long term. The patient and perhaps a caregiver will be instructed in the care needed, and then the visits are tapered off or ended. The expectation is that the patient and family will assume responsibility for care. This includes learning such things as injections, wound and ostomy care, and tube feedings.

Patients often go home expecting that a nurse will be coming to stay with them for an extended period of time, but this is not the case. Typically, the nurse or therapist won't visit until the day after discharge unless there are specific procedures, such as IVs, tube feedings, or frequent dressing changes, that require a same-day visit. Patients also participate in IV care, and the nurse is then available for site changes and problem solving. The nurse might visit monthly to change a Foley catheter or G-tube, but the family handles the everyday care or feedings.

Paying for Home Health Care

The home health agency will notify the patient when reimbursement will end, and the patient or caregivers may opt to pay privately to continue care. In most cases, further care is not needed, and the patient and family are prepared to continue on their own. If the patient's needs change, home health care could be utilized again if all criteria are met.

Some private duty nursing care can be reimbursed by Medicaid and private insurance. This type of care might include such things as ventilator care or other complex skilled care. Custodial care is not reimbursed by Medicare or Medicaid and only rarely covered under private insurance. This is an out-of-pocket expense. This level of care is available from private duty agencies (which might be part of the home health agency or a sister company) or by privately hiring individuals.

FACT

A doctor must order all the care and be willing to oversee and provide continuing orders for home health care. In most cases (Medicare especially), the patient must be homebound for the duration of the home care, and there must be a skilled need for nursing or therapy. If all these criteria are met, the care is usually covered by third-party payers (insurance, Medicare, or Medicaid).

Two of the most common inquiries to home health agencies are how to get custodial care and why it isn't covered by Medicare or insurance. Most patients can benefit from a home health referral if for no other reason than for a physical therapist for a home safety evaluation and a couple of visits from a nurse for follow-up teaching about medications and assessment of the underlying event or illness that caused the hospitalization. Then they can also refer to the medical social worker for a visit to explore resources and to set in motion short- and long-term plans for assistance and care.

Accessing Community Resources

Nothing seems quite as stressful to some patients and family members as facing the reality that the hospital is booting them out before they are ready to go. No matter how much time is spent on discharge planning, some are just not prepared. The patient usually doesn't believe that he would have to go so soon.

To soothe the patient's and family's nerves, some of the suggestions you can make to reinforce the discharge planning efforts include reviewing community resources they should enlist to help them through this crisis. Of course, their network of friends and family should be enlisted. This can be as simple as a list of people the patient could call and check in with regularly or a friend who could make a scheduled quick phone call to the patient once a day to remind her to take her meds.

Clergy and friends from church or other religious organizations can be good sources to network with to find caregivers and others willing to help with errands and transportation to and from appointments. They can also be a great source of emotional support to the family, as well as the patient.

The hospital may offer patient education classes and other community service education resources. The hospital may also be involved in low-cost medical transportation or hot meal delivery services. (These could also be available from the senior center.) Local chapters of organizations, such as the Alzheimer's Association, American Heart Association, MS Society, American Cancer Society, etc., may be appropriate resources as well. High schools and local colleges may be resources for hiring flexible part-time help for errands, shopping, cooking, and even some companionship opportunities. A nursing program at a local college might be an excellent opportunity for both patient and employee.

ESSENTIAL

For seniors, local senior centers and agencies on aging can help with other resources. Have the caregiver make a visit to the senior center site and pick up all the literature the agency has available. Encourage the caregiver to share information about his situation and ask for advice. These groups have a wealth of information and resources.

Discharge planning is a team effort. Remember that the patient is an important member of that team and needs to be involved in the entire process. Effective discharge planning will help the patient assume responsibility for his care and prevent unnecessary repeat hospitalizations.

CHAPTER 18

Documentation and Communication

Strong communication skills are as essential to nursing as any other skill. The ability to document clearly and concisely is an art, but one that must be cultivated by every nurse. Documentation provides a legal, written record of the health care provided, including the reason for it, the actual care given, and the outcomes. Documentation is an important means of communication between health care professionals. It provides information about the care provided and the patient's response, as well as a directive about the needs for future care.

Writing Skills

Nurses need to be able to read and write in the language of the country in which they are providing care. In the United States, that language is English. Throughout the country, however, there may be other predominant languages, such as Spanish, French, or a variety of Native American and Asian dialects and languages. In most instances, although these may be the languages of the patients, the official language of the facility will be English. To become licensed and practice as a nurse in the United States, you must be able to read and write in English.

ESSENTIAL

It is important to remember that the health care record is a legal document and that documentation is not optional. Nor is it trivial and unimportant. The cliché about no job being done until the paperwork is completed is perhaps more true of health care than almost any other profession.

Your documentation reflects the care you have or have not provided to your patient and is your only legal proof that you did or did not do something. Your documentation needs to be as important as the care you provide. Often, nurses feel that the hands-on care is all that is important and that the documentation is a waste of time. Foreign-trained nurses may have actually been taught that documentation is insignificant in their home countries. In the United States, this is never the case. These responsibilities should carry equal importance at all times because your documentation becomes a part of the patient's medical record.

The skill with which you write about your assessment and intervention, and the patients' outcomes will reflect on the quality of the hands-on care you provide. Your records must be clear, concise, complete, and accurate. Other health care providers will rely on this information to make decisions about the patient's continuing care and needs.

You need to represent the five senses to the reader. If a wound is ugly and disgusting, that no doubt conveys a message, but it does not accurately describe the wound. In fact, it could be judgmental. The following gives a much clearer description of the wound: "The old dressing was removed.

The R hip wound is now 3 cm by 4 cm by 0.5 cm. There is a 1 cm. strip of yellow slough along the entire right side that is well adhered and pink granulation tissue around the outer edges of the other three sides. There is a slight odor emanating from the slough, but the old dressing has no odor. There is a small amount of serosanguinous drainage on the inner aspect of the dressing. The patient is afebrile and experiences only slight (0–2/10) pain during the dressing change." You would go on to explain the new dressing procedure and sign your note with your name, credentials, date, and time according to your facility's policies.

Accuracy and Timeliness

In the previous example, you can see that the wound measurements were given, the odor was described, and the fact that the old dressing has no odor recorded. The patient was afebrile, and his level of pain experienced with the procedure was recorded. Too often, nurses will merely chart that "the dressing was changed per doctor orders." What does that record about the wound healing, any signs or symptoms of infection, and how the patient tolerated the procedure?

ESSENTIAL

Accuracy is essential. If you don't have a measuring device, you'd better get one immediately. For now, give approximations or compare it to the size of something similar, such as a quarter or fifty-cent piece, and state that they are approximations. Next time, be sure to measure accurately.

You wouldn't say that the patient's wound stinks. You would state that it has a very strong foul odor. If you can describe it more accurately, do so. In some instances, it might be a fruity odor or a smoky odor, or smells like ammonia. It is also important to pinpoint the slough. Is it covering the entire wound bed, scattered over it, or as the example said, just a thin strip along the one side? Is it loose and easy to debride or adhered to the wound for dear life?

Documentation needs to be done in chronological order. If some other staff member did something or observed something about your patient and has documented it already, then your documentation will be out of order. Be sure to document that this is the situation. Never document ahead of time. Also, be honest and don't document something you didn't do or didn't observe yourself. You can state that someone else (and identify them) stated that some event occurred with such and such outcome, but don't say it was your observation when it was not.

Timeliness of your documentation is also important. You want to document as soon as you can so that the event is fresh in your mind and you don't forget important aspects. Even with careful notes, if you wait until the end of the shift to do all your documentation, you may find yourself rushing to finish and even mixing up your patients' data.

In the event the patient is reporting something that you think is unsubstantiated, you must report it, but document that the "patient states. . . ." For instance, "The patient states she is having 10/10 pain in her right thigh region, however she is observed to move freely and actively about in bed and is able to stand and walk ten feet without any verbal or nonverbal expressions of pain, such as grimacing or splinting."

Pain is subjective, and indeed the patient might be experiencing this level of pain. However, your documentation of the unrestricted activity also adds to the picture so that the situation can and should be explored with the patient particularly if she is seeking more or higher doses of medication.

If the patient was verbalizing the pain at 2/10, yet she was sweating, her pulse was racing at 110 beats/minute and her blood pressure has suddenly shot up to 170/90 from 110/70, then again her symptoms tell a different story. Perhaps she needs to adjust her pain scale, or perhaps she has experienced pain that is far worse. Therefore, to her own best judgment, this is where she truly would rate the present condition.

In either of these scenarios, you should clearly see that without the additional information, an accurate picture is not provided with just numbers. Clearly, the patient has other issues, along with their experience and rating of pain.

Reporting Off

Information does no one any good if it's all stored in your head. You might be able to accurately document on each of your patients at the end of the shift, but what happens if you leave the floor for a break or a meal and haven't done any documentation? If something happens with any of your patients, the first place others are going to look for clues is in the chart. Beyond that, they're going to hunt down the person who is covering for you. If that person knows nothing, look out! Trouble is coming!

You don't want to be the one caught watching another nurse's patients when the doctor comes in and demands to know what is happening with his patients. Nor do you want to be left to decide if the present set of vitals represent a sudden change in condition or whether the patient has been this way for a while. Do you need to notify the doctor or is he aware of this already? The information is useless if it isn't documented and isn't communicated to coworkers and colleagues.

ALERT

Any time you leave the unit for any reason, you need to report off to someone. That will usually be your supervisor, but you should also report off to anyone who is going to keep an eye on your patients for you. Whenever possible, you should have your documentation up to date before you leave. That may not always be possible, so a verbal report is essential.

You don't want to be the brunt of the missing patient situation either. For example, a patient has left the unit to visit with his young daughter in the lobby. The doctor has authorized this, but his nurse didn't write the order for it before she left for her lunch break. The patient is with his daughter and ex-wife in the lobby when his impetuous new bride comes in and finds him missing from his bed. After searching the bathroom and other places on the unit where he might be hanging out, she is now half hysterical and making a big scene! You're covering for this nurse who actually left the facility to run an errand on her lunch break. She didn't tell you this patient had gone to the lobby, and it has only been five minutes since the nurse left on her break. She's not answering her cell phone. This could be a very long lunch break!

If You Didn't Chart It, You Didn't Do It

If you didn't chart it, you didn't do it. This phrase has been drummed into your head since your very first nursing course. And your instructors hovered to make sure you charted everything just as you did it. That was because you were working under their license. Now you're on your own, and things have gotten a little lax because you're always so busy and feeling overwhelmed.

You finally have a few days off, and your flight just took off for Hawaii for a long weekend. Suddenly you remember you forgot to document that you gave Mr. Jones his last step (enemas until clear) of the barium enema prep just before you left the hospital to get to the airport. Now it's too late; you can call when you land, but that won't be for several hours. You know that no one will believe Mr. Jones when he tells them he's done; this is the second time around, and he didn't prep himself right the first time. The doctor was furious, and several things had to be delayed.

ESSENTIAL

The medical record is your proof that you did or did not do something. Always document as soon as possible, especially when administering medications and treatments. Remember to include accurate information regarding site, route, and the patient's response or outcome. If the patient refuses a medication or treatment, be sure to record this information and that you have notified the doctor.

True to form, no one believes Mr. Jones, so he's mad at you and your supervisor is disappointed. The nurse who now has to stop what she's doing and prep him is mad as well. While no real harm has been done, everyone has been inconvenienced, to say the least. And when you call them several hours later, they're not happy with you all over again. Imagine if this was an entirely different scenario and medication was duplicated or skipped entirely because the medical record was incomplete and basically inaccurate. What if Mr. Jones decides to sue over this matter: How can you prove that you did give the prep?

You can go back and amend your documentation at any time as long as you can honestly state that you remember the event. You must clearly state that this is an amendment and include the time and date that you are amending the record. If you are changing a statement because it is erroneous, you can mark through it, initial it, and reference where to find the amendment. Make sure that the information being corrected is still legible. And again, make note in your amendment of the time and date of the new entry.

In the event that documentation is destroyed or lost and you have been asked to re-create it, be sure to make note of how accurately you remember the data and that this is a re-creation to the best of your knowledge. Again, date it with the new entry date and time. Always sign your name and credentials to any documentation you write.

Omissions Are Errors

Omissions of any type are errors. If you forgot to do something, it is as much an error as if you did the wrong thing. You need to report omissions and complete any incident reports or other documentation required by your facility. As with any other error or incident, you must always be honest and up front about the situation. Never try to cover it up. And don't be a tattletale and run to your supervisor about someone else's omission error. Bring it to the private attention of the individual and let her handle it: If she doesn't, then privately speak to your supervisor about your concerns.

If the omission is one of forgetting to document something and no repercussions have followed, then you can amend your documentation as previously discussed. However, if events occurred as a result, such as Mr. Jones having to have an extra set of enemas, then you must also notify the doctor and complete any required incident forms.

The incident report form is a confidential documentation of the incident, including who was notified and when and any resulting consequences or outcomes. This form is not a part of the patient's medical record. It does not get copied and placed in your personnel file either. It is kept on file by the facility, usually with the quality improvement department or the nursing administrator's office in case of any further events or an investigation.

ESSENTIAL

Your facility will have specific information about how the error is documented in the medical record. Usually this involves a brief statement of facts and no mention of any incident forms.

Legal Implications of Documentation

Remember that the medical record is a legal document. It must be factual and accurate. You do not want to include your personal opinions. You want to be precise, concise, clear, and comprehensive. You may record your observations but not your interpretations. You may also quote the patient, but be careful not to use something out of context. Always follow these tips, and your documentation will be an asset to the care you provide:

- Be accurate and honest.
- Document in a timely manner—only during or after providing the care.
- Provide complete information regarding assessment, nursing diagnosis, nursing interventions and the plan of care, and evaluation of outcomes.
- Be sure it is legible and in permanent ink.
- Be sure all information needed for any forms used is complete and accurate.

Never chart ahead of time. This is a trap that many nurses fall into particularly when the nurses use blocks of time to document so that a statement could cover two hours at a time. This happens on the night shift frequently when nurses document, for instance, that the patient "is sleeping comfortably" from 10 P.M. to 7 A.M. The patient slept through the night with no complaints and there was no reason to awaken them. So they lump together two-hour blocks and just repeat over and over that the patient was sleeping comfortably.

Well, that may be fine, except that Mrs. Kellerman got up at about 6:32 A.M. and went to the bathroom. Her nurse had just checked on her five minutes before and had gone to complete her charting and to give report. Mrs. Kellerman arrested on the toilet at about 6:35 A.M., but her nurse documented that she was still in bed sleeping comfortably at 7:00 A.M. By the time they found her at 7:20 A.M., she could not be resuscitated, and the doctor canceled the code.

Had the nurse accurately recorded that she had checked on Mrs. Kellerman at 6:25 A.M. and, indeed, she was still in bed at that time, there would not have been an issue raised. However, when the chart said that she was still asleep in bed at 7:00 A.M., the family got a little curious why so little effort was made to attempt resuscitation efforts and why they failed.

ALERT

Don't document something until you have actually done it, and when you document it, be accurate in your time frames. Erroneous documentation can have the same ramifications as other errors.

Don't chart medications before you give them either. You could be on your way to administer a medication and get flagged down to help catch a patient who's falling out of bed. In all the resulting commotion, you forget to deliver the medication, but you already documented that you've given it. An hour and a half later, the patient is really in pain and wondering what's taking so long with his pain medication. He asks his night nurse, and when she checks the chart, it shows he recently had a dose. She tells him, "It's not time yet." He's perplexed, but suffers through it. It isn't until days later when you're doing laundry that the medication cup falls out of one of your uniforms. By now you don't even remember whose it was and assume he got one when he asked again.

CHAPTER 19

Confidentiality

Nurses and other health care professionals have long been morally and ethically responsible to protect their patient's right to privacy and to maintain confidentiality. Implementation of HIPAA legislation has brought the issues of privacy and confidentiality to the attention of the entire nation, from individuals' access to health care and physician visits to purchasing prescriptions and hospital stays. Nurses have a primary role in helping patients to understand all their rights.

HIPAA

The Health Insurance Portability and Accountability Act (HIPAA) was passed by Congress in 1996. It took five years for it to become effective (April 14, 2001) and another two years before compliance was mandatory (April 14, 2003).

The original intent of the law was two-fold: portability and accountability. The portability functions to protect individuals from losing their insurance coverage when leaving or changing jobs and to prevent employers from imposing pre-existing condition clauses. The accountability portion provides the federal government with increased power with regard to fraud and abuse issues in health care.

Another impetus for HIPAA legislation was the need to create electronic health records and management systems that would require layers of security but would get medical records out of massive storage areas and into an area where they can be readily accessed to provide better and safer care for patients.

Of course, implementation has been costly and will continue to be costly for a while. HIPAA is an evolving process and a huge example of how legislation has to see far into the future to predict and account for possible changes. At the time this law was passed in 1996, the Internet and electronic information processes were basically in their early toddler stages. As technology advances, new and more complex implications have to be considered.

FACT

Prior to September 11, 2001, terrorism, bioterrorism, and threats of identity theft had very different meanings. Today, all those issues play a big part in protecting the privacy and confidentiality of health care records. The issue of accessing medical records for homeland security situations is also a factor that was basically nonexistent at the time HIPAA was legislated.

Nurses need to be up to date with all issues related to HIPAA and patient confidentiality and privacy concerns. This is an evolving process, not one you learn once and move on. Patients need to understand their rights and to participate in their health care. Nurses need to educate patients and, therefore, need to keep up to date with changes.

A lot of misinformation about HIPAA and its implementation has been abundant in the health care arena. Some misinformation derived from the fear of penalties and allowed rumors to abound. HIPAA "experts" emerged from every nook and cranny to provide seminars and publish materials in multiple formats that are available at exorbitant prices. Many fortunes have been made by less than reputable sources, which has made it more difficult for the truth to be spread by those who really understand the rules.

Recently some pretty hefty fines have been lodged for serious HIPAA violations where privacy issues were ignored. One of the more famous cases involved fifteen employees who were fired for looking at medical records for Nadya Suleman (The Octomom), the woman who gave birth to octuplets in California.

Understanding Your Facility's Policies

As electronic capabilities continue to grow and information technology takes a stronger role in health care facilities, the rules pertinent to enforcing HIPAA regulations will continue to emerge and change. It is vitally important that all staff be kept apprised of changes and that you have a good understanding of your facility's particular rules and policies.

A facility where you did much of your training may have had a very different philosophy and practice regarding HIPAA responsibilities than your present one does. There may have been practices that you were unaware of as well. Be sure you understand what your facility expects regarding HIPAA and privacy regulations.

For instance, one facility may have made it a hard and fast rule that it doesn't divulge a patient's presence in a facility at all. If you called there looking for a relative or friend, they would tell you they cannot tell you if the patient is there. The only way people calling in can talk to a patient is to know her room number and a code word or password. They might even have to use a different password to obtain information from the nurses about the condition of their relative or friend.

Another hospital requires that the patient officially notify the admitting staff if he wishes to withhold his name from the phone directory. Unless so noted, anyone calling in to ask if the patient is in this facility would be told that he is indeed a patient in this facility. This is in keeping with HIPAA regulations despite myths being circulated to the contrary.

In most instances, patients do need to designate who can be given information about their care or condition. In the event a patient is not able to consent, it can be implied that next of kin or a caregiver be recognized as a designated representative to whom information can be divulged. How the facility's exact policy is written will dictate the actual procedure.

Protecting Patients' Privacy

Health care professionals have a moral and ethical responsibility to protect the privacy of their patients, and now this has been mandated by federal law. This encompasses all aspects of patient care, from pulling curtains and using towels and sheets to protect the patient's modesty and dignity to refraining from discussing details about a patient in any circumstances where you can be overheard.

You have an obligation to protect the patient's information from being seen by anyone who has no need to know. That means not leaving electronic records open when you leave your seat by the computer. It means not leaving patient charts out and unattended for anyone to view.

ALERT

If you work in a setting outside of the hospital, such as in home care, you must always be in possession of any records you remove from your office, or they need to be securely locked in your car away from view. You must not leave them in another patient's home or in a public place. Nor should you allow your family or friends to have access to them.

Whenever you are discussing a patient with a colleague, you need to be discreet and away from the hearing of others. Don't mention names or specifics that could identify a particular patient if you can't avoid being overheard. Don't discuss your patients with your friends and family members. Never assume that even in an employee-only cafeteria that you are "safe" to discuss patients. Others have no need to know and could be friends or neighbors of your patient.

Remember that your patients have public lives, as well as private ones. Their neighbor might seem very concerned, but to the patient, she's a nosy gossip-monger. Your patients most likely live in this community. They are teachers and lawyers and real estate agents. The middle school physical education teacher doesn't need to broadcast that he has had prostate surgery; the prominent lawyer has the right to conceal his HIV status; and the award-winning realtor doesn't need her clients to know she has frequent bouts of Crohn's disease. Neither do they need to have their idiosyncrasies of coping shared with the community.

Dealing with Celebrity Patients

The media jumps at every chance to inform the world whenever any celebrity checks into or out of a drug rehabilitation center. When someone famous is ill, injured, or dying, the paparazzi and news media camp on the doorsteps of the local hospital hoping to get a photo or sound bite from other famous visitors. When you're the nurse caring for that patient, you could find yourself being hounded for information. Usually the facility will do everything possible to protect you, but occasionally, you may be approached.

Although the celebrity is quite grouchy and not as nice as you expected him to be, remember he's not well, and no one is at his best when he is ill. Don't judge him; allow him the same opportunity to get well as you would any other patients. Celebrities are human beings with the same fears and feelings as anyone else.

What happens if you come to work and find that you are assigned to care for Mr. Latest Heartthrob, who recently collapsed from pneumonia? You can hardly control your excitement and can't wait to tell your roommates! No, no, no—you can't tell them anything! No matter who the patient is, you must always protect his privacy.

Most often, it's when you have a celebrity's family member as your patient that the "jerk" emerges. Celebrities are used to getting their own way about other things in their lives just because of who they are. So when a celebrity has a friend or loved one who is ill, she seems to think that her status will get special considerations as well.

When her demands become unreasonable and she begins demanding miracles, things can get intense. Anyone who is being prevented from doing something because of an illness or injury is going to be angry; however, for some reason, it is usually the celebrity who demands that the impossible be done to make a bone heal in twenty-four hours! Watch out if you're the one who tries to explain the healing process to her! Beyond your unit, you cannot express how much you'll never pay to see another one of her movies again!

Maintaining Confidentiality

Arranging for care after discharge can be challenging, but the need to know allows you some latitude. For example, your patient is an elderly gentleman who lives alone in an old residence hotel. He was a stand-in for a famous actor when he was young, and he claims to have many pieces of memorabilia in his apartment. He will need a caregiver and a visiting nurse, and he could be very vulnerable because he's very trusting and has been scammed in the past. The elderly gentleman often refuses medical care if he has to leave his apartment and his cat unsupervised.

The agency needs to know that he is a celebrity and of his vulnerabilities so that they can choose wisely in providing his caregivers. But your family and friends have no need to know who he is. This is true for any information you glean from caring for any of your patients. You wouldn't share that the middle school teacher had a prostatectomy and that he has one of the more severe issues with urinary incontinence from it. Neither would you share that Mr. Heartthrob was so delirious from fever one night that he paced up and down in his room for an hour stark naked.

FACT

You have an obligation to provide the same level and quality of care to all patients regardless of their gender, race, creed, or public status. Your celebrity patient is not entitled to any better care nor to more attention than you would provide to any other patient. He might be more demanding, but that should not influence the care you provide.

Be Professional

It goes without saying that you are a professional. No matter how appealing that sum of money might be to snap a quick picture for the tabloids or to drop a tidbit of information about how nasty a celebrity can become in a hospital, you are a professional and have an obligation to protect the privacy of all your patients. By the same token, your patients who are not celebrities have the same right to privacy about their health status and care. You have the same obligation to protect their rights as you do for any well-known patients.

Social Networking—Facebook, Twitter, and the Future

Social networking is a fast-paced way to connect with your friends and colleagues and to follow celebrities 24/7. It can be a lot of fun connecting with people and reconnecting with old friends and family all over the world. But there are responsibilities to be aware of. Your boss may be watching. Your enemies may use what you say and do against you. Your patients may even end up as a "friend" on Facebook or "following" you on Twitter someday. If you're not careful, confidentiality can be compromised and things about you and your personal life exposed.

There are multiple security functions to help you control who can view your pages and photos and who can read your posts and comments. However, things you post on someone else's page or site may be visible beyond your control.

Written words and pictures can be misinterpreted, copied, altered, and pasted many places on the web. So be very conscious of what you post and who can see it. Remember that you are a professional, and yes, you are entitled to a private life, but once you post it on the web, it's not private any more.

Social networking is a great way to learn about educational, as well as employment, opportunities. In a matter of minutes, you can connect with other nurses, headhunters, employers, etc., all over the globe. It's a far cry from attending gatherings and mixers or depending on cover letters and word of mouth to find you that new job.

Have fun with social networking, but always be professional. If you need to vent, don't do it publicly. Nurses have been fired for postings on Facebook, Twitter, and on their own blogs. Writing can be cathartic, but then hit the delete button instead of posting it.

ESSENTIAL

Sites like LinkedIn are specifically designed for professionals to network business and career opportunities. They allow you to post your experience and skills and even to have colleagues write recommendations for all to read.

Be wary of HIPAA as well. You cannot post any identifying information about your patients online. Many nurses and student nurses have blogs and use them to give others an idea of what their day was like. Make sure you have a disclaimer on your pages stating that you have changed names, dates, medical conditions, and other identifying information in accordance with HIPAA. And don't slander or disparage anyone.

CHAPTER 20

Nursing Is a Lifelong Learning Experience

In the health care industry, learning is an ongoing process. As a nurse, you are required to continue your education in order to renew your license. Possibly the only exception is your first license renewal period. But after that you will have to take continuing education units in each renewal period as long as you wish to keep your license active to practice nursing. This varies somewhat by state. Check with your state board of nursing for exact details.

Soak Up Knowledge Like a Sponge

You will learn something new almost every day of your career. Look for opportunities to keep learning. Even procedures you have now done many hundreds of times can be learning situations if you have an opportunity to assist or observe another nurse. Everyone will develop his own style and process for procedures. What you learn can even be a "how not to do that" situation. Nonetheless, this can be as effective a learning experience as learning something new.

Subscribe to nursing journals and search the Internet for informative sites. Read everything you can about subjects you feel weak in. If you work on a specialty unit, subscribe to listservs and other e-mail discussion groups, forums, or chat rooms for nurses who share your interests and specialty. Facebook offers many different nursing groups. On Twitter, you may find nurses from all over the world who share your interests and some who have websites or blogs on the topic. Join nursing organizations and look for local chapters to attend events and seminars.

Listen to a news program every day whether it is on the radio or television, or read the headline stories on the web. Stay current with political climates and issues that affect your community and the world. Have an understanding of what stimulates and affects your patients' world. Be a responsible citizen of your community. Keep up to date with health care issues in the news, and know who and what is effecting changes.

In-Services, Seminars, and Journals

Take the opportunity to attend workshops and any in-services and classes offered by your facility. If a seminar is being offered that is applicable to your particular job description or unit, ask your supervisor if you can attend as a representative of your facility.

Become active in your facility by providing your staff educators with ideas and requests for in-services and seminars. Volunteer to sit on committees to choose and provide in-services and seminars. As you find valuable resources and information pertinent to your job, share it with your coworkers, and provide a copy to staff educators. They are almost always open to new ideas and subjects.

If you hear of or read about a new technique, treatment, or procedure, request that your staff educators provide you with more information and education to keep everyone up to date. Many times, seminars are broadcast via the Internet and over phone lines so that one fee covers as many students as can attend at a facility. Other times, there are group discounts available. Check out these possibilities to save money and expand your knowledge base.

FACT

Sometimes your facility will pay your fees and/or pay you to attend in-services or seminars (so you don't have to take a vacation day or other paid time off). You may have to report back to a small group or make a larger presentation to the facility in return, but this can be a terrific opportunity for you to expand your horizons as well.

Always subscribe to at least one nursing journal. Many offer online access now and can offer other benefits in addition to subscriptions, such as access to archived articles and search capabilities. Whenever possible, subscribe to one or two other journals as well. These could be either broad-based nursing journals or those designed for a particular specialty. They can give insight into other areas of nursing or support your skills and techniques in your current position. Find out which journals your facility receives and check with your local library. Some journals are free in your geographic areas just for subscribing.

Look for Opportunities to Improve Your Skills

New techniques and procedures are commonplace in the health care setting. Look for opportunities and ask for a chance to observe and then perform them. Talk to your nurse manager and staff educators and let them know of your interests. Be willing to come in on your own time occasionally to afford yourself a chance to observe and learn.

When an IV team is used to start and restart IVs and unit nurses don't have the opportunity to do so, this skill can be lost. If a crash cart team always comes when a code is called, floor nurses lose confidence and their skills at running codes. This can create a problem if for some reason the teams are unable to attend to a situation and the unit nurse must fill in. Some facilities address this issue, sometimes by rotating nurses through teams if they request it. Or the facility makes sure that nurses still show competency in these areas. If many of them have difficulty, they recommend that the teams be used only for backup for a while each year. Other facilities leave it up to the individual nurses to advocate for themselves and their individual needs.

ESSENTIAL

As you perfect your skills, you will gain confidence and become more and more adept at handling situations. Always strive to keep up your skills, and if you don't have opportunities to perform, be sure to observe and mentally participate. If possible, ask the team to let you try so you can keep up your hands-on skills.

Try to attend workshops and seminars that include hands-on opportunities or, at the very least, those that include video presentations. Sometimes you can purchase the DVDs or CDs for your personal library, and sometimes your facility may have an extensive library of multimedia materials for enhancing nursing skills and knowledge bases. The Internet may afford you additional opportunities for accessing multimedia materials. YouTube has a huge library of videos.

If you work in a teaching facility, you may have much more access and opportunity to observe and practice new techniques and skills. Take advantage of all that is available to you.

Keeping Up to Date with Pharmacology

Not every change in the realm of drugs is as dramatic as the COX2 inhibitors were a few years ago. Pulling Vioxx and Bextra off the market created quite a stir throughout the medical community, along with the controversy of leaving Celebrex on the market.

You can't watch much television or read a general-interest magazine without some sort of encounter with an advertisement from a group of lawyers recruiting you to join in the fight against a particular drug if you took it and suffered side effects.

The media also run many ads promoting drugs for almost anything that could possibly ail you. The lay public eats this up as they try to self-diagnose and demand medications from their physicians. The challenge for nurses today is to keep up with the drug information and be informed of issues, as well as new drugs coming to market. Nurses are at the forefront of patient education. They need to be informed and have access to the latest information in order to accurately inform their patients about the medications they have been prescribed and those they think they should have because they heard about it on TV.

ALERT

Nurses must use only the latest editions of drug books and software applications and ensure that old ones are destroyed. Don't pass them on to your family and friends. There is too much information that changes too rapidly to take a chance that a loved one would reference a several-years-old drug book with less than optimal results.

Electronic databases from reputable publishers and apps for PDAs and smartphones can provide you with the most up-to-date information. Learn to utilize these sources and access Internet pharmacology sites as well. And don't forget to ask the pharmacists. They can and should be your most valuable resource for drug information. That's their job and their field of expertise. They can break down the information into simple nontechnical terms so that you can provide your patients with all the information they need. Pharmacists can also give you some insight into the inside information about drug studies and why certain drugs have been pulled from the market or are being watched closely.

Patients frequently see more than one physician. Sometimes the doctors are aware and communicate, but most times, they don't talk even if they are aware that the patient is seeing someone else. What typically happens is that each physician orders different medications, sometimes to counteract the side effects of other drugs and sometimes independently for other issues altogether. Unless the patient obtains all her medications from one pharmacy, it is possible that no one is even remotely taking responsibility to coordinate her care, and many drugs can be duplicated or contraindicated. Only in recent years have pharmacists taken on this responsibility except possibly in small-town situations.

ESSENTIAL

Never assume that your patient doesn't require education about his medications just because he's been taking them for years. He might have a good idea and then again, he might not. Ask him what they're for and be prepared for the answer!

Patients can even be taking two versions of the same medication, such as Lisinopril and Zestril. Neither doctor knows what the other has ordered, and the medications have different names depending on the manufacturer. Only when the patient passes out from hypotension does anyone even consider that such a problem might exist. Nurses need to explore medication issues with patients, and they need to have all the latest information at their fingertips in order to best do this.

New Treatments and New Products

New treatments and products come to market all the time. This can be especially true in the line of products used for wound care. Wound ostomy nurses are your greatest resources for information about new techniques, treatments, and products. If you have a wound ostomy nurse on staff, be sure to consult her if you have a particularly problematic wound.

In rare instances, you may have a physician who objects to a wound ostomy nurse evaluating his patient, but the wound ostomy nurse is a nurse, and you don't have to have his orders for another nurse to see a patient. You will have to be diplomatic in making any suggestions or requesting any changes based on her evaluation, but you can always use the resource.

Medical supply vendors usually employ nurses as trainers and educators for their product lines. These nurses are available to facilities for in-services, seminars, and sometimes one-on-one instruction regarding the use, action, and properties of their particular products. Sometimes they meet with administrative staff and staff educators, who are then charged with disseminating the information to the unit nurses. In some instances, this works well, and, in others, staff may never even know that a new product exists unless they see it elsewhere.

FACT

Depending on how your facility works, you may need to do your own detective work to keep up to date on new products. Perhaps no one seems to have the time to devote to this or wants to take on the responsibility. You could find yourself with a new role.

Containing costs and improving outcomes are always primary goals in health care today. If a new product can help heal a wound faster and with fewer possible complications, then perhaps it should be explored and not ignored just because the vendor is an annoying little man!

There are always many new safety devices available, as well as assistive devices, that can help patients become more independent and self-reliant. Technology improvements have brought to market multiple at-home testing kits. Glucometers and home pregnancy tests were among the first of these to become popular and essential. Now there are many more that can detect urinary tract infections, coagulation levels, cholesterol levels, and help to determine when ovulation occurs. Keep your eyes and ears open. At some point, you'll need the information to instruct a patient about its use.

Health Care Is Constantly Evolving

It's hard to imagine that this could be an issue today, but there are nurses who believe that things don't change that much and that a technique they learned will always be correct. Never expect that what you learned in school will always be correct.

Take for example, newborns' and infants' sleeping positions. About twenty years ago, the theory was to place infants on their side or abdomen to sleep and to never place them on their backs. In this way, you would avoid any possibilities of aspiration. This was thought to avoid problems such as sudden infant death syndrome (SIDS).

About ten years ago, this whole theory underwent a drastic change, and now infants should only sleep on their backs to avoid the dangers of suffocation. Now you never place them on their abdomen or side.

ALERT

Nurses with many years of successful experience placing infants on their sides because of fears drummed into their heads that a newborn lying on his back might aspirate may have great difficulty incorporating this new theory into their practice. Unless an edict from administration demands compliance, some nurses may avoid following new practices because they are uncomfortable with the findings.

Remember techniques change. Nurses need to keep pace with advances in techniques and procedures.

How Health Care Reform Is Changing Nursing

The Patient Protection and Affordable Care Act was signed into law on March 23, 2010 by President Obama. The PPACA is probably one of the most debated and often misunderstood laws in history. It's no wonder; the compilation published by Congress is 974 pages long. It was designed to help reduce the soaring costs of health care by making it illegal to rescind insurance when a patient becomes ill with a major illness, such as cancer. It prohibits insurance companies from using pre-existing illness as an excuse not to cover children up to age nineteen. (By 2014, this will extend to all Americans regardless of age.)

It also says that a woman can choose to see an OB-GYN without a referral. Insurance companies cannot impose lifetime limits or caps on policies. And insurance companies must spend 80 to 85 percent of the money paid in premiums on your care and for improving your care and outcomes.

Along with the PPACA, a paradigm shift from a sick model for health care to a wellness and preventive care model is being implemented. This shift means that patients must assume responsibility for their own health status. If they are obese, it's at their own doing, and the physician and other health care team members are not responsible for the complications the patients develop.

Essentially, this will begin to remove the image that doctors are gods and can fix or cure any problem, and if they don't they are responsible and can be sued. Controlling the most outrageous and unwarranted litigious aspects can go a long way in reducing the high cost of health care. But the health care team is not being absolved of all responsibility. In fact, as mandated by law, quality and accrediting agencies are moving to make care even safer and more effective. Hospitals that don't show quality improvements and better outcomes for their patients can be fined and or receive lower rates of reimbursement overall.

As the backbone of the health care system, nurses will bear the brunt of much of these changes. In order for patients to assume responsibility for their own health status, they must be better educated in ways to achieve this, including diet, exercise, lifestyle changes, and their medical regime. Patient education is a big portion of the nurse's responsibilities.

Nurses will have to find better and more efficient ways to provide safer and better care to hospital patients. This includes learning how to use systems as they are implemented, such as bar codes as a form of identification of patients and having patients participate in marking surgical sites.

The lead accrediting agency, JCAHO, has a list of twenty-eight "Never Events" that hospitals have to report. These include such things as surgery on the wrong patient, removal of the wrong body part, infusion of the wrong blood type, instruments and sponges left in situ, and blood clots that develop post op.

Medicare has a policy to not reimburse for the specific care when these "Never Events" happen. Additionally, any care needed for complications of these errors will not be reimbursed. This leaves hospitals vulnerable to not only low ratings in performance but also to paying for the care for these errors as well. Most insurance companies are following suit, but not all states have mandated the Never Events, and patients can be billed for the care.

Nurses will bear the brunt of preventing these errors as well, and indirectly if budget issues from reduced reimbursement force hiring freezes and fewer skilled staff.

CHAPTER 21

Setting Future Career Goals

Where do you go from here? Look back on the past year, and explore all the new things you have learned and the experience you have gained. You are no longer that scared person you were when you first graduated. You are a confident, professional nurse now. Congratulate yourself. Say thank you to your family, friends, and coworkers who supported you throughout this transformation.

Advanced Degrees

Is it time to consider moving to the next level? Nursing is a field in which you will spend your lifetime learning. You will learn new things almost every day of your career as information and techniques change. Moving to the next level does not always mean moving toward a managerial position. It just means that you need to keep up with the times and accept more or different responsibilities to keep your skills fresh and keep yourself always prepared to make changes as life dictates them to you.

It also means examining where you want to go next with your career. Are you ready to move from a general unit to a more specialized one? Are you ready to obtain the next level of education? Are you an LVN/LPN ready to become an RN? Are you an ADN ready to pursue a BSN? Or are you ready to work on a master's or PhD? If you are staying abreast of the advances and needs in the nursing field, you will know that furthering your education is an important factor in managing your career.

Is there a certification you could achieve that makes you more of an expert in your field without necessarily having an advanced degree? These require some education and a certification examination but can lead to higher pay and better positions and make you better equipped to care for your patients and work well on a resume. The American Nurses Credentialing Center offers a list of nursing certifications. See *www.nurse credentialing.org/Certification*.

FACT

One thing for certain is that at least well into the next few decades, health care personnel will be in high demand as the population ages and demands better health care. Those who can help to educate others to assume these roles will be greatly needed.

Perhaps you want to pursue a degree in something besides nursing, perhaps health care administration, business, nutrition, communication, education, or even psychology. Think about where you want to be five years from now. People will often ask you that, and although the relevance may seem vague, basically they want you to think about whether you are being proactive and planning your career and your life or just sitting back and letting it happen. The specific job you hold five years from now may not even exist today, but if you know the general direction you'd like to take, then now is the time to begin to focus on that goal.

ESSENTIAL

It has been predicted for quite some time that LPNs would be phased out and the RNs would someday have to have at least a BSN. The nursing shortage crisis, although somewhat stalled with the economic downturn, has seemed to sideline some of this temporarily, and yet what may emerge from this crisis is a set of standards that brings this plan into reality despite the shortages.

Many educational programs allow even the most non-traditional student to pursue the next level advanced degree status. There are LPN to RN programs, LPN to BSN programs, RN to BSN, and RN straight to MSN programs. MSN options include NP programs or focus on such areas as clinical nursing, education, management, and health care administration.

NPs are predicted to be in very high demand, especially as the PPACA is implemented and many more Americans find themselves with access to health insurance and those with insurance already find more affordable aspects. NPs will be part of the plan to help reduce costs, as well as fill the need because of a shortage of physicians, especially in the family practice area.

Many of these programs offer students independent study programs and even offer credit for work and life experiences. Some offer distance education opportunities where part of the study is online with some actual classroom time or on-campus meetings for exams or presentations. Others offer an entirely online program.

Again, you must be sure that your program is accredited. Online education is a terrific option for those who are self-motivated. At this point, you have had clinical experience and will most likely continue to be performing hands-on care and always perfecting new skills. In that case, it's not like trying to learn to be a nurse strictly from a computer or a book.

Specialty Training and Opportunities

You may be perfectly satisfied with the level of education you have and the niche you have found. There is absolutely nothing wrong with this. Just keep your eyes, ears, and mind open to new opportunities. Aside from lengthy degree programs, in time you may find that you want to specialize in an area that the facility is willing to train you for. Internships and other training opportunities can be terrific ways to further your lifelong learning process at the moment and can offer you a chance to move into another area or to gain more knowledge and skills for the area you presently work in.

Let your supervisor and staff educators know what your goals are, and enlist their help in obtaining the training necessary to meet the requirements. In addition, you may want to focus your own continuing education units toward your goals as well.

ALERT

Don't overspecialize yourself so that you are pigeonholed the rest of your career. For instance, some nurses love ICU and intend to stay there for their entire careers. However, the stress and the constant adrenalin rush that this type of environment can produce can take a personal toll both physically and emotionally.

Some nurses are highly skilled technical clinicians, but sometimes they can't come down from the intensity to a slower-paced environment. One area they often have trouble with is in teaching patients to be independent and self-reliant. ICU nurses do so much for their patients, who are usually very dependent during their stay in these units, that they don't know how to let go and teach the patient to take care of himself. If you choose the ICU, just be sure to keep your options open by exploring other areas, for instance, with your continuing education courses.

On the other hand, generalists tend to feel inadequately prepared to take on a highly technical or specialized role. Take advantage of training opportunities that your employer offers. Even if you don't like the new role, at least you proved to yourself that you could make a move. Keep your options open. For example, you may be completely happy working on a particular unit and plan to stay forever, but along comes a new manager who makes your life miserable. Try as you might, you just cannot find a level of comfort and happiness with this new manager. You have to quit. But where can you go? This is all you know, and the openings are limited. If you had kept your options more open, you wouldn't feel so trapped.

Other Roles for Nurses

You will encounter many different attitudes about nurses. One of them is the strong belief by some that only hospital nurses are "real nurses." Another is that LPNs are inferior and not really nurses at all. Some specialty nurses, such as ICU nurses, feel superior because of their highly technical skills. Others think that quality improvement and utilization review nurses are not real nurses either. Sometimes nurse educators are viewed as teaching because they are inept at nursing.

ESSENTIAL

The truth is there will always be both good and bad nurses in any specialty, in any geographic area, and among graduates of the finest, as well as the most standard, nursing programs. The challenge is to encourage all nurses to raise their own personal standards and always strive to be the best they can be at whatever role they perform. In other words, nurses need to be professionals at all times.

All nurses are an essential part of the overall health care picture. Many times you'll find LPNs whose skills and bedside manners are impeccable and who best teach the new nursing grads and physicians how to perform the most technical procedures. The argument should never be about who is better but rather who is the most professional. The most professional nurse is the one who sees all nurses as necessary parts of the whole (a team); she recognizes the contributions of their individual special talents and skills to the team effort and that they strive to make a difference in someone's life every day. Whether their role is direct care or a supportive role behind the scenes, they are all necessary roles and are vital to providing patients with improved outcomes.

Hospital Opportunities

There are many roles for nurses. Inside the hospital arena, these include, but are not limited to, staff nurses, surgical nurses, midwives, lactation specialists, rehab nurses, nurse anesthetists, IV specialists, staff educators, supervisors, clinical specialists, clinical managers, quality and utilization specialists, nursing directors, and administrators.

Outside the Hospital

Outside the hospital, there are many roles, such as clinic nurses, office nurses, school nurses, forensic nurses, industrial nurses, case managers for insurance companies and workers' compensation, sales reps for drugs and medical supplies, clinical research nurses, diabetic educators, wound ostomy nurses, legal nurse consultants, flight nurses, childbirth educators, dialysis nurses, home health nurses, hospice nurses, and private duty nurses. There are managers and health care administrators and many, many more. Travel nurses fill vacancies in all areas, primarily in hospitals and clinics, but their roles are expanding as well.

Nurse Entrepreneurs

Nurse entrepreneurs are building a huge variety of independent businesses, ranging from consultants in many diverse areas of health care to aestheticians to foot care specialists. Nurse practitioners have hung out their own shingles in many fields for many years, such as mental health and women's health. These are expanding now, and hopefully Congress will see its way to recognizing the cost savings and other benefits of NPs and will allow for Medicaid reimbursement of their services.

The area of patient education leaves many opportunities for nurses to provide individual and small-group instruction on managing disease entities and care issues, such as diabetic teaching and managing chronic pain. The job you hold five years from now probably doesn't even exist today. Be sure to keep your skills current and learn about techniques and diseases beyond your own realm. Keep your options open.

Professional Organizations

Nursing is one of the most rewarding careers and at the same time one of the most challenging. By joining professional organizations, you will find that you are not alone in your struggles. You will have a huge network of peers with whom to share your interests and your ideas for helping to make nursing an even better experience for all. You will also have an opportunity to vent and commiserate. Most important, you will be tapped into one of the best sources of information about what's happening in nursing.

FACT

In addition to national nursing associations, there are state and, in some instances, local associations for nurses. There are also a large number of specialty organizations, such as the Oncology Nurses Association, the Home Care Nurses Association, the Emergency Nurses Association, etc.

Membership in a professional organization is not required, but it is highly recommended. The benefits are many, not the least of which is keeping on top of developments within the profession. Some of the benefits include:

- Networking opportunities
- Access to group insurance rates
- Educational opportunities
- Improving your marketability and showing your commitment to professionalism
- Access to mentors and mentoring opportunities
- Opportunity to promote and improve the nursing profession and other health care issues
- Personal and professional growth opportunities

What do these benefits mean to you? They mean that you are a part of the greater whole of the nursing profession. These benefits mean that you are actively involved in and concerned about making the most of your career and ensuring that others find their way to nursing as a profession too. They mean that you have access to the best perks for being a nurse, such as group rates for health, auto, homeowners, and malpractice insurance; credit cards; and loans. These benefits mean that you are connected to a large network of peers with whom you can brainstorm and commiserate and work to improve conditions for nurses, as well as health care issues in general.

Attend meetings, subscribe to the journals, and keep up to date with information on their websites. Many of these organizations also have a presence on Facebook and Twitter. Take the opportunity to attend a convention for your organization and meet nurses from all over the country or region. You will have a wonderful opportunity to attend workshops, visit with vendors, and network with peers.

ESSENTIAL

Membership gives you clout and makes a statement about your professionalism on a resume. It can give you an edge in competing for a promotion. And you will stay informed of the latest trends in health care issues.

Start by visiting the website of the American Nurses Association (*www .ana.org*), where you can access a great deal of information without being a member and investigate their membership benefits and information. All-Nurses.com has a comprehensive list of nursing associations both in the United States and internationally. You can access this information at *www .allnurses.com/Nursing_Associations/Nursing/USA*. Investigate a few associations and begin to join and become active in the organizations.

Networking

Unfortunately, many people believe that it is only necessary to network with peers when you are looking for a new job. This is only one of the times when you will need to network. The most successful professionals and those who are most satisfied and happy in their jobs find great rewards through constant networking.

Networking includes staying connected with your schoolmates and faculty members. It means spending a meal break with a coworker and getting to know more about him. It means joining listservs and following bloggers to share information about a common issue. In addition, networking means learning about other fields from everyone you encounter personally and professionally.

Networking today includes reconnecting with peers and old classmates and joining nursing groups through sites like Facebook. Following the tweets of nurses is networking. Twitter affords bloggers or organizers of grassroots efforts a platform for communication that can have huge impacts on the nursing profession to spread the news about their events and blog posts to followers everywhere.

FACT

Networking isn't just about going to a meeting where you know no one and trying to mingle. This is not something in most people's comfort zones, and they close their ears immediately when they hear the term *networking*. Stepping beyond your comfort zone is where you will find the rewards you seek.

Next time you attend an in-service or seminar, approach the speaker and exchange business cards. Ask about her role and how she got into this job. You never know when you might be looking for something entirely different to do and may want to contact her again. Stay in touch. Connect on Facebook or follow her on Twitter.

Get Business Cards

You don't necessarily need a business card that is imprinted with your facility's information; in fact, your boss might think you're being a bit presumptuous to ask for such a thing! All you need is a plain white card imprinted with your name, credentials, and contact information. If you don't want to broadcast your home address, simply include a phone number or even just an e-mail address. Invite them to friend you on Facebook or LinkedIn or to follow you on Twitter. You can add a simple graphic, such as a stethoscope or an RN emblem, but keep it simple and tasteful. Or use a simple design or color.

There are several computer programs for designing your own cards and printing them from your own computer. These are perfectly acceptable. If you don't have access to this software, there are a number of economical places online and off where you can have simple cards printed for a nominal fee. Always keep them with you and in a business card holder so that they are always clean and crisp. Hand them out!

Join your professional organizations and become involved. Find a coworker interested in joining or attending local meetings with you. You can attend as a guest. Branch out and meet a new person each time you attend. And share the information with your boss and coworkers.

Become involved with committees at work and let your supervisor know you are interested in volunteering for activities within the facility. Become a preceptor or mentor to the generation of new grads in your facility or on your unit. Volunteer to help with students when they are assigned to your unit. This will not only provide you with any number of new and interesting experiences, but it will also make you known throughout the facility and even the community as a valuable resource and willing subject. These opportunities will also build your confidence and allow you to measure your success.

Moving to Another Department

Perhaps when considering moving on to the next level, you will find that you would like to explore another area as well. This is part of fine-tuning your career. Keep it interesting and never let it get boring and old. Don't get trapped, and be prepared for a time when a new peer or manager can absolutely ruin your comfortable domain.

Making a move will be an exciting challenge, as well as a bittersweet one. You will have developed friendships and professional relationships with your coworkers that will be difficult to change and disrupt. However, growth always involves some degree of change. If your career isn't growing, it's most likely stagnating. This can lead to job dissatisfaction and burnout. Stay in touch and ask your colleagues to be happy for you.

ALERT

You don't want to make too many changes at any one time unless you thrive on stress. If you're continuing your education, you may want to stay put. However, if a change will provide you with better access to the patients or experiences to enhance your chosen area of study, you may need to consider making a move.

If your facility is offering training for the ICU and that's where you think you'd like to work someday, then perhaps you should jump at the opportunity. Or perhaps the pediatric ward has an opening, and the unit manager is willing to give you a chance.

Don't make changes just because another unit has an opening on the day shift; however, if changing is necessary for your personal life, you might need to consider it. Nurses often make the jump to home care just because they can work 8:00 A.M. to 4:30 P.M. and schedule patients around their children's school and extracurricular activities. This isn't always realistic or ideal either. You need to have a vested interest in the health care and professional opportunity that the change affords you.

Be happy in what you do, and you will be much better at it. If you don't like patients, consider roles where you don't have patient contact. And, of course, if you want more hands-on care, you certainly wouldn't look at positions that take you away from direct interaction with patients.

Re-evaluate your situation periodically, and always stay abreast of new trends in health care and how it will affect your role and the things you enjoy doing most as a nurse. Be open to change and embrace it. Set goals for yourself and specific timelines for achieving them. Be flexible, but don't compromise your needs and success.

CHAPTER 22

Taking Care of Yourself

Nurses spend their lives teaching others how to take care of themselves, but when it comes to the nurse doing this, oftentimes they are the worst patients. Take time for yourself to renew your energy and strength, as well as your soul. Nursing is a highly stressful job for all nurses, not just those who work in fast-paced environments, such as ERs and ICUs. Reward yourself for a job well done.

Don't Take It Home with You

Sometimes you will need to take your work home with you, especially early on in your career as you learn and perfect so many skills and talents seemingly all at once. But don't overdo it. Plan your time and use it wisely. Multitask whenever you can to save some free time for fun. For example, look up the information you need and print it out. Then while you're at the Laundromat waiting for the clothes to finish, read through the information.

Invest in a PDA or smartphone and a drug app or software database so that you have information at your fingertips. Don't spend hours looking for more information at home; have it available in your pocket. You can also put the whole *Merck Manual* in your PDA with a built-in search function, as well as nursing drug books, information about diagnostic tests, and so on. Smartphones have similar apps or Wi-Fi access to these with a browser.

Protecting Your Privacy

What would happen if everyone knew the private phone number of the White House? Well, scale that way back for you, but the effect is the same. You will have no private life the moment you give out your number! So don't do it. And resist the urge to friend patients and family members on Facebook.

ALERT

Never give out your home or cell phone numbers to patients or their family members. You may bond with many of your patients and their loved ones over the years, but you need to keep your private life private. Just tell the patients that your facility forbids you giving out private information. If the patient needs you, she can contact you through the facility, and if you're not available, someone else there can help her.

Living in the same community where you work, you will encounter former patients and family members from time to time. Sometimes you may find yourself having to hide in the vegetable section of the supermarket or the restroom at a restaurant to avoid them. Learn to smile, say hello, and keep moving. If they corner you, always refer them back to their physician for advice and information.

Making Time for Paperwork

Home care and community-based nurses often use a home office for paperwork. It's an easy habit to fall into, especially if you have children. You complete your visits and pick up the kids, rush home to start dinner, and work on your paperwork at the kitchen table. You get interrupted, and your children feel neglected, or you reprimand them for interrupting you. Or you delay the paperwork until they've gone to bed, and by then you're exhausted.

Try spending a half hour at the library or sitting in a fast food restaurant and doing some of your most important paperwork *before* you pick up the kids. Schedule the time just like a visit. Of course, you'll need to find a seat where you can protect the confidentiality of your work. If you have a baby-sitter and a home office, keep the babysitter a half hour longer and close yourself in your office. You'll find that then you can spend quality time with your family and not be so distracted. You'll even find that when you get to your paperwork later, there will be far less to do and you won't be so exhausted.

Be organized and make your free time a priority. Use your mornings or evenings (depending on your shift) to keep up with errands and housework so that your days off can be spent relaxing and having fun. To some extent, that isn't always going to be possible, but make it a priority.

Keys to Avoiding Burnout

Burnout, or caregiver fatigue, is a common disorder that affects many people who work in high-stress environments and provide services to others, such as nurses, doctors, firefighters, and police officers. It is most often associated with overextending yourself on a consistent basis. A feeling of being unable to control a situation contributes heavily to burnout as well.

Nurses are by nature overachievers. So it is not uncommon to find that nurses are at the point of burnout long before they recognize the symptoms. By the time they do recognize it, many nurses feel that being burned out means they hate nursing and need to find another field altogether.

This couldn't be further from the truth. You need to deal with the stress and find a way to cope or find another path to job satisfaction and a renewed joy in nursing. More important, you need to recognize the signs and avoid the burnout in the first place.

A nurse's job is extremely challenging, both physically and emotionally. Dealing with life-and-death situations every day takes a toll. Being responsible for someone's life and striving constantly to help improve his outcome make a tremendous load. Overextending, in terms of time and energy, is commonplace, especially in light of staffing shortages.

Burnout usually manifests itself in feelings of despair, depression, resentment, and frustration and a sense that you can no longer find anything positive about your job. You'd rather be having a tooth pulled without anesthetic than be at work. It's time to regroup, reprioritize, and re-examine your life and goals.

Think carefully and be honest with yourself. Perhaps your particular job requires skills and talents that you are still trying to master, and you're constantly being criticized or berating yourself for this. You need to set boundaries. You need to learn to say no and to make yourself an important priority in your life. You may need to seek some counseling if you can't shake the depression. Stay away from the negative people and find at least one positive thing each day. Some of the more simple ways you can avoid burnout include:

- Say no. You don't always have to accept an extra shift or additional patients.
- Set boundaries. Know your limitations and stay within that realm.
- Examine your priorities and be realistic about time frames.
- Slow down and eliminate something you don't absolutely have to do right now.
- Make time for yourself. Unwind before you get home or seek out a place to be alone for a few minutes.

- Leave work at work.
- Be organized, and clear the clutter and chaos from your home, your car, your mind.
- Manage your stress and take care of yourself.

The most important question you can ask yourself each time someone asks you or offers you something additional to do is Can I realistically do this without compromising myself? If you can't, then this is not the time to take on anything else.

If you have burned out, then you need to examine your life and make changes to improve the situation. You can't put off taking care of yourself. You need to start now to rebuild your life and your career. Start by making a list of all the things you do well and the things you like or would like about your job. Find a new niche. Perhaps you will return to this kind of job someday, but right now, you need something new and exciting and refreshing. You aren't doing yourself or your patients any good by staying in a job you hate.

Find Ways to Reward Yourself

Nursing is not a profession where you will have lots of praise and applause, especially not when you seem to need it most. Remember, sick people are not at their best. It may be weeks or months before they recognize the difference you made in their lives, and by then they are long gone from your life.

Once in a while, patients will say thank you, but even then sometimes it's for the trivial things and not for the things that were the hardest for you to do. Or they will be the kind of people who show their gratitude constantly and you can depend on them to say thanks. Many times, you will have gone the extra mile for many patients, and none of them will even know what it is that you have done, such as caught a huge error before they got the wrong medication or treatment. The ones you need a thank you from most are often the ones you won't get it from.

Set goals for learning new techniques and skills and reward yourself with treats or trinkets as you accomplish them. Keep a log of your skills and review it often to remind yourself of how far you've come, and you can use this log for your future marketability.

Keep a journal or make a box to hold little notes to write to yourself about special patients and how you made a difference in their lives. Be mindful of confidentiality issues, but use dates and clues to help you remember who they were. Keep copies of any thank-you notes you receive from patients and families. Don't forget to include any positive comments from your supervisor, doctors, and coworkers. Review these notes often, especially when you've had a particularly bad day or week.

ESSENTIAL

You need to create your own rewards. You need to hear the applause in your head. Pat yourself on the back for finally mastering a skill or technique. Recognize that you have gone the extra mile to make a difference today. And don't be afraid to share your accomplishments and joys with your supervisor and coworkers.

Rewarding yourself with items, such as a new uniform, shoes, stethoscope, and even a special pen, can bring a renewed sense of excitement about going to work for a while. These can seem trivial, but little things are easy and inexpensive and won't add to your stress load to accomplish.

Don't forget to reward yourself just for doing a job well. Have a massage or a spa treatment. Buy those tickets to the theater or concert; you're worth it! Take time to read or enjoy a hobby and don't feel guilty about letting the laundry pile up another day. Sleep in on your day off and enjoy a day of leisure once in a while. Take time to truly smell the roses. Surround yourself with the little things you love and that hold meaning and are important to you.

Managing Your Stress

Nursing is a stressful profession, and managing stress is essential. There are a number of formal stress relief measures, such as meditation, imagery, breathing exercises, and relaxation techniques, to help you de-stress. These all work well and should be incorporated into your daily routine.

Other activities that will help you de-stress are yoga or exercise and diversionary activities, such as reading, watching TV, listening to music, going to the gym, walking, and sewing and other needlecrafts.

You can develop your own feel-good program either formally or informally, but you need to make sure you use every opportunity possible to reduce stress in your life. Make stress relief measures a part of your daily routine before stress becomes a problem. Sometimes this can be best accomplished by eliminating activities that overextend you. You must take care not to try to do too many things at one time. Helping others is what nurses do, but there are times when you have to learn to say no and mean it. Take care of you so that you can continue to take care of others.

Join a club or group activity to explore a similar interest, such as scrapbooking or photography or creative writing. Exercise is important to your physical and mental health. Try jogging or walking if you don't like team sports. Or find adults' sports team that fit your schedule. Take those tennis lessons or piano lessons you gave up years ago. Consider and address your spiritual needs too.

Find support systems. The knowledge that you are not alone in your feelings needs to be reinforced from time to time. You need feedback to help ensure that you are well centered. Coworkers and friends from school are often excellent choices for some of your support systems because they share common issues and aren't as personally involved as your family would be. You can vent, and they will have the best understanding of what you are going through. Naturally, you need to be able to trust them. Family and friends are great support systems but sometimes they can add to your stress by being more concerned for or misunderstanding of your needs. Support systems will help to recharge your emotional and spiritual energy and help renew your physical energy and stamina as well.

ESSENTIAL

Don't forget that laughter can be the best medicine. It releases tension and heals your heart. If you can laugh at life's little challenges, you will understand that some things are just not as serious as they can seem. It might not have been a laughing matter at the time it happened, but several hours later, if you can see the humor in the most embarrassing incident, then you can let go of the stress and move on.

As a caregiver, you will constantly need to replenish your energy to continue to give. When you feel as if you have no more to give, that should be your clue that it's time to recharge your batteries. You do that by reducing your stress.

Your Personal Health Care

Nurses can be the worst patients and their own worst enemies when it comes to their own health status. It's usually easier to tell someone else how and what to do than it is to do it yourself, but nurses need to take care of themselves. With all the added mental and physical job-related stress taking a toll on their bodies, maintaining wellness is an important issue.

Just as you instruct your patients, you need to schedule routine exams and not skip appointments. It's not always easy to schedule them around work, but if you make a concerted effort, sometimes you can squeeze a couple of appointments into one day. Get your checkups and see the doctor if you're sick. It's important to have a physical once a year and to have a Pap smear and mammogram or prostate examination. You also need to see your dentist and have your teeth cleaned every six months.

Your car doesn't run very well if you never change the oil and then let the fluids run dry. Just about the time you really depend on it to get you somewhere, the old hose or worn tire will blow. The human body is a finely developed machine and if you don't keep it tuned, it will fail you.

ALERT

If you get sick, please be sure to see your physician by the third day. There are many nosocomial infections and diseases taking their toll on nurses these days. Methicillin-resistant staphylococcus aureus (MRSA) and vancomycin-resistant enterococci (VRE) are going to become even more troublesome. How many nurses have colonies of MRSA in their nasal passages? What will be the long-term effects?

Standard precautions and personal protective equipment when used appropriately can protect health care professionals and other patients from the spread of most diseases. How many nurses do you know who play

Russian roulette every day because they become complacent with hand washing and gloving?

Unfortunately, some nurses have become lax in their precautions. The spread of hepatitis C and MRSA and many yet unidentified nosocomial germs are on the rise. Nurses must be diligent in protecting themselves, as well as their families. The nurses are not just the ones being infected; they can be carriers as well and not just to other patients but to their own families and friends.

Just as you cannot provide the best of care when you are emotionally and physically drained from stress, when you are ill you will not be providing the best care either. Take the time to be proactive in your own preventive health care issues and set an example for your patients, friends, and family.

APPENDIX A

Glossary of Terms and Acronyms

ADLs: Activities of daily living: feeding, dressing, hygiene, and mobility.

ADN: Associate's degree nurse: an RN with an associate's degree in nursing.

APN: Advance practice nurse: an RN with an advanced degree or certification.

BSN: Bachelor's of science nurse: an RN with a bachelor's of science degree in nursing.

CCU: Cardiac care unit: a specialized intensive care unit for patients with acute cardio-vascular problems. (Can also be known as a critical care unit, which is a generalized intensive care unit.)

CHHA: Certified home health aide: a nurse's aide who has additional certification in home health care.

CNA: Certified nurse's aide.

Critical Thinking Skills: Ability to use deductive and inductive reasoning to assess and evaluate a situation and make decisions and problem solve based on assessment and analysis of the facts.

DOU: Direct observation unit: a step-down care unit; patients who still require monitoring and/or more intense care than a regular med-surg unit.

ED: Emergency department.

ER: Emergency room.

GN: Graduate nurse: a nurse who has graduated from an RN program but who has not yet taken or received notice of passing the NCLEX.

ICU: Intensive care unit.

LVN/LPN: Licensed vocational nurse-licensed practical nurse (California and Texas use the term LVN and other states LPN).

MAR: Medication administration record: a list and signed record of medications that a patient has been given.

Med-Surg: A medical-surgical unit of a hospital that cares for patients with acute medical problems and/or pre- or post-op surgical patients.

MRSA: Methicillin-resistant staphylococcus aureus.

MSN: Master's of science degreed nurse: an RN with a master's of science degree in nursing.

NA: Nursing assistant.

NCLEX: National council licensure examination: the board exam for nurses that allows for licensure as an LPN/LVN or RN.

NICU: Neonatal ICU: an intensive care unit for infants and premature infants requiring intensive levels of care.

Nosocomial Infection: An infection acquired in a health care facility.

NP: Nurse practitioner: an advanced practice degree for RNs.

NPA: Nurse Practice Act: The group of laws established by each state to protect the public and that define the scope of practice for RNs, APRNs, and LPNs in that state. (RN, APRN, and LPN NPAs are covered in separate documents.) The NPA includes the requirements for education for each level of licensed nurse.

OR: Operating room.

P&P: Policy and procedure: usually refers to a manual detailing the policies and procedures for care and administrative policies as determined by a facility.

PCA: Patient care assistant: an unlicensed person who has had some level of training in bedside patient care as described in the facility's job description.

PHN: Public health nurse: a certificate in public health nursing earned in a BSN program.

PPE: Personal protective equipment: can include gown, gloves, goggles, or face shield, cap, and booties to protect against splashing and contamination with bodily fluids and excrement or other chemical or hazardous materials.

RN: Registered nurse: a nurse who has received training as an RN and has passed the licensure examination.

Scope of Practice: The set of duties and responsibilities that each level of nurse is allowed to perform based on level of education, license they have been granted, and the specific laws and regulations of the state in which the nurse practices.

UAP: Unlicensed assistive personnel: an aide who has been trained by a facility to assist in the care of patients according to a job description devised by the facility.

VRE: Vancomycin-resistant enterococci: an intense strain of bacteria resistant to Van-comycin.

APPENDIX B

Additional Reading

Ball, Sally Perry. "POCT Today: Laboratory Testing at the Bedside Has Had a Significant Positive Impact on Patient Outcomes." *Advance for Nurses*, August 22, 2005, pp. 30–31.

Cardillo, Donna Wilk. *Your First Year as a Nurse: Making the Transition from Total Novice to Successful Professional.* (Roseville, CA: Prima Publishing, 2001).

Dunham, Kelli S. *How to Survive and Maybe Even Love Nursing School!* (Philadelphia, PA: F. A. Davis Company, 2001).

Eagles, Zardoya E. *Nurses Career Guide: Discovering New Horizons in Health Care.* (San Luis Obispo, CA: Sovereignty Press, 1997).

J. G. Ferguson Publishing Co. *Ferguson's Careers in Focus: Nursing.* 2nd edition. (Chicago, IL: J. G. Ferguson Publishing Co., 2003).

Finkelstein, Barbara, editor. *My First Year as a Nurse: Real World Stories From America's Nurses.* (New York: Signet, 1997).

Munoz, Cora and Hilgenberg, Cheryl. "Ethnopharmocology: Understanding How Ethnicity Can Affect Drug Response Is Essential to Providing Culturally Competent Care." *American Journal of Nursing*, August 2005, pp. 40–49.

Newell, Robert, editor. *Developing Your Career in Nursing.* (New York: Cassell, 1995).

Rogers, Carla S. *How to Get into the Right Nursing Program.* (Lincolnwood, IL: VGM Career Horizons, 1998).

Venes, Donald, editor. *Taber's Cyclopedic Medical Dictionary.* (Philadelphia, PA: F. A. Davis Co., 2004).

APPENDIX C

Websites

Nursing Associations

The following are links to Internet sites for various professional organizations for nurses. Search each site for additional information, resources, and links. For a comprehensive list of specialty nursing associations, visit allnurses.com: *www.allnurses.com*.

American Association of Colleges of Nursing
Educational resources for nurses
www.aacn.nche.edu

American Nurses Association
Professional organization for all nurses in the United States
http://nursingworld.org

National Association for Practical Nurse Education and Service, Inc.
Professional organization for LPNs and LVNs
www.napnes.org

National Council of State Boards of Nursing
Links to all state boards of nursing. Links to NCLEX testing information for RNs and LPNs
www.ncsbn.org

National Federation of Licensed Practical Nurses
Professional organization for LPNs and LVNs
www.nflpn.org

National League for Nursing
Organization responsible for the accreditation of nursing education institutions
www.nln.org

National Organization for Associate Degree Nursing
Professional association for ADNs
www.noadn.org

National Student Nurses Association
Professional association for student nurses
www.nsna.org

Nursing Journals and Professional Publications

The following are links to just a few of the online versions or subscription sources for nursing journals and publications. Some offer online access to archived articles and may also have blogs, RSS services, and e-mail updates. There are many more nursing publications available. Search the Internet for nursing journals or nursing publications. A more comprehensive list of publications can be found at the Nursing Center: *www.nursingcenter.com*. Many journals also have a presence on Facebook. Search for them and "like" their pages. They may also be on Twitter where you can "follow" them and receive updates.

American Journal of Nursing
http://journals.lww.com/ajnonline

LPN Journal of Nursing
www.napnes.org/jpn/jpn_subscriptions

Male Nurse Magazine
www.malenursemagazine.com

Nurse Zone
www.nursezone.com

NurseWeek
www.nurse.com

Nursing Spectrum
www.nurse.com

Advance for Nurses
www.nursing.advanceweb.com

Other Useful Websites

The following is a sample of the multitude of nursing websites available that provide resources, information, and forums for nurses to post questions and comments about nursing.

The Nursing Site
From Kathy Quan, RN, BSN, PHN, the author of *The Everything® New Nurse Book*, this site provides resources, links, and information for nurses, nursing students, and those who desire to become nurses.
www.thenursingsite.com

The Nursing Site Blog
Also from Kathy Quan, RN, BSN, PHN, this blog serves to update nurses on the nursing profession.
www.thenursingsiteblog.com

allnurses.com
A comprehensive site with forums and links to many resources for nurses, including a list of specialty nurses associations.
http://allnurses.com

American Assembly for Men in Nursing
A wealth of information about men in nursing today, as well as the history of men in nursing
www.aamn.org

College Board
Information on SAT and ACT college entrance exams, as well as links to financial aid and other college entrance information
www.collegeboard.org

Commission on Graduates of Foreign Nursing Schools
Comprehensive information and instructions for foreign nurses wishing to emigrate to the United States to practice nursing
www.cgfns.org

Epocrates

A site with nursing PDA and smartphone software databases and includes links to purchase and download the software. Apps available for iPhone, BlackBerry, and Android platforms, as well as others.
www.epocrates.com

FAFSA (Free Application for Federal Student Aid)

You can access and submit the application online
www.fafsa.ed.gov

Financial Aid

One of many financial aid information sites
www.finaid.org

Health Literacy Consulting

Helen Osborne, a health literacy expert, discusses the issues involving literacy in health care today. Links to many articles and resources.
www.healthliteracy.com

HomeHealth 101

A site with practical information for home health professionals
http://homehealth101.com

HouseCalls-Online

A site for home health professionals with links to resources and other home health sites
http://housecalls-online.com

Medical Wizards

A site for nursing PDA software and smartphone apps
www.medicalwizards.com

The National Nurse for Public Health

A grassroots effort started by Teri Mills, a nurse educator, in an oped to the *New York Times*. Now a bill is before Congress to provide a national nurse for America and national nursing leadership for nurses.

www.nationalnurse.org
www.nationalnurse.blogspot.com

Nursefriendly National Directories

Massive databases with information and resources for nurses
www.nursefriendly.com

NursingLink

Articles, information, links, and resources for nurses and nursing students about education, career choices, jobs, lifestyle, and professional information
http://nursinglink.monster.com

NurseTogether

Discussions, articles, links, and resources for nursing students and professional nurses
www.nursetogether.com

Nursing Center.com

A comprehensive site with links to journals, publications, nursing websites, and CEUs
www.nursingcenter.com

PDRhealth

A health resources and drug information site from the publishers of the *Physician's Desk Reference*
www.pdrhealth.com

Reality RN

Resources and discussion opportunities for students and professional nurses
www.realityrn.com

RN.com

Resources for nurses, including education, jobs, CEUs, and websites

www.rn.com

Support for Nurses

This site provides solution-focused articles, resources, and best practices to address the needs of nurses. E-Booklets and E-Toolkits for nurses and nurse educators.

www.supportfornurses.com

Ultimate Nurse

A forum and information site with numerous links to jobs and other nursing sites. Lots of travel nursing information.

www.ultimatenurse.com

WholeNurse.com

A large database of nursing links for resources, jobs, education, and other nursing sites

www.wholenurse.com

Index

A

Abuse, reporting, 211–12, 215
Acronyms, 271–73
Admissions, 210–11
Advance practice nurse (APN), 6, 9, 36
Aides, 2, 33–34, 87, 92, 139, 216
Alcott, Louisa May, 16
American Nurses Association (ANA), 7, 10, 23, 256
Appearance, professional, 12–14
Associate Degree in Nursing (ADN), 5, 36. *See also* Degrees
Associations, 255–56, 278–79

B

Baby boom, 27–28
Bachelor of Science in Nursing (BSN), 5–6, 31, 36–38. *See also* Degrees
Back injuries, preventing, 194–95
Barton, Clara, 15
Bedpan duties, 118–19
Best practice process, 145–46
Blogs, 237–38
Bodily functions, 20, 22–23, 150, 157, 192
Body mechanics, 194–95
Book resources, 275–76
Breaks, taking, 124–25
Burnout, avoiding, 52, 125, 263–65
Business cards, 257–58

C

Calling in sick, 87–88, 179–80, 197
Career goals, 249–59. *See also* Lifelong learning; Training
Care plans, 141–44
Celebrity patients, 235–37. *See also* Patients; Privacy
Certified Nursing Assistant (CNA), 2–4, 33–34, 51, 94
Changes in techniques, 245–46
Chart, documenting, 105–12, 226–27. *See also* Documentation; Medical records
Cheerfulness, 119–21, 185–87
Clinical pathways, 144–45
Clinicals, preparing for, 45–46
Code of ethics, 10
Communication, 221–29
    with doctors, 166–67
    of pain levels, 224
    reporting off, 225–26
    timeliness of, 223–24
    writing skills for, 222–23
Community resources, 218–19
Computer skills, 33, 200–201. *See also* Technology
Confidentiality, 231–38
    HIPAA and, 232–33, 238
    for patients, 10, 153, 156–58, 216, 231–38
    policies about, 233–34
    social networking and, 238

D

Day, planning, 101–3
Degrees
    advanced degrees, 2, 5–6, 9, 25–26, 31, 36–38, 250–51
    Associate Degree in Nursing (ADN), 5, 36
    Bachelor of Science in Nursing (BSN), 5–6, 31, 36–38
Delegating tasks, 11, 90, 115–17, 139
Departments, changing, 258–59
Diagnosing diseases, 95–97
Diploma Nurse Program, 5, 36
Discharge planning, 209–19
Diseases, diagnosing, 95–97
Dix, Dorothea, 15
Doctors, 165–76
    communicating with, 166–67
    dating, 173–75
    earning trust from, 167
    as mentors, 170–71
    observing, 172–73
    "old-boy" attitudes, 167–69
    patient education and, 171–72
    respect from, 166–70, 173
    training for, 18–20
Documentation, 221–29
    accuracy of, 223–24
    on chart, 105–12, 226–27
    legal documents, 106–7, 222–29
    legal implications of, 228–29
    medical records, 106–7, 222–29

Infections
    controlling, 191
    exposure to, 189–98
    preventing, 132
    spreading, 197
In-services, 240–41
Insurances, 58, 167–68, 212–14, 256

J

Jobs. *See also* Nursing
    annoying coworkers at, 68, 74–75
    asking for help with, 76–79
    calling in sick, 87–88, 179–80, 197
    cheerfulness at, 119–21, 185–87
    equipment for, 64–68, 200–201
    expectations of, 68–70, 108–10
    finding, 49–59
    firings, 182–83
    first day at, 61–70
    new employee at, 71–83
    office politics, 79–81
    orientation at, 72–74
    preparing for, 61–70, 75
    quitting, 182–83
    teamwork, 75–78, 81–83
Journals, 240–41, 279

K

"Know-it-alls," 82
Knowledge. *See also* Education
    absorbing, 240
    increasing, 203–4
    lifelong learning, 203–4, 239–47, 252–53
    patients and, 163–64

L

Labor laws, 124
Legal documents, 106–7, 222–29
Legal issues, 14, 124, 167–68, 228–29
Licensed Practical Nurse (LPN), 2–4, 8, 35–36, 38, 54–57, 87–91
Licensed Vocational Nurse (LVN), 2–4, 8, 35–36, 38, 54, 87
Lifelong learning. *See also* Training
    improving skills, 241–42
    opportunities for, 203–4, 239–47, 252–53
    seminars, 240–42
    workshops, 240–42
Lincoln, Mary Todd, 16
LinkedIn, 237–38, 258
Listening skills, 152–53

M

Malpractice insurance, 58, 167–68, 256
Mandated reporting, 211–12, 215
Master of Science in Nursing (MSN), 25, 31, 38. *See also* Degrees
Medical records, 106–7, 222–29. *See also* Documentation
Medication administration record (MAR), 129–30
Medications
    conflicts between, 132
    dosage of, 66, 77, 129–30, 213
    "Five Rights" of, 128–30
    safe use of, 132
    staying up-to-date on, 242–44
Mentors, finding, 170–71
Mistakes
    handling, 132–35
    learning from, 123–35
    omissions as, 227–28
    reducing, 206–7
    surviving, 134–35
Mobile devices, 65–66, 200–201

N

NCLEX
    passing, 26, 35, 54–56
    preparing for, 38–39, 46–47
Needles, fear of, 21
Needle sticks, avoiding, 196–97
Neglect, reporting, 211–12, 215
Networking, 256–57

We Have
EVERYTHING
on Anything!

With more than 19 million copies sold, the Everything® series has become one of America's favorite resources for solving problems, learning new skills, and organizing lives. Our brand is not only recognizable—it's also welcomed.

The series is a hand-in-hand partner for people who are ready to tackle new subjects—like you!

For more information on the Everything® series, please visit *www.adamsmedia.com*

The Everything® list spans a wide range of subjects, with more than 500 titles covering 25 different categories:

Business	History	Reference
Careers	Home Improvement	Religion
Children's Storybooks	Everything Kids	Self-Help
Computers	Languages	Sports & Fitness
Cooking	Music	Travel
Crafts and Hobbies	New Age	Wedding
Education/Schools	Parenting	Writing
Games and Puzzles	Personal Finance	
Health	Pets	